cool pla

Britain's coolest places
to stay, eat, drink...
and more

Punk Publishing

cool places

Britain's coolest places
to stay, eat, drink...
and more

Contents

Introduction   7

Boutique   26

City   50

Unusual   66

Pubs, inns & restaurants   90

Seaside   124

Coastal cottages   164

Countryside   178

Cottages for couples   218

Country cottages   228

Parties, groups & gatherings   256

Glamping   278

Lodges & cabins   312

Indexes   330

Acknowledgements   336

Introduction

Welcome to the first edition of *Cool Places: Britain's Coolest Places to Stay, Eat, Drink… and More* – a print version of the website that features the best places to stay around the UK and much more besides. We're your first stop for the best of British accommodation, whether you're looking for a night away, weekend break, holiday cottage or glamping experience. And we're unashamedly choosy, so you can be sure that the properties featured in this book are some of the best the UK has to offer.

What do we mean by 'cool'? Good question! You might think fashionable and hip – and we're all for that. But for us 'cool' simply means the kind of homespun, homerun hotel, B&B, pub or restaurant that we would go to again and would recommend to our friends. This book is different in that it celebrates everywhere from the tiniest one-bedroom B&B to the grandest country-house mansion, a single shepherd's hut to a self-catering castle, an unpretentious rustic pub to a posh restaurant with rooms. We also love unusual places to stay like converted windmills and railway carriages, yurts and tipis, hideaway hostels and forest cabins.

We definitely don't do bland, we don't like average or run-of-the-mill and we like to celebrate the fact that travelling anywhere in Britain is a million times better than it used to be, when accommodation of all kinds could be a dreary affair. Food was either fast or posh, everywhere shut at 11pm, and if you had children you were unwelcome pretty much everywhere. No wonder we couldn't wait to go on holiday abroad.

Even in those days, though, there was much about the UK to celebrate – amazing landscapes, wonderful beaches, ancient towns and cities, a rich and burgeoning cultural diversity and a wealth of attractions that meant there was always something to do, even on the rainiest of days. But in the last couple of decades Britain has added a new generation of enthusiastic hosts, passionate about providing high-quality, contemporary accommodation. Our cuisine is immeasurably better, too, often celebrating classic British dishes and local, seasonal ingredients, and – whisper it softly – you can take your children (and your dogs!) along and no one seems to mind.

So come and discover the hotels, B&Bs, glampsites, cottages, hostels and lodges that are doing things right. Some are new, plugging into a new-found sense of enthusiasm for holidaying at home; others are long-standing businesses that have simply upped their game and joined the 21st century. What they have in common is that they are thoroughly rooted in their region, most are independently owned and run, and they all represent a new and improved pride in British hospitality. Above all, they are Cool Places in our eyes, and we think you're going to love them.

www.coolplaces.co.uk

DESTINATIONS
Where do you want to go?

ARTIST RESIDENCE PENZANCE Quirky boutique hotel by the sea 130

ATLANTIC HOTEL Old-fashioned luxury and a spectacular seaside location 142

BARFORD BEACH HOUSE Fabulous high-end seaside holiday home... 166

THE BEACH AT BUDE Coastal chic by the beach 126

BLUE HAYES Sumptuous suites with sea views 140

BOSINVER FARM COTTAGES As good as family holidays get.. 248

BRYN COTTAGE Romantic Padstow cottage......................... 227

BUDDHA BEACH HOUSE Cornish Caribbean cottage retreat by the sea 169

BUDOCK VEAN HOTEL Beautifully situated resort hotel 150

COHORT HOSTEL Cool surf hostel in St Ives 149

COSTISLOST Boutique B&B with a wellbeing slant.............. 185

FALMOUTH LODGE Home-from-home seaside hostel......... 148

FILTER HOUSE Former Art Deco waterworks....................... 82

FLYING BOAT COTTAGES Stylish Scillies cottages............... 168

THE GREENBANK HOTEL Historic harbourfront hotel......... 138

THE GURNARD'S HEAD Gorgeous Cornish gastropub with comfy rooms and great food 101

HALZEPHRON HOUSE Unique clifftop B&B and self-catering cottages 176

LESKERNICK COTTAGE Fabulous off-grid Cornish cottage..... 250

LITTLE WHITE ALICE A perfect Cornish eco-retreat 241

MARINE POINT Bright contemporary apartment with sea views... 174

THE OLD COASTGUARD Relaxation and food, Cornish-style.. 131

THE OLD QUAY HOUSE Boutique hotel that's a grown-up stay by the sea.. 130

THE OLDE HOUSE Beautifully furnished Cornwall cottages with loads of facilities.. 238

PEBBLE HOUSE B&B Luxury B&B in a stunning location with tremendous sea views................................. 158

PENTIRE PENTHOUSE Designer luxury apartment with amazing sea views.. 168

POLTARROW FARM Family farm with B&B and self-catering cottages 241

RICK STEIN'S CAFÉ ROOMS Snug Padstow B&B.................... 60

THE ROSEVINE Perfect family seaside hotel with rooms and apartments 144

ST ENODOC HOTEL Seaside boutique hotel, spa and restaurant 131

THE SEAFOOD RESTAURANTRICK Rick Stein's flagship restaurant with rooms.. 118

SOLOMON'S ISLAND Eco-friendly remote seaside cottage. 175

TALLAND BAY HOTEL Quirky luxury hotel in an idyllic bay 30

TREGULLAND COTTAGE & BARN Contemporary self-catering cottages that are the last word in luxury....... 270

CORNWALL &
THE ISLES OF SCILLY

COTSWOLDS &
THE MIDLANDS

ABBOTS LODGE One fabulous suite on the edge of a picturesque Herefordshire village................................ 180

ARTIST RESIDENCE OXFORDSHIRE Contemporary country inn with boutique rooms and great food..........37

BROOKS VINTAGE HORSEBOXES To the-manor-born glamping...68

BROOKS COUNTRY HOUSE Shabby-chic Herefordshire country house hotel................................... 196

THE BULL HOTEL Reinvented Cotswolds coaching inn with boutique rooms and great food 112

CALCOT MANOR Country house hotel suitable for both adults and kids.. 210

THE CASTLE HOTEL Cosy, dog-friendly hotel in an artsy Shropshire country town......................... 188

CIDER MILL COTTAGE Delightful country retreat in Worcestershire for two..................................... 220

CRESTOW HOUSE Luxurious and intimate Cotswolds hotel.. 198

CROWTREE WIGWAMS Rural Lincolnshire glamping 325

CRUCKBARN Spectacular country bolthole deep in the Herefordshire countryside........................... 244

DANNAH COTTAGES Two romantic Peak District cottages with hot tubs 224

ELTON OLD HALL Peak District cottage ideal for big groups and families.................................. 265

THE GREYHOUND INN Pub with top-quality food and rooms.. 109

HEATH FARM Luxury Cotswolds cottages set in acres of beautiful grounds 252

KNOTLOW FARM Back-to-nature Peak District glamping with hot tubs.................................. 298

MANOR HOUSE Georgian country house B&B in the Peak District 202

OLD DOWNTON LODGE Off-the-track foodie hotel...... 192

THE OLD STOCKS INN Updated 17th-century coaching inn with rooms, food and self-catering 112

THE PAINSWICK Cotswolds manor house with boutique rooms 207

PORTLAND HOUSE Peak District house that's ideal for big parties.. 274

RED LION PUB & KITCHEN Ancient Oxfordshire pub with comfy rooms and good food........................... 109

SETT COTTAGE Cosy cottage for Peak District walkers ... 226

THE SHEEP ON SHEEP ST Contemporary Cotswolds restaurant with rooms 118

STAYING COOL AT THE ROTUNDA Chic suites in the heart of Brum.................................60

SYMONDS YAT ROCK LODGE Cosy and right-up-to-date self-catering lodges on the edge of the Forest of Dean....... 223

WALCOT HALL All kinds of Shropshire glamping in the woods..77

YHA ST BRIAVELS CASTLE Atmospheric castle hostel........88

BRISTOL HARBOUR HOTEL Cool Bristol hotel and restaurant......64

BROOKS ROOFTOP ROCKETS City centre glamping on the roof......77

THE CHAPEL An exquisitely renovated Somerset chapel **78**

THE CRICKET INN Seaside pub with fabulous views and rooms......113

HOTEL ENDSLEIGH Lavish Devon living at this boutique country hotel in the Tamar Valley......207

FINGALS APART Quirky apartments in a prime South Devon location......234

GODNEY ARTS HOUSE A super-stylish Somerset cottage......242

THE HORN OF PLENTY Boutique rooms and high-end food on the Devon-Cornwall border......208

HOWARD'S HOUSE HOTEL Wiltshire home-from-home hotel for foodies......198

LAVERSTOCK FARM Stylish cottages on a Dorset farm......240

LONGLANDS GLAMPING Luxurious glamping in a beautiful location on the edge of Exmoor......286

LOOSE REINS Equestrian glamping in the deepest Dorset countryside......306

LOWER KEATS GLAMPING Luxury Devon glamping in canvas safari lodges......306

MIDDLE STONE FARM Somerset glamping with hot tubs and a self-catering cottage......297

MILL STREAM LOFT Romantic Somerset hideaway for two......222

THE NEST TREEHOUSE Cosy Devon treehouse for two......76

OLD RECTORY HOTEL Stylish North Devon boutique hotel......38

PARK FARM HOUSE Somerset B&B with pool and tennis court......211

THE SALUTATION INN Cool Devon restaurant with rooms...100

SAUNTON SANDS HOTEL Family-friendly seaside luxury......132

SWALLOW BARN Luxury Somerset B&B......206

SOAR MILL COVE HOTEL South Hams hotel that's great for kids......136

TILBURY FARM Idyllic Somerset cottages and shepherd's huts......240

THE 25 Unique B&B that brings a touch of style to Torquay......36

DEVON &
THE WEST COUNTRY

NORFOLK & SUFFOLK

THE ANGEL INN Cosy Norfolk country pub 95

THE BILDESTON CROWN Suffolk coaching inn with
great food 102

THE BOATHOUSE Boutique rooms above a
waterside restaurant 98

THE BUCKINGHAMSHIRE ARMS Cosy inn in a
historic location 94

CLEY WINDMILL Converted windmill by the sea 80

CLIPPESBY HALL Broads campsite with sumptuous
lodges 324

CROSSWAYS FARM Welcoming B&B deep in
the country 185

DEEPDALE BACKPACKERS Brilliant North Norfolk
budget option 149

EAST VIEW FARM Eco-friendly Broads cottages 237

FIVE ACRE BARN Contemporary design and a
warm welcome 42

GREAT BARN FARM A perfect rural spot for large groups
to relax and unwind 266

THE GROVE CROMER A welcome so warm you
won't want to leave 146

INCLEBOROUGH HOUSE Big Georgian Norfolk house
for parties 275

IVY GRANGE FARM Luxury Suffolk glamping 284

MAGAZINE WOOD Charming country B&B 184

MAIDS HEAD HOTEL Historic and re-energised city hotel 58

MILSOMS KESEGRAVE HALL Country-house hotel with a
boutique feel 46

THE OAKSMERE Suffolk hotel for jaded city-dwellers 202

RECTORY MANOR Just like staying with your poshest
friend in the country 203

THE ROSE & CROWN Old-school gastropub with rooms 104

THE SAIL LOFT Beachside Suffolk restaurant with rooms 128

SALTHOUSE HARBOUR HOTEL Cool boutique hotel
overlooking a marina 58

SIBTON WHITE HORSE Proper local pub in rural Suffolk 120

STRATTONS HOTEL Quirky contemporary design and
great food 36

STOKE BY NAYLAND LODGES Light-filled lodges
overlooking the golf course of this Suffolk resort hotel 317

STONE'S THROW COTTAGE Charming Norfolk
Coast cottage 170

THE SWAN AT LONG MELFORD Stylish rooms and
excellent food in this classic Suffolk village 119

WARDLEY HILL CAMPSITE Relaxed back-to-basics
glamping 292

THE WAVENEY INN Riverside pub with rooms and
much more 122

THE WHITE HORSE Great North Norfolk coast food
and rooms 110

THE WINDMILL SUFFOLK The ultimate stargazing escape
for lovers 86

WIVETON BELL North Norfolk gastropub with rooms 101

INTRODUCTION **17**

THE ANGEL AT HETTON Country-chic accommodation and food in the Dales 114

ANOTHER PLACE, THE LAKE Contemporary lakeside country house 203

BRIMSTONE HOTEL Boutique luxury and sublime surroundings 37

BROWNBER HALL A country B&B to dream about 48

BUTTERCRAMBE SHEPHERD'S HUT Romantic shepherd's hut on a farm 316

CAMP KÁTUR Glamping on a beautiful Yorkshire estate 308

THE DEN AT HUSTHWAITE GATE Cottage retreat with spillover camping 264

FAWCETT MILL Large country cottage in the Howgill Fells 258

GRASMERE GLAMPING Romantic walkers' glamping 290

HIDDEN RIVER CABINS Woodland cabins with hot tubs 322

THE HIDEAWAY @ BAXBY MANOR Off-grid countryside glamping 304

LAKESIDE HOTEL Full-service luxury Lakeland hotel 216

LOW MILL GUEST HOUSE Restored mill and boutique B&B in the Yorkshire Dales 28

THE LODGES AT ARTLEGARTH Slick lodges with hot tubs 320

LORD CREWE ARMS Cosy country hotel with great food 184

MILLGATE HOUSE Lavish Georgian townhouse B&B 204

MOSS HOWE FARM Yurt glamping with hot tubs in the Lake District 310

NUMBER ONE ST LUKE'S An award-winning Blackpool boutique B&B 156

PINEWOOD PARK Western-style glamping in Yorkshire 290

THE QUIET SITE Eco-friendly Lake District glamping – perfect for families 288

RANDY PIKE One-of-a-kind Lakes B&B 32

ROWAN LODGE Scandinavian-style lodge with hot tub 321

SHANK WOOD LOG CABIN Off-grid Cumbria log cabin with hot tub 324

SPLIT FARTHING HALL North Yorkshire women's retreat 216

STOW HOUSE Exceptional Yorkshire Dales B&B 186

TICKTON GRANGE Family-owned country house hotel 212

WANDERLUSTS GYPSY CARAVANS Gypsy caravan tours in the Lakes 302

WOODMAN'S HUTS Handmade shepherd's huts 320

YHA BLACK SAIL Remote hostel amid the highest Lakeland peaks 214

YHA BOGGLE HOLE Family-friendly seaside hostel 148

YHA GRINTON LODGE Grand accommodation at budget prices 76

YHA THE SILL HADRIAN'S WALL Fabulous new Dark Skies hostel 217

NORTHERN ENGLAND

SOUTHEAST ENGLAND

ALKHAM COURT FARMHOUSE Luxury Kent farmhouse B&B... **200**

THE ALMA INN Historic harbourside pub with great food **100**

ARTIST RESIDENCE LONDON Boutique rooms in the
    heart of London...**52**

CAREYS MANOR HOTEL New Forest country house
    hotel.. **211**

THE CAVALAIRE Friendly and very comfy Brighton
    boutique B&B **157**

DRIFTWOOD BEACH HOUSE Cool and welcoming
    Whitstable B&B.. **157**

THE DUKE WILLIAM Kentish pub with superb food
    and rooms... **217**

FAIR OAK FARM A unique Sussex estate with a diverse
    variety of accommodation.. **272**

THE FARMHOUSE AT REDCOATS Easy-to-reach country
    hotel and wedding venue with a great restaurant.................... **199**

THE FOX AT WILLIAN Updated country pub with
    good food **95**

THE GATE HOUSE Bijou Kentish castle for two **227**

GRAYWOOD CANVAS COTTAGES Luxurious 2-storey
    yurts.. **291**

GREEN FARM KENT Self-catering spa and yoga retreat **246**

THE HADLOW TOWER Magical Gothic tower in Kent **70**

HOUSE OF AGNES Funky Canterbury boutique B&B **45**

THE LITTLE BARN Secluded Isle of Wight holiday cottage.......... **236**

MAISON TALBOOTH Country house with high-end
    restaurant... **119**

MONTAGU ARMS Cosy New Forest country hotel with
    great food **199**

NUMBER ONE PORT HILL Quirkily elegant contemporary
    guesthouse..**40**

NUMBER ONE WAVECREST Self-catering cottage with
    Whitstable's best views **175**

THE OLD RECTORY Boutique Hastings hotel **156**

THE ORIGINAL HUT COMPANY Cosy Sussex shepherds'
    huts **314**

THE PIER AT HARWICH Stylish harbourside hotel...................... **162**

THE POINTER Comfy rooms and proper field-to-fork
    cooking in a pretty Buckinghamshire village..........................**94**

RAILWAY RETREATS Stay in a railway carriage in Sussex.............**83**

ROCKSALT ROOMS Folkestone restaurant with rooms **116**

SEASCAPE Large holiday cottage with sea views **265**

A SECRET GARDEN Log cabin glamping with hot tub ....

SEVEN Boutique hotel that makes Southend's lights
    shine brighter... **161**

SOLENT FORTS Your own private island in the Solent **83**

SWALLOWTAIL HILL Idyllic glamping in
    Amazing Spaces... **307**

THE SUN INN A proper pub with in Constable Country.................**96**

TAPNELL FARM Large holiday cottages and lots of facilities **276**

TOM'S ECO LODGE Comfy Isle of Wight glamping **328**

THE WIFE OF BATH Boutique rooms and Spanish-inspired food **108**

ACHMELVICH BEACH HOSTEL Your own slice of hostel paradise.. 160

AIKWOOD TOWER A spectacular castle in the Scottish Borders.. 260

AVIEMORE GLAMPING Cute and cosy glamping pods in Scotland's winter sports capital 307

BROOKS HOTEL EDINBURGH Affordable luxury in Edinburgh's West End.. 59

CAIRNGORM LODGES Eco-friendly lodges deep in the woods 318

COMRIE CROFT As good as glamping gets, with katas and tipis and a bunkhouse too........................ 294

CRISPIE ESTATE Two comfy cottages on a stunning Loch Fyne estate.. 275

CROFTHOUSE AT THE ROUNDHOUSE Pine-clad open-plan living in the Highlands................................. 274

EAST CAMBUSMOON FARM Luxury and eco-friendly self-catering cottages near Loch Lomond.............. 254

GREYSTONES Stylish B&B with stunning views over the harbour in Oban... 152

HARVEST MOON HOLIDAYS Treehouses, safari tents and a cottage by the sea.................................. 321

HOLYROOD COTTAGE Small cottage that makes a romantic city break bolthole for two............................ 226

HUNTINGTOWER LODGE Contemporary guesthouse in the Highlands.. 190

LAGGAN Off-grid west coast cottage that's only reachable by boat... 236

LAZY DUCK Cool, elemental glamping in cabins, lodges and a bothy.. 325

LOG CABIN SCOTLAND Log lodges in spectacular lochside surroundings 326

LOWER POLNISH Ultra remote Scotland escape for star-crossed lovers 223

94DR Modern Edinburgh guesthouse with super-friendly hosts.. 56

PLANE CASTLE Fabulous Scottish castle steeped in history that's perfect for a large gathering 268

ROULOTTE RETREAT Adults-only Caravans of Love in the Scottish Borders... 84

ST HILDA SEA ADVENTURES Sea cruises around Scotland's Western Isles... 134

THE THREE CHIMNEYS Skye's legendary restaurant with rooms 34

WHEEMS ORGANIC FARM Orkney glamping and self-catering.. 300

SCOTLAND

WALES

AROS YN PENTRE GLAS Quirky Pembrokeshire glamping in a cabin and a converted Bedford bus............ 296

CAERFAI FARM COTTAGES Comfy coastal holiday cottages 169

COSY UNDER CANVAS Dome glamping in a glorious mid-Wales location 282

DENMARK FARM Self-catering eco-lodges in the heart of southwest Wales 317

THE FELIN FACH GRIFFIN Gastropub with rooms in glorious Brecon Beacons surroundings 92

FFOREST FIELDS Cottages and glamping in the heart of Wales 237

FOREST HOLIDAYS BEDDGELERT Adventurous family holidays in Snowdonia, just one among many Forest Holidays locations around the UK 316

FFYNNON Boutique rooms in a romantic Snowdonia guesthouse 45

GRAIG WEN Beautiful Snowdonia yurts and holiday cottages 297

HENFAES ISAF Welsh farmhouse on the edge of Snowdonia 232

MANOR TOWN HOUSE Seaside B&B with views to die for 154

PENRHIW PRIORY Historic Pembrokeshire hotel with boutique rooms 44

RED KITE TREE TENT Perhaps the future of glamping as we know it? 291

ROCH CASTLE Spectacular Pembrokeshire castle with just six boutique rooms 74

THE SLATE SHED Super comfortable boutique B&B in Snowdonia 182

SMUGGLERS' COVE BOATYARD Riverside glamping and holiday cottages 264

SNOWDONIA GLAMPING HOLIDAYS Glamping barns with wood-burners 296

TOP OF THE WOODS Boutique Pembrokeshire glamping 280

TREBERFEDD FARM Eco-friendly self-catering in both cottages and wooden eco-cabins 230

TWR Y FELIN HOTEL A contemporary Welsh hotel par excellence 62

TY MAMGU Romantic self-catering for two on a working organic farm 222

YHA SNOWDEN PEN-Y-PASS Stay right at the base of Snowdon itself in this historic hostel 206

BOUTIQUE

What's boutique? Designer fabrics and original art? Mismatched antiques, bold colours or retro decor? We reckon you'll know it when you see it, whether it's in a large hotel that's had a stylish makeover or a highly personal B&B. Either way, don't settle for ordinary when you can enjoy exceptional – from gorgeous rooms with private hot tubs to artisan toiletries and homemade cake.

Randy Pike, Cumbria

Low Mill Guest House

A special place to stay in the heart of the Yorkshire Dales

"Small but special" is what one award citation said about Low Mill, and it's bang on. Just 3 rooms keep your stay on the intimate side, but what wonderful rooms they are, fashioned from an 18th-century watermill on the gushing riverside in Bainbridge, in the heart of Wensleydale. There is no mistaking the building's heritage – owners Neil and Jane have restored the lot to working order, so the grindstones and cogs form a dramatic backdrop in the eye-popping guest lounge, while the wheel itself lies underneath the dining room (a tour by Neil, who did the work himself, is very much part of the experience).

There's a story to tell in every lavishly appointed room – the old 'Store Room' sits under gorgeous beams, while the 'Kiln Room' retains its vintage ceramic floor tiles where the grain used to be spread to dry. And if you think you've been-there-done-that as far as boutique goes, be prepared to swoon at 'The Workshop', which is an absolutely massive space running the length of the building, complete with winding gear and pulleys, wood-burner and free-standing copper bath. Low Mill is a chic affair all round, from polished wooden floors and exposed stone walls to cheeky fabrics and designer bathrooms, and it's iPod-docked, wifi-ed, flat-screen-TV-ed and fluffy-bath-robed up to its eyeballs. But style aside, there's comfort and fun here too, whether it's in the deep bedside rugs or the leopard and tiger standing guard in the lounge. Mornings see serious breakfasts, strong on local produce; 2 or 3 evenings a week are reserved for home-cooked suppers; while outside is a riverside terrace where you can lay in wait for the visiting herons. Small but special indeed – well said *Yorkshire Life*.

NORTH YORKSHIRE Bainbridge Leyburn DL8 3EF
01969 650553 lowmillguesthouse.co.uk
HOW MUCH? Store Room from £110, Kiln Room £130, Workshop £180. Dinner, 2 courses £22, 3 courses £28.

"We hope a stay with us will show our guests why we love this building, the local area and the produce it provides."

Jane McNair, Low Mill Guesthouse

What's nearby?

THE KING'S ARMS, ASKRIGG This historic old pub famously doubled as the Drovers' in TV's All Creatures Great & Small, and very cosy it is too, with good local ales, nice food and lots of dogs.

HARDRAW FORCE WATERFALL England's highest single drop waterfall and mighty impressive. Drop into the comfy Green Dragon for a pint afterwards.

WENSLEYDALE CREAMERY "We'll go somewhere where there's cheese!" says Wallace to Gromit, and we all know which cheese he had in mind!

Talland Bay Hotel

A unique luxury hotel tucked into an idyllic bay

Bang on the South West Coast Path, the Talland Bay Hotel is about pure relaxation. Forget the trappings of spa treatments, indoor pools and sports facilities – here the focus is on glorious sea views, sub-tropical gardens, fine Cornish cuisine and lounging around in a quirky but luxurious environment. The 19 rooms and 4 suites have been individually decorated – there's an airy seaside feel throughout, a rolltop bath in one, a sleigh bed in another – and many have gorgeous views of the ocean and direct access to a patio, terrace or garden. There's also a pretty big collection of local and international artwork, both in the rooms and dotted around the gardens as well. Together with a fine-dining restaurant, there's a swanky brasserie in the sea-view conservatory (where the dishes are a little lighter but no less divine) and a very comfy bar too, which, like the rest of the hotel, is dog-friendly. Just as well: this is prime territory for strolling with your faithful hound, a short walk away from glistening Talland Bay – childhood haunt of national treasure Dame Judi Dench, incidentally – from where the South West Coast Path runs east to Looe (a little over 3 miles) and west to Polperro (2 miles).

Sweeping up a grand tally of awards, including 'Best Small Hotel in Cornwall' a few years ago, and 'Best South West Restaurant' in 2017, this former family home proves that location, style and cuisine are all you need to relax and embrace the natural beauty and lifestyle this part of the world offers. The fab clifftop location and ocean backdrop would also look pretty good in wedding photos... just saying.

CORNWALL Porthallow PL13 2JB 01503 27 667
tallandbayhotel.co.uk
HOW MUCH? Double rooms from £160 to £250 B&B – or £240 to £330 including dinner.

"We love this quiet corner of Cornwall, which is a fabulous place to escape and unwind."

Jack Ashby Wright, Talland Bay Hotel

What's nearby?

COLWITH FARM DISTILLERY Cornwall's first plough-to-bottle gin distillery, and now the producer of Talland Bay's very own blend.

POLRUAN Ancient fishing village with a maze of backstreets meandering up the steep hill and breathtaking views over the estuary to Fowey.

SAM'S ON THE BEACH Fowey's Sam's Bistro is an institution but it doesn't have the views and beach location of this new Sam's, down on lovely Polkerris beach.

Randy Pike

A one-of-a-kind boutique bolthole in the Lakes

There are boutique B&Bs – and then there's the glorious, one-of-a-kind Randy Pike, a designer bolthole that's also the home of local restaurateurs Andy and Chrissy Hill. Three suites have been carved out of their Victorian gentleman's residence on the Wray Castle estate, and they are simply stunning ensembles, featuring hand-carved beds, designer fabrics, rococo touches and absolutely massive luxurious bathrooms (variously described as nearly the size of Belgium, Luxembourg "or another small European principality" – you get the idea, these are big bathrooms).

Individual they most certainly are, but the suites do have some common features, with flatscreen TVs, tea and fresh coffee and complimentary drinks, wonderful wooden floors and great views looking out over the woods around the building. Andy makes his fab music collection available on the in-room iPod sound systems, there is a warm welcome on arrival and private gardens to stroll in which come complete with their own Dr Who Tardis, plus a further place to stay, the amazing Juniper House. This is basically another spacious suite with a vast bedroom and views over the lake, equipped with an Alexa speaker, big squashy sofas, a minibar and Nespresso machine. They bring breakfast to your door so you don't even have to move.

Transfers are also offered down to their excellent Grasmere restaurant, the Jumble Room, which serves up hearty seasonal food in a relaxed and rather bohemian environment. There are plenty of B&Bs around nearby Ambleside, but for a different kind of stay in glorious surroundings, Randy Pike really does stand out from the crowd.

CUMBRIA 2 Randy Pike Ambleside LA22 0JP
01539 436088 randypike.co.uk
HOW MUCH? Double rooms with breakfast £200 a night, weekends £225 – 2-night minimum at weekends. Juniper House £300–£325 a night.

"We love to share the beauty of the Lakes and to look after you while you rest, relax and repair."

Andy Hill, Randy Pike

What's nearby?

WRAY CASTLE A stunning Gothic Revival castle on the shores of Lake Windermere, with turrets, towers and informal grounds, a 15-minute stroll from Randy Pike.

BRANTWOOD John Ruskin's magnificent country home above Coniston Water: beautifully preserved interiors, dramatic gardens and an excellent café.

TARN HOWS If the mountains seem too high and forbidding, then it has to be a stroll around Tarn Hows – a gorgeous lake owned and maintained by the National Trust.

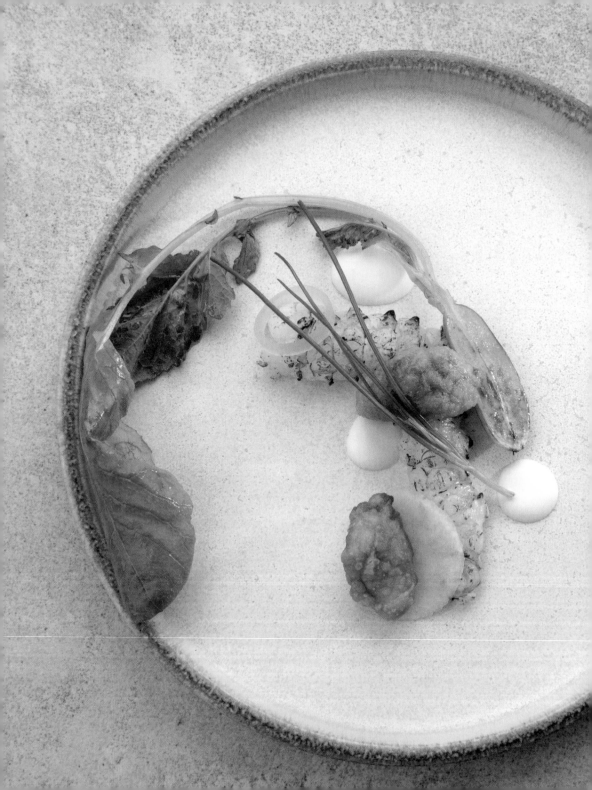

Once upon a time restaurants in Britain were odd places, serving mediocre dishes, usually with French names, consumed off white tablecloths in hushed silence. Seems like a long time ago, doesn't it? But if eating out in the UK is so much better than before, then much of it is down to people like Shirley Spear at The Three Chimneys on the Isle of Skye.

She and her husband Eddie moved into this seashore crofter's cottage in the mid-1980s, and through a mixture of sheer determination and self-taught cooking forced their way on to the culinary map. No one bats an eyelid now at Shirley's mission to revive Scottish cuisine using great local ingredients. But back in the dark ages this was an extraordinary idea, and The Three Chimneys far ahead of its time. It's now the sort of fine-dining establishment that you go to for a treat, the kitchen run by Professional Masterchef finalist Scott Davies, but Shirley and Eddie are still involved and regularly travel the country as ambassadors of Scottish cooking. Shirley's favourite dish? A simple plate of fresh prawns served with locally-grown salad leaves, though oddly one of her original and most popular desserts (hot marmalade pudding) is not based on local ingredients at all (though you'd be hard-pressed to find a more traditional product than marmalade). You can stay at The Three Chimneys in one of 6 lovely suites with sea views, flatscreen TVs, wifi , Bluetooth and lovely bathrooms. A table is automatically guaranteed upon booking – and you really couldn't do much better if you were looking for a short break to celebrate a special occasion.

THREE CHIMNEYS Colbost Dunvegan, Isle of Skye IV55 8ZT 01470 511258 threechimneys.co.uk. Double rooms with breakfast £360 a night; dinner from £68 pp.

Strattons Hotel

Vanessa and Les Scott opened Strattons well over 20 years ago now, and were remarkably ahead of the curve in coming up with what is now almost the epitome of a British boutique hotel: an attractive historic building, a great restaurant and comfortable rooms that are both contemporary and welcoming – and often a little bit different. Tucked away in a courtyard away from what passes for the urban hum of Swaffham, there are 8 rooms in the main house, varying from the extravagant opulence of the Boudoir and Red Room to the funky lines of the Seagull and Portico Room, with its bathtub and mermaid mosaic. Add in 2 slick self-catering apartments in a converted printworks across the garden and further rooms and suites in a converted cottage, and overall you couldn't be more comfortable, surrounded by the fruits of Les and Vanessa's magpie-like travels and ultra-vivid imaginations. The restaurant is fab and the on-site café CoCoes does excellent coffee and cooks up a storm at lunchtime, so you won't go hungry.

NORFOLK 4 Ash Close Swaffham PE37 7NH
01760 723845 strattonshotel.com
HOW MUCH? Double rooms with breakfast from £99 a night, suites from £131, apartments from £154.

The 25

The 25 is like no B&B you have ever stayed in, an adults-only luxury guesthouse that is helping to drag Torquay into the 21st century by pure style. Owners Andy and Julian used to run a country house hotel, and their experience and attention to detail shows in everything they do – from the high standard of design to the cleanliness of the rooms and above all the nothing-is-too-much-trouble attitude. Breakfast is fabulous, with everything from kippers to eggs Benedict, and the 6 rooms are each a different size and styled with a specific colour palette: one has zebra stripes, another is decorated with a large mural of an orange gerbera. All have Netflix, Amazon Echos, ultra-fast wifi complimentary iPads and Nespresso machines; the 4 luxury rooms also have super-king-size beds, and they all have contemporary en-suite bathrooms with posh toiletries, power showers and fluffy bathrobes and slippers. The owners don't allow dogs but they do like dog lovers, who will be charmed by their miniature Schnauzer (Patsy), who is occasionally on reception duty.

DEVON 25 Avenue Road Torquay TQ2 5LB
01803 297517 the25.uk
HOW MUCH? Double rooms from £129 a night including breakfast, up to £179 for the largest suites.

Artist Residence Oxfordshire

Nestled in the Oxfordshire countryside, just a few miles west of Oxford, this is the ultimate boutique country inn – with 5 bedrooms tucked away in the eaves, a further 3 bedrooms in the outbuildings, plus a shepherd's hut in the garden. The rooms really set this place apart, with large, comfy beds, powerful showers and the sort of vintage-tinged decor we've come to expect from the quirky Artist Residence group. All have wifi, flatscreen TVs, Nespresso coffee machines and mini fridges stocked with local goodies – and there are Bramley toiletries in the bathrooms, some of which have standalone rolltop baths. The rooms range in size, from the compact 'Rabbit Hole' through the larger (dog-friendly) 'Farmhouse Loft' rooms to the spacious 'Stable' with private terrace and 'Barn Suite' with a 4-poster. Downstairs in the Mason Arms you can enjoy all the best things about a good country pub – an open fire, local ales, armchairs to lounge about in, homemade bar snacks, and a dining room menu that hits all the right buttons.

OXFORDSHIRE Station Road South Leigh Oxford OX29 6XN 01993 656220 artistresidence.co.uk
HOW MUCH? Double rooms from £120 a night, suites from £210 – all including breakfast.

Brimstone Hotel

If you love the Lake District but lazily write it off as being somewhere for the dufflecoat and rucksack brigade, then you should think again. The region has changed quite a bit since the days of Wainwright, and nowhere more so than the Brimstone Hotel, one of a new breed of local boutique hotels, housed in a slate-clad building perfectly in keeping with its surroundings. Situated in one of the region's most beautiful valleys, and with some great walking on its doorstep, it has everything that people come to the Lakes for, but the approach is as contemporary as it gets, with an emphasis on comfort, good food and creating a welcoming home-from-home. Its 16 rooms are large, decorated in cool and contemporary colours and oozing with gadgets, although ironically the best rooms also boast a suitably retro open fireplace. There's a spa and a lovely indoor pool, plus a decent restaurant, Stove, across the way. All in all, this is a hotel that is firmly anchored in the Lakes, yet is thoroughly up to date.

CUMBRIA Langdale Estate Great Langdale Ambleside LA22 9JD 01539 438062 brimstonehotel.co.uk
HOW MUCH? Double rooms with breakfast £275–£375 a night.

The Old Rectory Hotel

A stylish boutique hotel in a quiet corner of Exmoor

There are a lot of small hotels in England, so you have to have done something pretty special to win 'best small hotel' of the year from Visit England – as the folks at The Old Rectory Hotel did a few years back. Boutique hotels are two-a-penny these days, but Huw Rees and Sam Prosser got it right when they found this place back in 2008 – not only is its location second-to-none, with spectacular views across the Bristol Channel towards Wales, but the thoughtfulness with which they went about the whole project is impressive. The result is 10 comfortable rooms furnished in a contemporary style, decked out with fresh flowers, large bathrooms, wifi and everything else you could possibly need. Beyond the rooms, the hotel fosters the atmosphere of a convivial country house party, with afternoon tea in the comfy downstairs sitting room, early evening canapes and an excellent dinner in the restaurant, whose motto is local all the way, with fish from day boats, meat from nearby farms and fruit and veg from their kitchen garden.

Outside, the location couldn't be more peaceful, and there are lovely gardens in which to enjoy it; for the more energetic the steep wooded valleys and high cliffs of Exmoor National Park are on your doorstep – you're just 500m from the South West Coast Path. Beyond lies the coastal resort of Lynton and Lynmouth – take a ride on the Cliff Railway that joins them, the highest and steepest totally water-powered railway in the world. In the other direction, you'll find the rightly renowned beaches of North Devon. Not bad in terms of local attractions, then, but above all a lovely country house retreat to come back to at the end of the day.

DEVON Martinhoe Exmoor National Park EX31 4QT 01598 763368 oldrectoryhotel.co.uk
HOW MUCH? Double rooms with breakfast from £180 a night, DB&B from £220 a night. Usually a minimum 2-night stay at the weekend.

"With just birdsong, jaw-dropping scenery and the South West path, you couldn't choose a better place if you're looking for somewhere to soothe the mind."

Huw and Sam, The Old Rectory Hotel

What's nearby?

BARRICANE BEACH Our fave beach in an area of brilliant beaches – rocky and sheltered, and with a Sri Lankan beach café to enjoy at the end of the day.

SAUNTON SANDS Three miles of beach and surf that featured in the Robbie Williams's single 'Angels' – plus the massive dunes of Braunton Burrows behind.

LUNDY ISLAND This wind-blown island is the ultimate escape. Just be prepared to share it with thousands of seabirds, seals, dolphins and basking sharks.

Number One Port Hill

A unique, quirkily elegant contemporary guesthouse

Forming part of an elegant Georgian terrace, a short walk from the centre of the pleasant market town of Hertford, Number One Port Hill is the home of music biz exec Annie Rowley, who luckily for the rest of us runs it as an eclectically furnished and very comfortable 3-bedroom guesthouse. Its very homely style, packed full of antique furniture, gilded and ornate mirrors, random sculptures and arrangements of flowers in big urns and vases, makes it a unique place to stay – and there's always a lovely warm welcome to go with it.

Above all, Annie and and her business partner Emily Sheridan have made Number One Port Hill into the kind of guesthouse you want to spend some time in. Among places to relax there's a comfy 1st-floor sitting room full of knick-knacks, books and magazines, and a courtyard garden that's as over-stuffed with plants and flowers as the house is with furniture. The upper floor is home to 3 guest bedrooms, the largest of which is a spacious and comfortable room with a gilded antique bed, satellite TV and its own bathroom across the hall, which has a big bath and walk-in shower and locally made toiletries. The other 2 bedrooms are cosier but also very well kitted-out, with en-suite shower rooms and toiletries; and all 3 rooms have good tea and proper coffee, complimentary mineral water, sweets, biscuits and other snacks. Finally, Annie is a keen cook and her ground-floor dining room – full of fine crystal and china – plays host to an excellent breakfast buffet and a generous Full English, made with local sausages and bacon. Annie sometimes provides dinner as well, and hosts monthly supper clubs that take in anything from Malaysian cuisine to their popular 'psychic suppers'.

HERTFORDSHIRE 1 Port Hill Hertford SG14 1PJ 01992 587350 numberoneporthill.co.uk **HOW MUCH?** Room 1 £160 a night, rooms 2 & 3 £130 a night – all with breakfast.

"We pride ourselves on our attention to detail and expert local knowledge – and it's a pleasure to create the perfect stay."

Annie Rowley, Number One Port Hill

What's nearby?

SHAW'S CORNER Situated in a picturesque Hertfordshire village, George Bernard Shaw's house and garden look much the same as when he died here in 1950.

HATFIELD HOUSE Still the home of the Marquess of Salisbury, this Jacobean house is the centre of a large estate that features wonderful country walks.

HENRY MOORE STUDIO & GARDENS Moore's studio is not only open to the public, the gardens here also contain 20 of his monumental bronzes.

Five Acre Barn

Cool contemporary design and a warm welcome

Housed in an award-winning barn conversion, midway between Aldeburgh and Thorpeness, Five Acre Barn is a boutique B&B par excellence, with a modern extension designed for London escapees David and Bruce that makes for a very comfortable – and very contemporary – place to stay, and a great-value one too, with prices that compare extremely well with other options in what can be a pricey area.

Furnished in an eclectic, retro-ish style, with Scandinavian influences and lots of of eBay purchases in between, it has 5 guest rooms, 4 of which are suites really, with separate sitting rooms and mezzanine floors with king-size beds with cotton sheets and duvets. You can enjoy the soaring ceilings of each room's cool, crisp living area, equipped with Freeview TVs and good wifi, and later on climb the stairs and lie on your bed and gaze at the big Suffolk skies through the large roof lights, drawing the solar-powered blinds once it's time to go to sleep. Bathrooms are small but well thought out, 2 with wet rooms and showers, 2 with baths, and stocked with Bramley toiletries. Outside, each room has its own stretch of decking with access to no less than five acres of garden and woodland, where you can spot rabbits, lots of birds and even the odd muntjac deer. The 5th room – the 'Garden Room' – fills one storey on its own and has a fully accessible shower and a luxurious bathroom. Breakfast is a relaxed affair, made to order in front of guests in the Barn – delicious and convivial. You could if you wished spend the rest of the day chilling out in the Barn, and it's certainly tempting – there's a Sonos music system, comfy sofas, games and books and a wood-burner that will make you almost wish for a rainy day.

SUFFOLK Aldeburgh Road Aldringham IP16 4QH
07788 424642 fiveacrebarn.co.uk
HOW MUCH? Double rooms with breakfast from £100 to £160 a night.

"Come and explore the beautiful Suffolk Coast... or just make yourself at home: relax, put the kettle on and your feet up!"

David Woodbine, Five Acre Barn

What's nearby?

THORPENESS With a toytown quaintness reminiscent of the 1960s TV show The Prisoner, you can walk here on foot in 30–40 minutes from Five Acre Barn.

THE RED HOUSE Just a mile from Five Acre Barn, this was home to England's greatest 20th-century composer, Benjamin Britten, and is preserved as a museum.

THE LIGHTHOUSE Reckoned by most locals to be Aldeburgh's best and most consistent restaurant, this place is always busy and always good.

Penrhiw Priory

Situated on the edge of St Davids, Pembrokeshire, Penrhiw is from the outside an impressive and imposing monument to Victorian grandeur. As soon as you set foot inside, however, it is clear that the building has been restored to exacting contemporary standards: suede wallpaper and contemporary artworks set the scene for a boutique venue that nestles in acres of private gardens, surrounded by woodland paths, river and meadow. There are just 7 en-suite bedrooms and a spacious ground-floor suite, all of which come with robes and slippers, aromatherapy toiletries, satellite TV and iPod docking stations. Breakfast is sumptuous (including unmissable Welsh laverbread) and there is a complimentary evening transfer for dinner to Penrhiw's sister hotel, Twr y Felin, which boasts the fab Blas restaurant. It's only a short stroll into St Davids – Britain's smallest city – with its cathedral dating back to the 6th century, and you can also walk to beautiful Whitesands Beach, rated by many as one of the finest beaches in Europe.

PEMBROKESHIRE St Davids Haverfordwest SA62 6PG
01437 725588 penrhiwhotel com
HOW MUCH? Double rooms with breakfast from £190 a night.

Bank House

The old port of King's Lynn is one of England's most historic towns, with more listed buildings than York and a unique waterfront district lined by Hanseatic warehouses and medieval mansions. It's also home to one of North Norfolk's best boutique hotels in the Bank House, which occupies a handsome Georgian former banker's house right on the quay – a creakily grand and evocative old place that has been done up with a dash of contemporary style and has a choice of 12 distinctive rooms. It was refurbished by Jeannette and Anthony Goodrich who took the place over around a decade ago after cutting their teeth on the excellent Rose & Crown in Snettisham (see p.104). Most of the rooms enjoy marvellous views over the river – although the large Captain's Room and Bath Room are definitely the ones to go for if you can. The restaurant is a lovely haven at night, overlooking the water. Ask if you can also have a peek at the downstairs cellar, which dates back around 8 centuries and can be booked for private parties.

NORFOLK King's Staithe Square King's Lynn PE30 1ED
01553 660492 thebankhouse.co.uk
HOW MUCH? Double rooms £115–£220 a night including breakfast.

Ffynnon

This old stone rectory would be a lovely place to stay wherever it was, but its location in Dolgellau, at the foot of the Cader Idris mountain and not far from the sea, makes it extra special. Its 6 bedrooms are thoughtfully decorated in a manner that's designed to be both in keeping with the Victorian property but artfully contemporary at the same time, with wifi, iPod docks, DVD players and PlayStations (they have a library), and all individually decorated so that each is as different from the last room as you could imagine, varying from the cultured orientalism of Annis to the cool simplicity of Hazel. You have robes and slippers in your room, free-standing baths or enormous showers – sometimes both – and there's a hot tub in the garden too. Facilities include a range of popular in-room beauty and wellbeing treatments, and the hotel also serves dinner Thursday–Monday nights if you're feeling lazy. Not for nothing is Ffynnon located on Love Lane – it's about a romantic a small hotel as you could wish for.

GWYNEDD Love Lane Dolgellau LL40 1RR
01341 421774 ffynnontownhouse.com
HOW MUCH? Double rooms with breakfast £160–£220 a night.

House of Agnes

This is one of our favourite Canterbury boltholes, an exceptionally well-run, funky and friendly boutique B&B that was featured – and highly praised – on Channel 4's *Four in a Bed* series. Once a restaurant, and a nightclub before that, it's situated in a historic house said to be mentioned in 'David Copperfield', and has 9 quirky, individual rooms in the main house and 8 in a converted stables overlooking a beautiful and surprisingly large walled garden. Each bedroom in the house is decorated according to a theme – mostly cities – meaning you can choose between spending the night in Mumbai, Marrakesh or Tokyo, to name just the most exotic destinations. They all have wifi, flatscreen TVs and DVD players and tea- and coffee-making facilities and decent-sized bath or shower rooms. There's an honesty bar and a cosy lounge with books and board games, and the breakfasts are excellent and generous – plus they'll prepare a takeaway breakfast for early departures. In short it's a very nice and rather unique place to stay in the heart of the city.

KENT 71 St Dunstans Street Canterbury CT2 8BN
01227 472185 houseofagnes.co.uk
HOW MUCH? Double rooms with breakfast from £85 to £130 a night.

Milsoms Kesgrave Hall

A country-house hotel with a relaxed boutique feel

Situated on the eastern edge of Ipswich, this rather grand building used to be a school and was also once owned by the local Tolly Cobbold brewing dynasty, but nowadays Kesgrave Hall is a country-house retreat that's part of the small but perfectly formed East Anglian boutique hotel group, Milsoms.

It sits in expansive grounds, sheltering just 23 rooms, around half of which are in the main house, with the rest situated in the former headmaster's quarters and various outbuildings. Guest rooms are sumptuous and on the glam side, even in the smaller, standard rooms, with sound systems, satellite TV, super-fast wifi, and complimentary soft drinks and snacks. Upgrade to the so-called 'Top Rooms' and expect a bit more woo and wow – we're talking massive beds, free-standing bathtubs in the room, walk-in showers and plenty of space to lounge.

Downstairs there's a bar and lounge that are relaxed rather than stuffy, and the brasserie is deliberately accessible (no reservations, no dress code), staying open all day and featuring stripped pine tables, an open kitchen and a quirky way of ordering – just write what you want on the pad provided. Brunch isn't just for weekends at Kesgrave Hall, which is great if you've done a midweek bunk from work, while summer means drinks on the outdoor terrace, a read of your book and a stroll in the grounds, making sure you're back in time for a proper afternoon tea, served from 3pm to 5pm every day. Like we said, cool, relaxed and boutique, and all super-friendly too.

As for the location, it's just off the A12, so very easy to get to, and also very well situated for exploring the delights of the Suffolk Coast.

SUFFOLK Hall Road Kesgrave Ipswich IP5 2PU
01473 333741 milsomhotels.com
HOW MUCH? Double rooms with breakfast from around £125.

"We're handy for both the Suffolk coast and delightful market towns like Framlingham and Newmarket, the home of horse racing."
Sue Bunting, Milsoms Kesgrave Hall

What's nearby?

JIMMY'S FARM The farm of Jamie Oliver's mate and TV celebrity Jimmie Doherty, where kids get a chance to feed the sheep and build a den while the grown-ups enjoy the farm shop and restaurant.

FELIXSTOWE FERRY The nice end of Felixstowe – a quaint riverside hamlet with Martello Towers, a wet fish shop and a decent pub at the end of the Deben estuary.

RAMSHOLT ARMS A dog-friendly place with a large terrace, this riverside pub enjoys a fabulous setting looking across the Deben, and serves decent food too.

Brownber Hall

The sort of country retreat most people dream about...

Hidden away in a remote corner of the Howgill Fells, Brownber Hall is about as comfortable a country retreat as you could wish for – a thoroughly up-to-date version of a traditional guesthouse, run by a welcoming couple who are in love with this beautiful region and everything it has to offer – the gorgeous walks on their doorstep and the stunning countryside of the Yorkshire Dales National Park. The Grade II-listed Victorian mansion retains original features galore – tiled fireplaces, wooden floors, stained-glass windows – which combine beautifully with the couple's artfully eclectic rugs and kilims, shabby-chic sofas and other furniture rescued from local antique shops and bric-a-brac markets. The owners' contemporary art collection lines the walls and would be the envy of many a gallery, but otherwise the feel is deliberately that of the home of your luckiest countryside friend. Bedrooms have large windows and beautiful country views, yet are very cosy, individually decorated with antique furnishings and contemporary beds created by a local blacksmith. Bathrooms are spacious, sleek affairs with underfloor heating and powerful showers. Owners Peter and Amanda are full of advice on the best local walks and pubs but if you want to just loaf about indoors there's an honesty bar stocked with local beers and wines, bookcases filled to overflowing and plenty of board games for rainy days. There is also a restaurant, which serves homemade pizzas and other Italian goodies (Peter used to have a mobile pizza van in London in a previous life) and for breakfast they make their own granola, sourdough bread and marmalade. Er, they also bake a cake every day for tea. Let's face it, it's unlikely that even your most devoted country friend would be able to manage all that!

CUMBRIA Newbiggin-on-Lune Kirkby Stephen CA17 4NX 01539 623208 brownberhall.co.uk
HOW MUCH? Double rooms with breakfast from £95 a night.

"We recently got described as 'Hackney in the Hills', which we thought was hilariously apt!"

Peter and Amanda, Brownber Hall

What's nearby?

BLACK SWAN, RAVENSTONEDALE Eden Valley inn that has won an almost criminal number of awards, serving some of the best food in the area yet retaining a proper pubby feel.

THE HOWGILL FELLS Brownber Hall sits in the Howgill Fells, a beautiful region of scenic hills that's also home to England's highest waterfall, Cautley Spout.

SEDBERGH This is North Yorkshire's very own 'Book Town', with a concentration of browsable shops and a popular literary festival every October.

CITY

Who doesn't like a city
break? There are no fewer than
59 official cities in the UK, and
there's a brilliant British weekend to
be had at every one – from Stirling to
St David's and from Bristol to Hull.

Staying Cool at the Rotunda, Birmingham

Artist Residence London

Your very cool home bang in the centre of London

We're big fans of the Artist Residence hotel group, which also has places in Brighton, Cornwall and Oxfordshire. They're good-value, well run and strive to be different, so we weren't surprised at all when their flagship London property won the Good Hotel Guide's 'London Hotel Of The Year' a couple of years ago. The 10-bedroom boutique hotel features individually decorated guest rooms, a basement cocktail bar and its own all-day-dining restaurant, Cambridge Street. Room decoration is delightfully random, with reclaimed floorboards, a mix of furniture that blends vintage and contemporary, and – naturally – a good selection of art on the walls. They also have fast wifi, air conditioning, flatscreen Freeview TVs and digital radios, well-stocked fridges, Nespresso machines and complimentary tea, coffee and biscuits. The beds are big and bouncy, and all the rooms have powerful rainfall showers, while the larger rooms and suites also have free-standing baths and walk-in showers, super-king-size beds and seating areas.

Pimlico may not be London's most interesting district, but it is a proper neighbourhood and you are super-central, very well located for public transport and also within walking distance of any number of major London museums and sights. The hotel has also been deliberately designed for people to hang out in, so once you're done with exploring the city you can sup cocktails in the bar and eat well in the hotel's busy restaurant – maybe even enjoy a spot of ping-pong in the basement games room. It's your choice – and this is your very cool home in the centre of London.

LONDON 52 Cambridge Street SW1V 4QQ
0203 019 8610 artistresidence.co.uk
HOW MUCH? Double rooms and junior suites £235–£255 to £410–£440 a night, not including breakfast.

"We like to think that staying at Artist Residence is like staying at a quirky friend's house – comfy, welcoming and a little offbeat."

Justin and Charlotte, Artist Residence London

What's nearby?

SAATCHI GALLERY London is packed with great museums free to the public but this nearby iconic gallery is perhaps the best complement to the Artist Residence, with cutting-edge contemporary work.

TATE BRITAIN Its South Bank sister gets all the plaudits, but the Tate's original home is the place for seeing British art, most notably its prized collection of Turners.

PASSIONATE ABOUT...
BEES

It's almost 20 years since Steve Benbow was sitting in London pining for the lanes and hedgerows of his native Shropshire. In those days he was a photo-journalist, but as a frustrated country boy he was inspired to re-create a little bit of the countryside in the city. So – encouraged by a bunch of bandit urban beekeepers he had met in New York – he set up some beehives on the roof of his funky flat in Tower Bridge.

Who knew, but bees thrive in the relatively warm, relatively green environment of London, where there are lots of trees and a diversity of plants unharmed by industrial farming methods, and before long Steve was adding more hives, and producing jars of complex, citrussy London honey. The London Honey Company – as it became known – has moved on quite a lot since those early days, setting up home in Bermondsey and spreading its hives around the country. It also also looks after hives for other people – for example, the Tate and the V&A – and produces honey on their behalf. Steve remains passionate about bees and the company still has plenty of hives in London, not least on a barge not far from his old Tower Bridge flat. Its sells honeycombs, honey in jars and all sorts of related products online (and on Saturdays from its southeast London HQ), and its honey features regularly on the menus of high-end London restaurants. It also runs regular beekeeping courses and in general flies a very active flag for urban beekeeping. Those New York bee bandits would be proud...

LONDON HONEY COMPANY Arch 7 Spa Business Park Dockley Road London SE16 3FJ 0207 394 7072 thelondonhoneycompany.co.uk

94DR

A sharply designed guesthouse with super-friendly hosts

Owners of 94DR, Paul and John, are the ideal hosts – friendly and incredibly knowledgeable, with a clear love for their city. They've created a stylish haven, a place to relax after sightseeing in Edinburgh, with 6 individually designed bedrooms named after malt whiskies, plus an additional 3–4 bunk space, aptly called 'Wee Dram', that can be booked alongside the Lagavulin or Tamdhu bedroom to provide the perfect family suite. They even have books, DVDs, games and an Xbox to help keep the little ones entertained.

The B&B takes its moniker from the property's address, and is modern yet traditional – period features mixing with soothing grey decor and high-quality fabrics. The bathrooms have power showers and underfloor heating, some with cast-iron rolltops. Stay in a 'Couture' room and enjoy a huge bed, seating area and uninterrupted views to Arthur's Seat; opt for 'Bespoke' and you get natural wool and tweeds. Breakfast takes centre stage, and no wonder, given Paul is a trained chef. Take a seat in the bright and airy orangery, then go ahead and order your Full Scottish or Eggs Royale. Produce is seasonal, local and organic, and there are daily specials to choose from. Prefer to sleep in? Breakfast boxes can be brought to the room, plus they also hold pop-up evening dining experiences twice a month.

A leisurely stroll (alternatively catch a bus or borrow one of the B&B's bikes free of charge) leads you to any number of Edinburgh attractions – the Castle, elegant New Town, the winding lanes of the Old Town, or the shops of Princes and George Streets. Back at 94DR, sit back with a drink from the honesty bar and let Paul and John recommend a restaurant for dinner.

EDINBURGH 94 Dalkeith Road Edinburgh EH16 5AF
0131 662 9265 94dr.co.uk
HOW MUCH? Double rooms with breakfast from £80.

"Staying with friends is how we want our guests to feel… we want to share our enthusiasm for Edinburgh and all it has to offer."

Paul and John, 94DR

What's nearby?

ARTHUR'S SEAT A craggy former volcano surrounded by the rugged moorland of Holyrood Park. Climb to the top for unsurpassed views of Edinburgh and around.

CRAIGMILLAR CASTLE Edinburgh's 'other castle' is well worth a visit, a grand old dame that is one of the finest ruined castles left standing in the country.

AIZLE RESTAURANT It's a 10-minute stroll to this thoroughly original restaurant. Select your ingredients and see what the chef comes up with!

Maids Head Hotel

This ancient hotel claims to be the oldest in the country, dating back to the 1100s, and without question it enjoys one of Norwich city centre's best positions – right by the cathedral, on the edge of the city's most atmospheric quarter, and very handy for its best shops, restaurants and pubs. Norwich is not blessed with loads of hotels, with the result being that those that are here often don't have to try too hard. The Maids Head is an exception, under new ownership and determined to raise its game, with an excellent 2-AA-rosette restaurant, a lovely wood-panelled bar and recent refurbishments to a lot of its 80-odd rooms. The good-value rooms are all shapes and sizes, varying from nicely furnished, contemporary, spacious doubles to more characterful beamed affairs, some with 4-posters. Bathrooms are good sizes, and whichever room you stay in comes with Freeview TV, tea- and coffee-making facilities, air-con and wifi – plus they've introduced iPads to guest rooms for in-house services and internet access.

NORFOLK 20 Tombland Norwich NR3 1LB 01603
209955 maidsheadhotel.co.uk
HOW MUCH? Classic double rooms from £90 a night,
including breakfast.

Salthouse Harbour Hotel

You might not immediately consider Ipswich as a weekend break destination. But this large boutique hotel, housed in an imaginatively converted old warehouse in the town's resurgent Waterfront district, might just make you change your mind, with 70 large, slickly designed rooms, many of which look out over the marina – squint, and on a sunny day you could be in Antibes. The public areas are classy but never dull, complete with eccentric modern furniture and splashes of colour, while the rooms cleverly blend the building's maritime legacy with a quirky, modern sensibility. The bathrooms are large and well-appointed, with power showers and high-end toiletries, while the rooms have cafetieres and nice coffee, flatscreen TVs, and some rooms have their own balconies. We reckon also that the ground-floor restaurant is one of the best places to eat in town, serving great-value set menus and light dishes at lunchtime, and more ambitious fare in the evening. Time – perhaps – to think again about Ipswich?

SUFFOLK Neptune Quay Ipswich IP4 1AX
01473 226789 salthouseharbour.co.uk
HOW MUCH? Double rooms with breakfast from £140
a night.

Brooks Hotel Edinburgh

Located in Edinburgh's funky West End, this contemporary, comfortable and yet well-priced city centre hotel is housed in a period property and has the warm welcome and comforts you ould expect from a privately-owned, family-run hotel – which, er, is what it is! It has no less than 46 guest rooms, all of them impressively kitted-out in bold colours and furnished with a mix of carefully chosen antiques and modern furniture – itself a good reflection of the neighbourhood vibe. The beds are comfy, there's a scattering of contemporary art, and bathrooms are equipped with fluffy towels, high-end showers and toiletries and powerful hairdryers. The hotel has an attractive courtyard at its heart, which is the perfect place for summer lazing while enjoying a drink from the downstairs honesty bar, and there's also a cosy lounge and handsome dining room in which to enjoy breakfast, which includes award-winning haggis from a local butcher. Not bad considering you're only a 5-minute walk from Princes Street.

EDINBURGH 70–72 Grove Street EH3 8AP
0131 228 2323 brooksedinburgh.com
HOW MUCH? Double rooms with breakfast £88–£119 a night.

University Rooms Cambridge

Students, eh? Hanging out with their mates, not much to do, loafing about in beautiful university cities like Cambridge, where they have the pick of the best places to stay, right in the heart of the city. The good news is that you too can stay in one of these beautiful old colleges during summer and other holidays, and you don't need to be a student – anyone can book. It's usually far cheaper than a city-centre hotel and, while we're not talking luxurious digs, you get to feel like you're one of the elite, at least for a few days. It's hard to say which college you'll end up in, but the rooms are generally comfortable and conveniently located. You'll eat in the college's dining hall (basically think Harry Potter), use the bar and stroll through the historic courtyards and gardens on your way to a day's sightseeing or a spot of punting on the river. It's a brilliant concept and really popular. And if you're heading to England's other principal historic university city, you should consider staying at University Rooms, Oxford.

CAMBRIDGESHIRE Cambridge University Colleges
universityrooms.com/en-GB/city/cambridge
HOW MUCH? Rates for double rooms start at around £40 a night.

Staying Cool at the Rotunda

Chic apartments for a sleek Brummie stay

The serviced apartments at Staying Cool may just be one of Birmingham city centre's best-kept secrets – as discreet as you like, with no signage indicating that it's a place to stay. And, in fact, Staying Very Cool at the Rotunda would be a more apt description, as the accommodation here is of rock-star quality, housed within the city's most iconic building – now a Grade II-listed landmark. With nearby Selfridges as your 'corner shop', and British designers given free rein in the classy interiors here, these are Instagram-ready city breaks in waiting.

The Rotunda's circular shape lends these idiosyncratic upper-floor apartments a 'cheese wedge' design, while the floor-to-ceiling windows make for great panoramic views of the city. The stylish bespoke furniture keeps everything refreshingly light and airy, even in the smaller studio apartments, and they all boast proper pocket-sprung king-size beds and high-end fixtures and fittings – Poggenpohl kitchens with dishwashers and washer/dryers, Illy espresso makers, Bose speakers, ultra-fast complimentary wifi and Sky TV… plus aromatherapy bathroom products and complimentary breakfast cereals.

The staff and service are slick and professional, and you also couldn't be more central for the many delights of England's second city, a sprawling metropolis that has been through a dramatic renaissance over recent years. It's not the first place you think of for a weekend away but its wide range of sights and great choice of restaurants make Birmingham well worth considering – and there's no better place from which to discover the multiple delights of Brum than Staying Cool.

BIRMINGHAM 150 New Street B2 4PA

0121 285 1250 stayingcool.com

HOW MUCH? Mini apartments (studios) from £99 a night, Clubman (1-bed) apartments from £129, Maxi (2-bed) from £179, Penthouse (2-bed with balcony) from £299.

"I never get tired of the views from this fabulous landmark. Everyone in Brum knows the Rotunda, and our interiors give a nod to its 1960s heritage. Chic and unique!"

Tracey Stephenson, Staying Cool

What's nearby?

THE DISKERY If you want shell out for some rare shellac, the self-proclaimed 'oldest record shop in the UK' is likely to have it. Well worth a browse.

CHUNG YING GARDEN A firm local favourite, this long-established Chinese claims to have the largest dim sum selection outside of Hong Kong.

MUSEUM OF THE JEWELLERY QUARTER A former workshop of jewellers Smith & Pepper, left much as it was when the workers left in the 1980s.

Twr y Felin Hotel

A contemporary Welsh hotel par excellence

Situated on the edge of Britain's smallest city, this former windmill dates back to 1806 but is anything but rustic, with public spaces that are seriously – and very deliberately – chic, with minimalist grey and black furnishings, subdued lighting and a wealth of contemporary art, most of it commissioned specially for the hotel and inspired by the St Davids Peninsula. The 21 guest rooms are similarly contemporary, and have robes, slippers, aromatherapy toiletries, satellite TV, Nespresso coffee makers as well as a mini fridge. The best room in house is the Windmill Tower suite, spread over 3 stories, with a spacious bedroom and lounge and a spiral staircase that takes you to the original observatory, located on the highest floor of the hotel and giving you spectacular 360-degree views of the whole peninsula, including the nearby coastline at Caerfai Bay. You couldn't be anywhere else in the world, and indeed Twr y Felin revels in its 'Welshness': the menu of its Blas restaurant (literally 'Taste' in Welsh) features local specialities such as Welsh lamb, crab, Laverbread and great Welsh cheeses.

All in all, Twr y Felin is a rare thing – a place where you can immerse yourself in Wales but in the most contemporary of surroundings. It's a good base for St Davids, a quaint sort of place, full of indy shops and cool cafés and galleries that makes a perfect venue for a weekend away. But it doesn't take long to see the city and the hotel is also well situated for exploring the best of Pembrokeshire – drop by the Oriel y Parc Visitor Centre opposite the hotel to pick up info on the region around, including the 186-mile long-Pembrokeshire Coast Path (just a 10-minute walk away from the hotel), and make the most of what is a breathtaking part of Wales.

PEMBROKESHIRE St Davids SA62 6QT
01437 725555 twryfelinhotel.com
HOW MUCH? Double rooms with breakfast from £200 a night.

"Contemporary luxury, fine dining and the warmest of Welsh welcomes – plus endless miles of coast path to explore."

Paula Ellis, Twr y Felin

What's nearby?

CAERFAI BAY Recently voted among the world's 100 best beaches, this is a beauty: clear jade-green water laps golden sands and steep cliffs make it a real suntrap.

THE SHED, PORTHGAIN An informal fish-and-chip restaurant in the renowned village of Porthgain, with great local fish and shellfish, landed daily and served within hours.

BLUE LAGOON Former slate quarry flooded by the sea, with improbably turquoise blue waters, into which brave thrill-seekers fling themselves regularly.

Bristol Harbour Hotel

Luxury, comfort... and a fair dash of style

In a city not really known for luxury hotels, the Bristol Harbour has arguably already taken the city's hotel scene to a new level. Bang in the city centre, having been fashioned out of not one but two of the city's landmark bank buildings – the Edwardian former Midland Bank and the splendid old Lloyd's Bank building, grade II-listed and inspired in the mid-19th-century by Sansovino's famous Library in Venice – it's as urban as Bristol gets, close to the busy Waterfront and within easy walking distance of pretty much everywhere in the city centre. The hotel's magnificent facade is carried through into the interior, built as a homage to the solid virtues of the banking world but now making a different sort of statement – of luxury, comfort and a fair dash of style.

The hotel has 42 guest rooms – most of them spacious and well-appointed cocoons in which you want to spend time, enjoying the views across the city centre and their big, comfy beds, Nespresso machines and en-suite bathrooms with rainfall showers and White Company toiletries. The Jetty restaurant is a crisp and contemporary place for dinner, with a tempting, mainly seafood- and fish-based menu that's moderately priced and attracts its fair share of non-residents. Afterwards you can retire to the funky Gold Bar for cocktails in between admiring the fabulous Sansovino Room, which is without question one of the city centre's most spectacular interiors, much used for weddings. Finally, the former bank vaults house a small gym and the hotel's spa, complete with plunge pool, hydrotherapy pool, sauna and steam room – perfect to round off a pampered weekend city break.

BRISTOL 49–55 Corn Street BS1 1HT 0117 2034445 bristol-harbour-hotel.co.uk
HOW MUCH? Superior double or twin rooms from £125 to £139 a night, deluxe doubles £145–£159, suites from around £200.

"Our hotel is the perfect platform to explore Bristol: from street art to street food, harbour to bridges, the city is buzzing with life."

Grant Callaghan, Bristol Harbour Hotel

What's nearby?

BANKSY TRAIL He doesn't live here any more, but Banksy has left a trace nearly everywhere; download a map from visitbristol.co.uk and see what you can find.

ST NICHOLAS MARKET The largest collection of indy retailers in the city, including a fantastic food section selling cheese, Moroccan tagines, charcuterie and more.

RIVERSTATION Former police station with a posh restaurant serving Modern European food and a bar that does a mean cocktail. The city's best terrace too.

UNUSUAL

Bored of boutique, tired of tipis? We're always on the look-out for unusual places to stay, from historic castles and windmills to travelling circus wagons, hideaway horseboxes and the odd Napoleonic fort or railway carriage.

Roch Castle, Pembrokeshire

Brooks Vintage Horseboxes

Glamping in the grounds of a Georgian manor house

One of the first things Carla and Andrew Brooks did when they took over the Pengethley Estate in 2016 was drop the word 'hotel' from the title. They wanted to give this handsome, Georgian manor a more homely feel, and while today they still offer comfortable hotel accommodation and a good restaurant food, it's all done with a studied air of informality that really defines the place. It's an atmosphere that also lends itself to the quirky style of the vintage horsebox glamping they have outside. If you want hotel-style facilities but all the fun of a glamping holiday, this Herefordshire haunt is just the place to come.

Set in a walled courtyard yards from the main house, the trio of 1970s horseboxes mirrors the dynamics of the hotel. Inside, the warm wood panelling of the bedsteads and the textures of the soft furnishings and wooden side-tables echo the decor in the hotel rooms, while the functionality of the fold-away bunk beds allows for extra space. Small touches like the equestrian-themed paintings on the wall and luxury toiletries show a real eye for detail. The horseboxes, of course, are only one part of what makes this place so special. The National Trust owns much of the land, but 15 acres still belong to the hotel and include not only a heated outdoor pool and a sauna in a walled garden but also their very own 2-acre vineyard. The very drinkable Pengethley Estate White is best enjoyed in the setting of the hotel dining room, where glampers are served breakfast and dinner each day as they gaze through the floor-to-ceiling bay window at the gorgeous views beyond. By no means your average glamping holiday.

HEREFORDSHIRE Brooks Country House Pengethley Park Near Ross-on-Wye HR9 6LL 01989 730211 brookscountryhouse.com
HOW MUCH? From £79 to £129 for 2 with breakfast.

"Guests love our vintage horseboxes: they are cute, comfy and quirky — and perfect if you love horses too."

Carla Brooks, Brooks Vintage Horseboxes

What's nearby?

LOUGHPOOL INN It's a mile or so through the meadows to this ancient and ineffably quaint, dog-friendly old pub, which serves local ales and excellent food.

CANOEING THE WYE There's nothing like paddling to make you feel like you're in the middle of nowhere with all the time in the world.

GOODRICH CASTLE The Wye Valley is castle country, and this originally Norman structure ticks all the boxes when it comes to evocative fortress ruins.

The Hadlow Tower

A magical Gothic tower in the heart of Kent

The word 'cottage' is used to cover all sorts of holiday properties in the UK, but in the case of The Hadlow Tower it doesn't quite do the job. One of the country's tallest and best-preserved Gothic follies, if there is a more fairytale place to stay in England (let alone Kent) then we have yet to find it. This 50m-high tower – also known as 'May's Folly' – has been converted into a unique 4-bedroom holiday home and has genuinely 360-degree views over the Kent countryside from its Rapunzel-like heights. It was built in the mid 19th century as part of a grand Gothic castle, the rest of which was demolished in the 1950s; an exhibition space on the ground floor has displays on the building's history and renovation. The Grade 1-listed tower now has accommodation spread over no fewer than 5 floors, connected by two spiral staircases and even an elevator that runs from bottom to top. There is a well-equipped kitchen and dining room on the first floor, a small bedroom, family bathroom and sitting room with log-burning stove on the second floor, plus a twin bedroom and two further doubles with en-suite bathrooms on the upper floors. The views are predictably fabulous from up here, and although guests can't actually go to the top of the tower, it is open to visitors every Thursday between April and September. There's a welcome pack of basic items to greet you on arrival, but you can also hire a chef for the night if you can't be bothered to cook, and owners Christian and Rebecca will even even lay on a string quartet or a magician for your entertainment if that is your desire. Could there be a better or more romantic place for an impromptu – and surprisingly easy – escape from London?

KENT Hadlow Castle High Street Hadlow Tonbridge TN11 0EG 07740 199928 thehadlowtower.co.uk
HOW MUCH? Weekly prices from £3000, weekends from £2000.

"The tower looks very different depending on the light, but the one thing that is constant is the smile on our guests' faces when they arrive and look up!"

Christian Tym, The Hadlow Tower

What's nearby?

HEVER CASTLE As the home of everyone from Anne Boleyn to the Astors, this moated Tudor manor house is packed full of fascinating history. Beautiful grounds too.

ALL SAINTS CHURCH TUDELEY No ordinary parish church - adorned as it is with 12 stained-glass windows by Marc Chagall, swirling with rich colour.

THE SPOTTED DOG Perhaps the perfect village inn, with great food, real local ales and a garden with stunning views over the surrounding Weald.

PASSIONATE ABOUT...
PADDLING

Mark Wilkinson – otherwise known as 'The Canoe Man' – is the ultimate rat-race escapee: he gave up his job as a financial advisor a decade ago to paddle the Norfolk Broads and hasn't looked back since, offering a wide range of mainly canoe-based activities from a range of locations on both the northern and southern Broads.

You can of course just rent a canoe and go your own way, and Mark offers straight canoe and kayak rental from a network of 6 hire sites across the Broads; and he will happily give you the lowdown on the best routes. But he also offers guided canoe and wildlife trails, bushcraft experiences and overnight canoe trips, either camping or staying at local B&Bs, as well as running a variety of themed trips, varying from Swallows & Amazons adventures for kids to river snorkelling and stand-up paddle-boarding. He even offers canoe tours of nearby Norwich – and also has plenty of bikes for rent from the CanoeMan headquarters by the bridge in boaty Wroxham, in the heart of the Broads National Park.

The watery wilderness of The Norfolk Broads is Britain's newest national park, but it's an unusual one in that it is best appreciated from the water. Mark's canoes are not only one of the most soothing ways to do this but they will also take you to places that other craft can't go.

THE CANOEMAN 10 Norwich Rd Wroxham Norfolk NR12 8RX 0845 496 9177 thecanoeman.com

Roch Castle

A spectacular Welsh castle

Frankly, there are few places to stay in Britain as gobsmackingly awesome as Roch Castle. It's a 12th-century Welsh castle – and looks like one, perched high above the Pembrokeshire landscape, with panoramic views over St Brides Bay and the Preseli Hills. Step inside to find the historical footprint intact, with the feel of a real castle but with luxurious contemporary interiors – so much so that the hotel was named as Wales' best B&B in 2018's National Tourism awards. There are just 6 en-suite bedrooms within its massive walls, all pared back and ultracontemporary but also making the most of the building's weird curves and funny-shaped windows, with wooden floors, stark modern bathrooms, satellite TVs, robes and slippers. The jewel of the castle, the Sun Room, located on the 4th floor, has floor-to-ceiling glass walls, an al fresco viewing platform and well-stocked honesty bar you can help yourself from. Breakfast is made to order, with Welsh laverbread and locally made honey on the menu, while for dinner there is a complimentary transfer to and from the excellent Blas Restaurant at their sister hotel Twr y Felin in St Davids.

Overall the atmosphere is intimate and secluded, and with so few rooms you can really feel like the castle is yours for the duration of your stay – and no request is too much trouble. The castle is surrounded by acres of private grounds, or, if you can bring yourself to leave, there are 186 miles of coast path to explore, not to mention the wildlife-rich islands of Ramsey, Skomer and Skokholm, which lie just off the coast. All in all, it is the ideal place for a fantasy castle break.

PEMBROKESHIRE Roch Pembrokeshire SA62 6AQ
01437 725566 rochcastle.com
HOW MUCH? Double rooms with breakfast from £220 a night.

"Spectacular and dramatic, Roch Castle offers an experience like no other, with a warm Welsh welcome thrown in."

Paula Ellis, Roch Castle

What's nearby?

NEWGALE BEACH One of the longest beaches in Wales, this 2-mile sweep is popular with surfers and just about anyone who knows a top beach when they see one.

ST DAVIDS Named after the patron saint of Wales, this is officially the UK's smallest city – and worth a visit for just that, plus its magnificent cathedral.

SKOMER ISLAND Wildlife reserve with huge numbers of seabirds, plus seals and the occasional dolphin, but it's the puffins for which it is best known.

The Nest Treehouse

Tucked away in a quiet corner of Devon woodland, The Nest is the ultimate romantic retreat, a luxuriously crafted treehouse suspended 9 metres above the ground in the branches of a 130-year-old English oak tree. With a wood-burning stove, it's a cosy place to stay – the perfect honeymoon hideaway, Valentine's Day or birthday treat, or just a peaceful venue for couples who fancy a hermit-like break in a beautiful yet accessible part of the country. The treehouse has a double bed, living area and fully equipped kitchen and bathroom; there is plenty of wood for the stove, a TV and DVD and lots of games and books for rainy days, but no wifi, which is quite in keeping with this place. The only tweets that are likely to disturb you here are those of the dawn chorus. It's an environmentally friendly option, with recycling and composting on-site, and it is easily accessible by train from nearby Honiton; produce is available from a nearby farm. In short you could spend a lovely break here, emerging occasionally to sit on the balcony and enjoy an al fresco meal or glass of wine while savouring its peace and solitude.

> **DEVON** Combe Raleigh Near Honiton EX14 4UJ
> 01404 549430 treeholidays.co.uk
> **HOW MUCH?** Minimum 2 nights from £298 – rates include logs, electricity, gas, towels and linen.

YHA Grinton Lodge

The YHA snagged an absolute beauty when it bought this 200-year-old former gentleman's shooting lodge high above Swaledale in North Yorkshire. The views from most of the rooms are breathtaking – right across the heather-clad moors and down the dale – while the building has retained much of its grand period detail, including castellated walls and a set of antlers in the lounge. Most of the rooms follow the usual hostel configuration, sleeping 2–8 people, and while showers and toilets aren't en-suite there are enough to go around at busy times. Some of the rooms and bathrooms are actually pretty nice – certainly better than you have any right to expect at these prices – and there's no institutional feel at what is one of the Yorkshire Dales National Park's best budget options. They also let you camp in the grounds, while in a bosky grove next door there is a series of wooden camping pods. The nearest pub is a 15-minute walk downhill in the hamlet of Grinton, and there are wonderful off-road bike routes on your doorstep.

> **NORTH YORKSHIRE** Richmond Swaledale DL11 6HS
> 0345 3719636 yha.org.uk
> **HOW MUCH?** Dormitory beds from £10 a night, private rooms from £29, pods from £39.

Walcot Hall Glamping

Walcot Hall is a fabulous country estate, perfectly placed for exploring the beautiful Shropshire Hills but also a glorious place to stay in its own right, with a Georgian house at its heart and, in addition to a number of comfy self-catering cottages, no fewer than 10 different glamping hideouts spread around the 30-acre woodland site. There are a wide range of options – 4 yurts, a couple of shepherd's huts, a romantic gypsy caravan, 2 'showman's' caravans, even a converted fire truck. Some of these have their own facilities, the yurts share a converted henhouse loo, others use long-drop toilets in the woods. All are exquisitely fitted out in a rustic, comfy style with huge beds, kitchenettes, BBQs, woodburners and the like. The village pub – the Powis Arms – is owned and run by the Hall and serves good food (and has camping during summer), while the grounds have a couple of lakes, fishing and rowing boats to play in – plus a nearby stables that can take you out for a hack on the local bridleways. Glamping heaven.

SHROPSHIRE Walcot Hall Lydbury North SY7 8AZ
01588 680570 walcothall.com
HOW MUCH? Glamping options from £120 to £200 for a 2-night weekend.

Brooks Rooftop Rockets

Despite the name, these shiny, bubble caravans did not rocket their way on to this Bristol rooftop – they were hauled here by a crane – but their compact rooftop garden could hardly be more central. Part of the excellent Brooks Guesthouse, which occupies the rest of the building, they're the shining, spitting, image of their American counterparts but redesigned inside to more modern specifications, with flatscreen TVs, iPod-compatible radios and an en-suite bathroom with a blissfully powerful shower, and overall a modern decor that echoes the teal interiors of the bedrooms and bar downstairs. This is an upmarket B&B, after all, so expect fresh towels, posh toiletries and hospitality trays with fresh organic juices. The cityscape views are fab, and it's a quick tumble down the stairs and out on to St Nicholas Street, a hot spot for the city's independent shops, cafés and boutiques. The guesthouse has an honesty bar, with local ales and ciders, wines and snacks, and breakfast is served in the dining room downstairs every morning.

BRISTOL St Nicholas Street BS1 1UB 0117 930 0066
brooksguesthousebristol.com
HOW MUCH? Rockets start at £99 a night for 2 people, including breakfast.

The Chapel

Exquisitely renovated chapel in a picturebook village

Situated in the picture-book-pretty village of Ubley, a little way south of both Bristol and Bath on the edge of Somerset's Mendip Hills, this exquisitely renovated late-19th-century Methodist church is a one-in-a-million find. Not only is it a brilliant conversion of a beautiful old building, oozing character and mod cons all at the same time, it's also as comfortable a holiday cottage as you could find. It does a great job of retaining the innate character of the chapel, with a mix of rich Victorian colours, accented with copper and brass, and a vast main living space complete with the original organ and pulpit and stained-glass windows. A cast-iron candelabra hangs from the ceiling, adding a contemporary character but one which is perfectly in tune with the building. Even the glass-and-steel mezzanine has a sense of Victorian engineering, and similarly blends old and new, with a perfectly pitched baby grand piano and Sonos sound system that will appeal to musicians and music-lovers alike. There's also a 52-inch flatscreen TV with YouView, wifi throughout, and a spacious kitchen suited to both cooking and enjoying big dinners. Upstairs in the rafters there are 2 sumptuous double bedrooms and a period-style bathroom with a copper rolltop bath and a generously proportioned rainfall shower. The Chapel really is the perfect country bolthole for 2 couples or a small group of friends who fancy somewhere a little bit different to stay while still enjoying a touch of modern-day luxury. It's also a perfect place from which to explore a beautiful part of Somerset, surrounded by the Mendips, and with a nearby footpath so you can leave your car keys in the drawer.

SOMERSET The Street Ubley BS40 6PD
07813 850872 ringobellscomptonmartin.co.uk
HOW MUCH? From £200 a night in low season to £250 a night in high season.

"A truly unique space, The Chapel offers a luxury weekend with a difference, deep in the Somerset countryside."

Luca Leonard, The Chapel

What's nearby?

MENDIP HILLS You can walk right into the Mendip Hills from The Chapel – and why wouldn't you? Surprisingly rugged in places, they are the jewel in Somerset's crown.

RING O' BELLS Situated in nearby Compton Martin, this cosy country pub is owned by the same people as The Chapel, and serves local Butcombe ales and good food.

CHEW VALLEY LAKE You can sail, walk, birdwatch and more at this local beauty spot, which is the largest stretch of inland water in the Southwest, no less.

Cley Windmill

A gorgeous converted windmill by the sea

It was a brilliant idea to turn this old windmill into a B&B – and a very successful venture it has proved to be too. Fabulously restored by Julian and Carolyn Godlee over a decade ago, the windmill sits among the reedy marshes on the edge of the village of Cley and is simply charming, with a sublime location right on the edge of the Norfolk Wildlife Trust reserve of Cley Marshes, perfectly placed for the delights of the rest of the North Norfolk Coast.

There are 8 guest rooms in all – 6 in the windmill itself and 2 in outbuildings – plus the Dovecote, a 2-bedroom self-catering cottage, and the Old Cart Shed, a self-catering suite sleeping 2 adults and 2 children. The rooms are all different, and well furnished in a sympathetic country-chic style, with rugs, kilim cushions and whitewashed walls, and equipped with en-suite bathrooms. The upper Wheel Room isn't for the faint-hearted, as you have to climb a ladder for access, but it has spectacular views over the coast and marshes. Immediately below, the Stone Room has its own private section of the windmill's circular balcony, making it an exciting place for a family of 4 to sleep.

The outbuildings are equally comfortable and well-appointed, and also have access to the mill's ground-floor sitting room and beamed dining room where they serve great breakfasts and 3-course evening meals too if you want them – there are plenty of good places to eat along this coast but it's nice not to have to get in the car for a change. The mill is also licensed for weddings, and you can book the whole place if you fancy a rather fabulous house party... indeed there might just be nowhere better to spend a memorable New Year's Eve with friends.

NORFOLK The Quay Cley-next-the-Sea NR25 7RP
01263 740209 cleywindmill.co.uk
HOW MUCH? Double rooms with breakfast £77–£99 per person; self-catering cottage £425–£570 a week. Evening meals £32.50 per person.

"This lovely windmill never fails to take your breath away. It's a unique and magical place to relax and unwind – we just love it!"

Carolyn Goodlee, Cley Windmill

What's nearby?

CLEY MARSHES Literally on your doorstep, the salt and freshwater marshes, reedbeds and coastal shingle at Cley have the evocative beauty so typical of this coast.

ANCHOR INN Just the other side of Blakeney, this is one of the best places to sample Morston's wonderful mussels, along with other good food and local ales.

WIVETON HALL CAFE Is this 'Normal for Norfolk'? Well luckily for us, it is on this part of the coast, with lovely lunches and weekend breakfasts. Dog-friendly too.

Filter House

This spacious single-storey property is an Art Deco gem – originally a pumping and filtering station for the local Cornish water board and rescued from dereliction just over a decade ago. Quiet, secluded and brilliantly located for some of the best bits of Cornwall, it overlooks a small tree-fringed lake and a large garden abounding with wildlife, which frequently makes incursions from the woodland beyond. Some of the original features remain, including the fabulous Crittall windows, but otherwise the property has been sensitively restored with 1930s-era furnishings that can make you feel as if you have stepped into an Agatha Christie mystery. There are 3 spacious bedrooms, a music room with piano, a vintage kitchen decked out in black and cream and a 1930s-style bathroom. More contemporary features include a washer/dryer, decent wifi, satellite TV, a Bluetooth music system and underfloor heating, making the house a perfect retreat even in the winter months and on rainy days.

CORNWALL Ladock Truro TR2 4PG 01637 878725
periodholidaylets.com
HOW MUCH? From £650 to £1400 a week.

A Secret Garden

Chris and Michelle Whalley are quite a team – specialists in creating comfortable and quirky glamping experiences, the latest of which is their very own Secret Garden, Located in the small village of Blean, near Canterbury, this tiny cabin hideaway has its own private and very secluded garden, alongside a popular treehouse and log cabin. Designed to blend in with the garden and its leafy surroundings, it's a cosy and romantic retreat for couples, with a comfortable king-sized pocket-sprung mattress tucked into the framework of a wooden pod complete with glass walls and glass ceiling. A wood-burner and underfloor heating keep you toasty, there's a gas hob for making a cup of tea or basic meals, and a welcome pack with breakfast stuff and other goodies, including a bottle of Prosecco to enjoy in the 2-person hot tub. There is a flushing toilet and a shower equipped with Neal's Yard toiletries and fluffy towels, and when night falls you can light the outdoor firepit, barbecuing your dinner and toasting marshmallows to your heart's content.

KENT 8 Honey Hill Blean Near Canterbury CT2 9JP
07739 850975 kent-cottage-holidays.co.uk
HOW MUCH? Prices from £168 a night, including a generous welcome pack.

Railway Retreats

Overlooking the platform at Northiam – a stop on the popular Kent & East Sussex Railway – Railway Retreats gives you the chance to sleep in your very own converted railway carriage, right up close to the track of a working steam railway. It's an excellent base from which to explore this part of Kent and East Sussex – you can just jump on the train to nearby Bodiam Castle or Tenterden and Chapel Down vineyard. But it's also a unique place to stay, and definitely more of a first-class than a third-class experience. The beautifully converted carriage sleeps up to 6 people in comfort, there is a fully functional kitchen, an open-plan lounge and dining area and a glass balcony for an elevated view of the steam railway and the surrounding countryside. Of 2 double bedrooms, one has an en-suite bathroom, plus there's a bunk bedroom for kids and a family bathroom. They've recently added other options too – a brake van and a goods wagon that can each sleep 2 in cosy comfort, making this place a romantic retreat as well as a perfect choice for young families.

EAST SUSSEX Station Road Northiam TN31 6QT
01797 253850 railwayretreats.co.uk
HOW MUCH? £300–£450 for two nights, £375–£900 a week – depending on season.

Solent Forts

If you've ever been on a ferry to the Isle of Wight, you'll have passed the Solent Forts, built during Napoleonic times to defend the south coast and now arguably one of the most unique places to stay in the UK, refurbished to a high standard with not a hammock or a ship's biscuit in sight. Spitbank Fort has 8 huge suites, all of them spectacular, with super-king-size beds, amazing bathrooms and uninterrupted views of the Solent, while just across the water is No Man's Fort, which is 3 times the size and has no fewer than 22 bedrooms. It's a slightly odd feeling knowing that you can't just up and leave, but that's really the point. You can eat in the restaurant, and afterwards relax in one of several bars or gather on deck around a firepit and gaze out to sea – there's a large heated pool on Spitbank and 2 hot tubs on No Man's Fort. There are also lots of activities on offer, including rib rides, fishing, kayaking or even practising the art of 'sabrage' – that's how to open a bottle of champagne with a sabre for those who didn't go to public school!

HAMPSHIRE Solent Ports Office Gunwharf Quay
Portsmouth PO1 3TZ 023 9280 9767 solentforts.com
HOW MUCH? Double rooms from £299 a night, or take a fort exclusively from £8000.

Roulotte Retreat

Adults-only 'Caravans of Love' in the Scottish Borders

Always thought you had a bit of gypsy blood in you, or are you just a little caught up in the romance of drifting around the world in a traditional hand-carved wooden caravan? Well Roulotte Retreat may just be for you. The same goes for yoga lovers and just plain lovers at this seriously sexy retreat in the Scottish Borders, which also offers yoga, walking, horseriding and cycling, and is an ideal adults-only getaway for 2, or for groups of friends.

There are 7 sumptuous roulottes (traditional French wooden caravans) to choose from, 6 of them sleeping 2 people and one for up to 4. They each have their own highly individual colour and decor scheme, and all are immaculately hand-finished and boast bags of character. There are just enough creature comforts, like a proper en-suite shower and toilet, kitchen and sumptuous bedroom, but no TV, leaving you free to focus on relaxing in your cosy hideaway in a wildflower-strewn meadow and getting to know each other a little better. Two of the roulottes – Gitana and Zenaya – have their own secret hot tubs so that you and your beloved can soak under the stars – and you can see plenty of those in the dark skies in this part of the world. Finally there's also an option for larger groups – Horseshoe cottage and Ruby, a bowtop Romany caravan –located in their own wild woodland garden and ideal for a longer break. Children are also allowed to stay in the cottage, as are dogs.

The owners also host small weddings for couples looking for something unusual for their special day – indeed for romantics who wish to run away to get married, you can elope here and they will help you organise a completely magical stress-free event.

SCOTTISH BORDERS Bowden Near Melrose TD6 0SU
0845 094 9729 roulotteretreat.com
HOW MUCH? Prices start at £105 a night.

"Our vision was for somewhere to escape and enjoy time and space together – just the two of you or with friends. It's just magical."

Avril and Alan, Roulotte Retreat

What's nearby?

MELLERSTAIN HOUSE One of Scotland's finest stately homes and a rare example of a house worked on by William Adam and his more famous son Robert – indeed it's one of the most complete examples of Adam's work in the UK. There are fabulous period gardens too, and 3 holiday cottages in the grounds.

THE HORSESHOE INN Historic inn that styles itself as an en vogue 'restaurant with rooms', serving superb food based on local ingredients.

ABBOTSFORD HOUSE The renovated former home of Walter Scott is a fantastic memorial to Scotland's best-known writer– and it has an excellent café to boot!

The Windmill Suffolk

The ultimate romantic stargazing escape

Everyone loves a windmill, so we were especially excited to discover this converted historic corn mill, which towers over the rural fields of Suffolk. It's a labour of love that sits at the end of the garden of Natalie Roberts and her very handy husband Steve, one of the last windmills to be built in England and a stunning conversion that has been shortlisted for a number of architectural awards. The furniture has been curved to follow the contours of the building, making it a quirky as well as a very contemporary place to escape to, just 2 miles north of the tourist honeypot of Lavenham but a world away in terms of peace and quiet. You can retire to your rooftop eyrie at the end of the day and enjoy 360-degree views from its supremely comfy top-floor room, complete with curved sofas, telescopes for star-gazing and a wine fridge to keep the traipsing up and down stairs to a minimum. There's also a 47-inch TV (curved, naturally), should you get bored with the views.

There truly are worse ways of spending the evening than gazing out over the Suffolk countryside as the sun goes down – and down below there are 2 highly contemporary double bedrooms with a sumptuous bathroom in between, well stocked with Elemis toiletries and a gorgeous oval bath and rainfall shower in which to enjoy them. A ground floor room completes the picture, kitted out as a curvy kitchen-diner with all the high-end utilities you could possibly need – plus there's an outdoor terrace for a lazy start to the day before trekking off across the fields. Rural bliss, then, less than a 2-hour drive from London.

SUFFOLK Lavenham Road Cockfield IP30 0HX
01284 828458 thewindmillsuffolk.com
HOW MUCH? From £650 for 2 nights to £1750 a week for 2 adults.

"Whether you are looking for a romantic hideaway or fun-filled time off with friends, there's nowhere quite like our windmill!"

Natalie Roberts, The Windmill Suffolk

What's nearby?

BURY ST EDMUNDS Head up to Bury for its ruined priory, wanderable old centre and lots of good places to eat, notably the Angel Hotel or tiny Pea Porridge.

THE GREYHOUND Our favourite among Lavenham's many pubs, an unpretentious place but one that serves really good food. Perfect for a romantic brunch.

ST PETER & ST PAUL One of the great 'wool churches' of East Anglia, Lavenham's huge parish church is a fantastic example of the Perpendicular style.

YHA St Briavels Castle

A haunted castle on the edge of the Forest of Dean

It's not every day you get to stay in a Grade I-listed historic monument, let alone one that's over 800 years old. Yet at St Briavels you not only get all this but at a budget price too, as well as a tremendous location on the edge of the Forest of Dean. The nice thing about YHA St Briavels is that you're always aware that you're staying in a castle, with characterful rooms that pay great respect to the building, from the mysterious 'Oubliette' room (ask about the contents of the dungeon below) to the State Apartment with its so-called 'King's Seat', as well as 2 spacious dormitories at the top of each of the castle's 2 towers. So in many ways, it's a boutique hostel experience, but in others it''s one of the YHA's more basic hostels, with bunk beds and shared bathrooms, and no private rooms at all. There is also no TV, and wifi is only available in the public spaces, so you really do have to make your own entertainment – which is not that hard in a building straight out of Camelot. To that end, the chapel has been turned into a family lounge, with dressing-up, toys and books, while the main banqueting hall is an amazing dining space that hosts medieval banquets and communal supper clubs.

It's a great spot for families above all. Beyond the castle's sturdy walls, the Forest of Dean and the beautiful Wye Valley are just a few miles distant, with lots of outdoor activitirs, plus there are excellent kids' attractions within easy driving distance, from the homespun Puzzlewood theme park to the old mine workings of Clearwell Caves, plus a branch of the high-wire adventure outfit, Go Ape.

GLOUCESTERSHIRE St Briavels Lydney GL15 6RG
0345 371 9042 yha.org.uk
HOW MUCH? Dorm beds from £14.99, private rooms from £79.99, family rooms from £69.99.

"St Briavels is an excellent base for exploring the Forest of Dean and Wye Valley."

Lucy Duszczak, YHA

What's nearby?

CLEARWELL CAVES Mines rather than caves, but well worth exploring, either on regular tours or in smaller groups that go deeper.

PUZZLEWOOD A lovely woodland site full of magical paths, nooks and corners that is said to be the inspiration for Tolkien's Middle Earth, no less!

GEORGE INN St Briavels' village pub welcomes dogs, has an atmospheric old interior and a nice garden and serves large portions of homely pub grub.

PUBS, INNS & RESTAURANTS

Cool Places loves to celebrate the survival and revival of that great British institution, the pub, and in particular those places that offer rooms, food and drink and do it wonderfully well. Quintessential village pub, old coaching inn, city tavern, restaurant with rooms – whatever it's called, if it's good, it's cool as far as we're concerned.

Artist Residence, Oxfordshire

The Felin Fach Griffin

No better place to do nothing in glorious surroundings

'The simple things in life done well' is the motto of this rather special inn – and we reckon it's perfectly suited to this gastropub with rooms, situated on the edge of the Brecon Beacons National Park. It lives up to its billing in every way possible. There are 7 very comfortable rooms above a restaurant that is one of the best in the region. It's also a proper pub, with all that that implies, serving well-priced, well-kept local ales – a bit of a haven for local drinkers and a welcoming place for everyone else, with a roaring fire in winter. And dogs and children are very definitely welcomed.

The rooms are all different in size and style, but all have big beds, Roberts Radios, homemade biscuits, fresh flowers and posh toiletries. There are no TVs, and they make a thing of that, so embrace the good old days and read a book. Served in the library, breakfasts are delicious, and a good indicator of the quality of the dinner you'll enjoy – namely seasonally influenced dishes and ingredients from the Welsh borders, whether it's beef or lamb, local cheese, or herbs, fruit and veg picked from their own kitchen garden. There's no shortage of things to do during the day either, to work up that appetite, from a hard day's walking to book-browsing in Hay or just pottering around nearby Brecon, Abergavenny or Crickhowell.

Really we can't think of many places that are better for a Welsh country weekend away – and if you like the style, it's good to know that the owners use the same motto for the other hotels they run in Cornwall – the Gurnard's Head near Zennor and Old Coastguard in Mousehole.

POWYS Felin Fach Brecon LD3 0UB 01874 620111
felinfachgriffin.co.uk
HOW MUCH? Double rooms £135–£175, including breakfast; DB&B £192.50–£232.50.

"At the foot of The Brecon Beacons, we are a welcome sight for travellers – still to this day watering and feeding those exploring this stunning landscape."

Charles Inkin, Felin Fach Griffin

What's nearby?

LLYN Y FAN FACH Accessible by way of a hike uphill alongside mini cascading waterfalls, this dammed lake is one of the most magical sights in Wales.

CRICKHOWELL This small market town has a boho vibe and plenty of indy shops and restaurants and is often featured among the Top 10 best places to live in Britain.

ABERGAVENNY FOOD FESTIVAL *The Guardian* famously reckoned that "Abergavenny is to food, as Cannes is to film" – and every September, it is!

The Pointer

There are many reasons to consider The Pointer as a brilliant place for a break from London. First of all, it's not far to come – about an hour by car from certain parts of north London; it's situated in a pretty hilltop Buckinghamshire village; and they have 4 comfy guest rooms in a cottage across the street, stylishly decorated in a rustic yet contemporary fashion, with roomy bathrooms with robes, nice toiletries and powerful rainfall showers that you won't want to get out of. Dogs are allowed in the ground-floor rooms, and the restaurant is a pure field-to-fork place to eat, with a short, always-changing menu deliberately focused on produce from the farm – rare-breed beef and pork, suckling pig and lamb and fresh seasonal vegetables; they even have their own butcher's shop next door. It's all beautifully presented and the service fab, with an emphasis on high-quality fresh ingredients, and, above all, taste – and the menu changes often enough to make it worth coming back regularly. Which you will want to do.

BUCKINGHAMSHIRE 27 Church Street Brill HP18 9RT 01844 238339 thepointerbrill.co.uk
HOW MUCH? Double rooms from £160 a night including breakfast.

The Buckinghamshire Arms

Location, location, location. The Bucks Arms would be a nice pub wherever it was, a cosy old building serving excellent food to hungry locals and tourists, and with 4 great-value rooms upstairs for those who want to stay over. In fact it sits right outside the Jacobean splendour of Blickling Hall in North Norfolk, so it is a bit more special than that – 2 of its rooms enjoy views over the hall's grand frontage while the other 2 look out over the vast expanse of Blickling's country park and grounds. Part of the same group that owns the Black Boys in nearby Aylsham and the Recruiting Sergeant in the Broads, the rooms are simply furnished but generous sizes, all with en-suite bathrooms, and 3 have 4-poster beds just to help you get into the spirit of this historic location all the more. The pub serves excellent breakfasts and a full menu at lunch and dinner times – smoked haddock rarebit, a lovely Cromer crab salad or just good steaks, burgers and fish and chips – which is just perfect after strolling Blickling's sumptuous grounds.

NORFOLK Blickling Aylsham NR11 6NF 01263 732133 bucksarms.co.uk
HOW MUCH? Double rooms with breakfast from £100 a night.

The Fox at Willian

Situated in a pretty Hertfordshire village, this revamped pub does everything a country inn should do: it has a set of guest rooms, recently decorated in a crisp contemporary style; it serves excellent food that's very moderately priced; and it's not a bad place to pop into for a pint either. The Fox's style is the same as its brethren in the excellent Anglian Country Inns group, with 8 rooms in all – 5 'garden rooms' and 3 rooms in the main building, one of which has a free-standing bath. All have king-size beds, good wifi, Freeview TVs, air-conditioning and bathrooms with aromatherapy toiletries and rainfall showers. Dogs are allowed in the garden rooms, where they get treats, bowls and suchlike, and the pub serves a simple bar menu and a slightly fancier menu in the spacious and airy restaurant behind. Both are relaxed places to eat, with stripped floors, Lloyd Loom chairs and lots of light, and the food is excellent. It's the perfect escape for tired folk from the Smoke to recharge their batteries at the weekend.

HERTFORDSHIRE Willian SG6 2AE 01462 480233
foxatwillian.co.uk
HOW MUCH? Double rooms from £85 to £130 a night, including breakfast. Dogs £10.

The Angel Inn

The Stammers family have run the Angel Inn since 1913, first as tenants and more recently as owners since Brian Stammers finally bought the pub in 1994, It's now run by son Andrew and daughter Lorraine, and was Norfolk Pub of the Year a few years ago – and quite right too, for they get all the essentials right at this 17th-century coaching inn, right by the A12 just south of Norwich. It's not big, and not clever, but just a great family-run country pub with comfy rooms run by passionate folk who couldn't make you feel more at home – providing hearty and wholesome pub grub in the bar and dining room and managing to maintain the function and feel of a proper village local at the same time. As a village, Larling was somewhat messed up by the dualling of the A12 years ago, but the pub survived and thrived and is nowadays one of the most welcoming places to eat, drink and sleep for miles around, serving generous breakfasts that are as excellent as their lunches and dinners, and adding a few tent pitches in the field across the road during the summer.

NORFOLK Larling NR16 2QU 01953 717963
angel-larling.co.uk
HOW MUCH? Double rooms with breakfast from £90 a night.

The Sun Inn

A proper pub in the heart of Constable Country

If you're the sort of person who likes a proper pub, preferably situated on a proper village high street and serving good local ales alongside hearty, locally sourced food, then there's a good chance that The Sun Inn will be your kind of place. Situated in the picturesque village of Dedham on the Essex–Suffolk border, The Sun Inn also has a set of cosy rooms upstairs which means that you don't have to go home at the end of the evening, and can wake up refreshed and ready not only to enjoy The Sun's excellent breakfast but also to explore the countryside around. The pub has bikes for the use of guests and can arrange boat trips on the river, and the rooms are a mixture of contemporary and traditional and very comfortable. Most have been recently refurbished and have comfy beds, wifi and posh toiletries in the bathrooms. Each room is different; some are very spacious with large en-suite bathrooms and all but one have king-size or super–king-size beds. Downstairs, the Italian-influenced food is also a central part of the offering, with lunch and dinner served every day; the menu changes monthly and they add a roast on Sundays, and you can enjoy your food in the pleasant beer garden outside on sunny days. But The Sun is also very much the pub, with plenty of locals regularly dropping by for a pint, with or without their thirsty dogs.

In short, we can't think of too many nicer – or easier – places for weary city folk to stay than Dedham, and The Sun Inn does very much what it says on the tin: good food, comfortable rooms, and a warm welcome. What more could you ask for?

ESSEX High Street Dedham CO7 6DF 01206 323351
thesuninndedham.com
HOW MUCH? Doubles rooms with breakfast £145 a night, DB&B £200 per room.

"We want The Sun Inn to be an honest, authentic and welcoming pub that constantly evolves – an antidote to bland!"

Piers Baker, The Sun Inn

What's nearby?

FLATFORD MILL An easy walk across the meadows from Dedham takes you to the site of Constable's most famous painting – or you could get there by a boat on the river.

MUNNINGS MUSEUM On the edge of the village, the former home of Alfred Munnings shows the work of this underrated Victorian painter.

BETH CHATTO GARDENS The glorious lush and diverse gardens of the celebrated gardener and plantswoman, who died in 2018, are just a short drive away.

The Boathouse

Boutique rooms and woodland lodges by the water

Mike and Belinda Minors run the excellent Waterside restaurant a few miles up the road, so they know a thing or two about feeding hungry punters in beautiful Broadside locations. Thus it made perfect sense for them to take over this rundown pub on the banks of Ormesby Broad a few years ago and transform it into a restaurant, wedding venue and boutique B&B, with some well-appointed self-catering woodland lodges for good measure.

The large bar overlooks the water, and there are comfy chairs by the fire if all you want is a drink. But it's the rooms upstairs that we like best of all, because waking up here is the best way to enjoy the Boathouse's perfect position by Ormesby Broad. There are 6 rooms in all, funkily furnished, cosy, well-appointed and well-priced, and 4 have views or partial views over the water. There are 2 suites, one of which is very spacious with a downstairs sitting room and upstairs bedroom, and all are decorated to a high standard, with free wifi throughout, tea- and coffee-making facilities in each room and beautifully decked-out bathrooms. Downstairs the restaurant is large but has a few cosy nooks, while the wedding venue is a self-contained unit off to the side, with its own waterside decking and gazebo and eating area – great if you're getting married here, but even better if you're not and don't want to be knee-deep in wedding guests in the bar or fighting for a table for dinner. Finally, the lodges have lovely oak floors and rustic cedar panelling and are comfy 2-bedroom affairs, equipped with a sitting room and kitchenette and verandahs from which you can watch the sun setting over the water in the evening. Broadland bliss, we reckon.

NORFOLK Ormesby Broad Eels Foot Road Ormesby St Michael NR29 3LP 01493 730342
theboathouseormesbybroad.co.uk
HOW MUCH? Rooms and suites £80–£135 a night, plus breakfast from £6.95. Lodges sleep 4, 6 and 8 people and cost £125 to £175 a night depending on the lodge and time of year.

"We love the location of the Boathouse nestling on the banks of stunning Ormesby Broad and are proud to be the owners of such a truly unique Norfolk venue."

Mike Minors, The Boathouse

What's nearby?

HORSEY MERE As far east as you can go by boat and still be in the Broads, this lovely expanse of water was celebrated by John Betjeman in his poem 'East Anglian Bathe'.

FAIRHAVEN WATER GARDEN A glimpse of the swampy wilderness that makes up much of the Broads, with creeks and shady paths leading down to its own Broad.

WINTERTON-ON-SEA A wonderful sandy beach (open to dogs year-round), backed by dunes that stretch all the way to Horsey, and with a decent beach café too.

The Salutation Inn

Inn, Restaurant with rooms? The Salutation is both those things, really, a classy revamp of a 17th-century pub built around an excellent fine-dining restaurant and a relaxed café. The food is great – it's the reason many visit – but they're also right on the money with the whole shelter-for-the-night bit, with 4 bright, spacious rooms and 2 suites, all turned out in crisp tones, featuring very comfortable beds (handmade locally) and en-suite bathrooms with upscale toiletries. There's no bar any more, but we like the first-floor 'Galley', where guests can grab a tea, coffee or a snack at any time of day or night, and – along with the excellent service – this is the kind of touch that makes it no surprise that the Salutation won *Food & Travel* magazine's 'Best UK B&B' award recently. Topsham itself is a nice place to stay, an old heritage port, handy both for Exeter and the coast at Exmouth, while the GlassHouse cafe in the Inn's courtyard makes a cheery port of call from breakfast through to afternoon tea.

DEVON 68 Fore Street Topsham Exeter EX3 0HL
01392 873060 salutationtopsham.co.uk
HOW MUCH? Double rooms with breakfast from £135 a night, suites from £195 a night.

The Alma Inn

Bang in the centre of Harwich's port, this salty old inn has been updated without losing any of its backstreet charm. The pub is still a proper local, but the food is some of the best you'll find plus a handful of rooms upstairs makes it a comfy place to stay too. There are 5 rooms plus a 2-bedroom family suite that is sympathetically renovated in line with the character of the building: re-purposed ships' timbers complement the beams and creaky floors, and the exposed brick walls with sea-faring charts place you firmly in maritime Essex. As for the food, the Alma deliberately doesn't describe itself as a gastropub, but the tucker is great – with local oysters and lobsters (they chalk their various sizes on the board every day), fish and chips and seafood sharing platters, along with a variety of well-hung, locally sourced steaks – like the lobster, enjoyed very simply with chips. They also make their own sausages, which can also be enjoyed as part of an excellent Full English the next day.

ESSEX 25 King's Head Street Harwich CO12 3EE
01255 318681 almaharwich.co.uk
HOW MUCH? Double rooms £95–£115 a night including breakfast; 2-bed suite £150 a night.

Wiveton Bell

Just a mile from the North Norfolk coast, the lights of the Wiveton Bell are a beacon of welcome on a dark winter's night, while in summer both the pub and garden are a magnet for walkers, birdwatchers and everyone else enjoying this beautiful part of the country. It's also got 6 irresistible rooms to tumble into once you've exhausted the joys of its beamed bar and restaurant, each with big beds, stylish shower rooms, flatscreen TVs with Freeview and all sorts of room treats (including a small bottle of Prosecco for you to feel properly pampered on arrival), mineral water and juice, and a continental breakfast hamper delivered to your room each morning along with a choice of newspaper. Perhaps the nicest thing about the Bell, though, is that the owners are keen to maintain it as a proper pub, somewhere locals and visitors stop by with their dogs. As such, it's a thoroughly relaxing place to stay – walking, cycling, and of course eating. The food they serve is locally sourced, seasonal and delicious, and they have 2 AA rosettes to prove it.

NORFOLK Blakeney Road Wiveton Blakeney NR25 7TL
01263 740101 wivetonbell.co.uk
HOW MUCH? Double rooms £100–£150 a night, including continental breakfast.

The Gurnard's Head

A short walk inland from one of the most wild and rugged sections of the South West Coast Path in Cornwall, this is the sort of place where you can kick off your muddy boots by the roaring fire and sip a glass of wine while the dog snoozes at your feet. A glance at the art hanging on the walls hints that it's also a pub with an eye for the finer things in life, with a menu that makes the most of what the boats land and the farmers grow. All this before you've even padded upstairs to find a Vispring bed draped with Welsh wool blankets and shelves stacked with novels to distract you from the moorland views. The briny air, hearty food and high comfort levels encourage such a deep sleep that you might not stir until the cows pass to be milked in the morning, but don't stress – breakfast is a lazy affair and you won't be in a hurry to leave. Dogs and children are welcome – cots and dog treats are provided at no extra cost. It's worth knowing also that the same people run the excellent Old Coastguard on the south coast of Cornwall near Penzance.

CORNWALL Near Zennor St Ives TR26 3DE
01736 796928 gurnardshead.co.uk
HOW MUCH? Double rooms with breakfast £125–£150 a night, DB&B £180–£205. Family rooms £190–£245.

The Bildeston Crown

A contemporary Suffolk coaching inn with great food

This 15th-century coaching inn has been a local landmark for centuries, and a foodie destination for well over a decade. In its day Bildeston was one of Suffolk's wealthy wool towns, and although this is hard to discern in what is nowadays a peaceful village, the inn's comfortable upstairs rooms and excellent food mean the tradition continues to this day.

As you might expect in a building of this vintage, its 12 guest rooms come in all shapes, sizes and designs – an individuality that owners Chris and Hayley Lee have decided to emphasise with a variety of decorative styles, from traditional to contemporary. All the rooms have big comfy beds, tea- and coffee-making facilities, complimentary mineral water, Freeview TVs and wifi – and, unusually, there's also a lift, so they are all accessible if you have trouble with stairs. All the rooms have baths but 3 have separate walk-in showers as well. Downstairs there are 2 bars, but the Crown is really more a restaurant than a pub these days. They serve the same menus in the bar and the slightly more formal restaurant, and you can choose between an excellent selection of classics and a more seasonal and refined 'select' menu. They also do an excellent value set lunch, or if you really want push the boat out you can go for the 7-course tasting menu at £80 a head.

All in all it's really the perfect place to enjoy a weekend break, with comfortable rooms, great food – and, with Lavenham and Long Melford just a short drive away, the chance to explore this quiet, picturesque and very historic part of western Suffolk.

SUFFOLK High Street Bildeston IP7 7EB 01449 740510 thebildestoncrown.com
HOW MUCH? Double rooms from £100 a night, including breakfast.

"We love West Suffolk because it's a great foodie destination, with farm shops which are still farms, weekly markets and amazing artisanal producers."

Hayley Lee, Bildeston Crown

What's nearby?

MUSEUM OF EAST ANGLIAN LIFE Windmills, barns, workshops and other salvaged buildings from across the region, dotted around a wanderable riverside site.

KERSEY This old wool town could just be Suffolk's prettiest village, with a tumbledown forded main street and an archetypally enormous parish church.

GREAT FINBOROUGH 'Teenage dreams, so hard to beat' – so says the inscription on John Peel's grave which is a poignant detour for all music fans.

The Rose & Crown

The best kind of gastropub with rooms

Run by the people behind the excellent Bank House in King's Lynn, this ancient inn has been around since the 14th century, and in some ways is still a traditional village boozer. But it's also well known as a place to stay, and we reckon it is everything a pub with rooms should be – a delightful old inn with 16 pretty and very comfortable en-suite guest rooms and a cracking bar downstairs.

The inn does what inns do – hidden corners, low ceilings and beams – but the rooms are all bright and Norfolk seasidey and come with good-quality beds and linen, wifi, Freeview TVs, fluffy towels, power showers and Molton Brown toiletries. Children and dogs? No problem – pooches pay a modest extra charge, as do kids under 12 to share their parents' room. The walled garden is a sunny spot for drinkers, while the pub has a great reputation for food, serving the same menu throughout the pub and a couple more contemporary restaurant areas at the back, with an emphasis on local, seasonal ingredients – fish and seafood from King's Lynn and Brancaster, meat and game from local estates – and serving a good old Sunday lunch that draws punters in from miles around (you'll need to book for this). Breakfast attracts non-residents who want to fuel up before walking or cycling, and they serve tea, coffee and excellent cakes all day.

The other nice thing about The Rose & Crown is that it's so handy for some of the most alluring stretches of the North Norfolk Coast and the pretty villages nearby – including Docking, Bircham and Ingoldisthorpe, all of which are lovely links in a country walk or cycle ride.

NORFOLK Old Church Road Snettisham PE31 7LX
01485 541382 roseandcrownsnettisham.co.uk
HOW MUCH? Double rooms £120 a night including an excellent breakfast. Children £20 a night, dogs £15.

"The Rose & Crown is a quintessentially English village inn, and I'm so proud that we continue to welcome locals and visitors as we have for 600 years."

Jeannette Goodrich, The Rose & Crown

What's nearby?

SANDRINGHAM Home of several generations of British monarchs since it was built by the future Edward VII in 1870, and much of the palace is open to the public.

SNETTISHAM RSPB Stretching along the banks of The Wash in a series of lagoons and mudflats, this is home to some of Britain's most impressive wildlife spectacles.

BIRCHAM WINDMILL Lovely old mill with a bakery selling bread and cakes made with its own flour. There's also an art gallery, tea room and more.

PASSIONATE ABOUT...
CHEESE

Jonny and Dulcie Crickmore are big fans of cows but not – surprisingly – most dairy farms, which they claim are often environmentally unfriendly places whose cows unleash clouds of methane and which clock up thousands of food miles transporting their milk to the other side of the country. So when they decided to diversify the family dairy farm in Suffolk they decided they would try to be a little bit different – aiming to be a bit kinder to the environment and to keep everything as local as possible.

They've yet to do anything about the farting cows, but the farm now runs on solar power; their Montbéliarde cows eat grass and homegrown hay and are not forced to produce unsustainable amounts of milk; plus their milk is super-healthy and ideal for cheese-making. Most importantly, say Jonny and Dulcie, their cows are happy, which means that they will produce the very best milk! Not all of the milk is processed on the farm, but much of it forms the raw ingredient for their own dairy products – principally creamy raw milk butter and the farm's fabulous Baron Bigod brie-style cheese, the only raw milk brie made in the UK. Raw milk and its products are not for everyone, but Baron Bigod is appearing increasingly often in specialist cheese shops and on restaurant cheeseboards, and production has increased 8-fold since they started making it. The cheese is also sold at the farm from what is the country's first raw milk- and cheese-vending machine (we kid you not!). If you're in the area you'd be mad not to stop by for a pack of butter or chunk of Baron Bigod – it really is that good.

FEN FARM DAIRY **Flixton Road Bungay Suffolk NR35 1PD**
01986 892350 fenfarmdairy.co.uk

The Wife of Bath

Named after one of the best-known of Chaucer's *Canterbury Tales*, this restaurant with rooms is the latest addition to of Mark Sargeant's small Kent-based chain and has 6 stylish bedrooms that make for a soothing place to stay in the country, with exposed timber beams that blend with contemporary furniture, colourful works of art and muted tones on the walls. We particularly like Sir Thopas: sup on the glass of sherry left out as a check-in treat and admire the capacious, high-ceilinged space. In the light and airy restaurant downstairs inspiration is taken from Spain, and the menu features dishes such as octopus and Iberico pork, plus you can enjoy an array of scrummy tapas at the rustic bar (think crispy squid, Manchego croquetas and salt cod fritters). Breakfast is a real delight – choose from a hamper full of goodies delivered directly to your door or head to the restaurant for a Spanish cooked breakfast. There's much to do in the local area – check out the Nature Reserve in Wye, jump on the train to Canterbury or explore the Kent Downs on foot.

KENT 4 Upper Bridge Street Wye TN25 5AF
01233 812232 thewifeofbath.com
HOW MUCH? Double rooms from £95 per night including breakfast.

The Townhouse Stratford

Right in the heart of Stratford, this 400-year-old hotel is quite a venue – a buzzy pub and restaurant that has 12 very comfortable en-suite bedrooms. Situated just a few minutes' walk from pretty much everything you might want to see in town, all of the hotel's rooms have been recently refurbished in a contemporary style, with super-king-sized beds, crisp cotton sheets and deliciously fluffy duvets, and bathrooms with high-pressure rainfall showers and Noble Isle toiletries; some also have free-standing baths. All the rooms also have tea- and coffee-making facilities, including Nespresso machines, mineral water, biscuits and – a nice touch – a small decanter of port! All in all, it's both a cosy and contemporary place to stay in a great location – plus it has the added bonus of the excellent bar and restaurant, serving good-quality food at prices most people can afford, and giving a busy, urban feel to the place. Perfect for both a weekend break, or just an overnight DB&B on a theatre trip.

WARWICKSHIRE 16 Church Street Stratford-upon-Avon
CV37 6HB 01789 262222 stratfordtownhouse.co.uk
HOW MUCH? Double rooms with breakfast £105–£205 a night.

The Greyhound Inn

Located in Letcombe Regis, a pretty downland village, The Greyhound is the type of place that welcomes you with open arms. Owners Martyn and Catriona took over the Grade-II-listed Georgian property a few years ago and refurbished it as a proper pub that serves top-notch food, plus it has 8 tastefully decorated bedrooms above. Each of the rooms is individually decorated and comes complete with pocket-sprung mattress, flatscreen TV, homemade biscuits and Bramley bath products. Don't want to leave Fido at home? Bring him with you – 3 rooms are dog-friendly, and if you're after a family suite, that's no problem either. Downstairs the regularly changing menu features an array of locally sourced produce, with imaginative dishes such as twice-baked Cheddar soufflé (a popular mainstay), and they also do fish and chips and a good burger too. It's an ideal spot for walkers – the Ridgeway and National Trust's White Horse Hill are close by – after which it's back to the pub for a pint in the bright, airy bar followed by dinner in one of the cosy dining rooms.

OXFORDSHIRE Main Street Letcombe Regis OX12 9JY
01235 771969 thegreyhoundletcombe.co.uk
HOW MUCH? Double rooms with breakfast from £90.
a night.

Red Lion Pub & Kitchen

The former local of *Wind in the Willows* creator, Kenneth Grahame, and thriller writer Dick Francis... who wouldn't want to drop by the Red Lion for a drink? It's a classic 17th-century inn, tucked away in the tucked-away village of Blewbury at the foot of the Berkshire Downs. Recently spruced up by Phil and Arden Wild, it's an undeniably cosy spot, with a flagstoned floor and log fire, but it's for the excellent food that most people come – and the fact that there are 3 comfortable en-suite bedrooms, so you can easily slope off upstairs and make a proper weekend of it. It's a great place to stay for lots of reasons: the rooms are comfy and the village is enchanting; the food is a very moderately priced combination of British and French classics, mixed up with an Oxfordshire twist – and there's lots to do in the area. It's a good spot for walkers, but there's also plenty of interest for car and train fanatics in Nuffield Place, home of one of the pioneers of the British motor industry. If none of that floats your boat, you can just stroll or cycle the lanes in and around the village.

OXFORDSHIRE Chapel Lane Blewbury OX11 9PQ
01235 850403 theredlionpubandkitchen.co.uk
HOW MUCH? Double rooms £95 a night, including
breakfast.

The White Horse

Great food and comfy rooms on the North Norfolk coast

Backing straight on to the marshes, lagoons and creeks of the North Norfolk coast, the views don't come much better than from the sea-facing rooms of this long-established gastropub with rooms. It has 7 airy, attractively decorated en-suite guest rooms in its main building and 8 garden rooms in a flint extension behind, with grass roofs to blend with the marshes beyond – plus their own outdoor terraces. All of the rooms are spacious and contemporary, with a blue-green decor inspired by the seascape beyond, and the top-notch 'Room at the Top' has its own viewing telescope with which you can take in the best of the coastline. Whether you stay in the main building or the garden rooms, all have large comfy beds, Freeview TVs, digital radios and wifi, and tea- and coffee-making facilities. Downstairs, it's a regular pub at the front but at the back the emphasis is on food, with a menu that boasts plenty of locally caught seafood – oysters and mussels in season, lobster, fish and chips and beautiful fresh sea bass – along with excellent local steak with chips, all washed down with ales from the Brancaster Brewery down the road. Table service is spot-on too, and you can enjoy all this while savouring the views from their glass extension or the curvy terrace outside.

But while the food and service may be great and the welcome warm, it's the location above all that makes the White Horse special – the Norfolk Coast Path runs by the bottom of the garden, making the pub an ideal location for walkers and cyclists, and indeed their dogs, who are allowed in the garden rooms. The White Horse has been here a while, but it remains one of the best places to stay on what is a very well-catered-for stretch of coast.

NORFOLK Main Road Brancaster Staithe PE31 8BY
01485 210262 whitehorsebrancaster.co.uk
HOW MUCH? Double rooms with breakfast £150–£230, weekends £160–£240, cheaper out of season.

"We are so lucky to be situated in such a beautiful location and love offering our guests a real taste of Norfolk living."

Rob Williamson, The White Horse

What's nearby?

JOLLY SAILORS Brancaster's local, owned by the same folk as The White Horse and with its own brews on tap.

SCOLT HEAD ISLAND You can tour the creeks of this nature reserve by boat from Brancaster Staithe to see terns, curlews and other waders.

HOLKHAM BAY The ultimate Noth Norfolk beach, with endless golden sands backing onto a ribbon of sand dunes and a beautiful stretch of pine forest.

The Old Stocks Inn

Situated in the pretty market town of Stow-on-the-Wold in the heart of Gloucestershire, this refurbished 17th-century coaching inn has 16 stylish bedrooms that seamlessly mix original features with contemporary design – think original beams, soothing colours and views down to the town square or across the attractive walled garden. Most of the rooms are packed full of character and vary from luxury doubles with giant TVs and complimentary minibars to a super-cool family option with a double bed, triple bunks and a games console. The on-site restaurant dishes up local and seasonal British cuisine – the likes of hearty 12-hour braised rib of Longhorn beef with creamed potato and king oyster mushrooms – and there's also a quirky café filled with upcycled furniture. There is also a very cool self-catering cottage for rent nearby – Parson's Barn – and the area is full of things to do, ranging from adventure days at Batsford Park falconry centre, to a leisurely walk down to Broadwell (be sure to stop in at The Fox Inn for a pint and a snack).

GLOUCESTERSHIRE The Square Stow-on-the-Wold GL54 1AF 01451 830666 oldstocksinn.com
HOW MUCH? Double rooms from £129 a night including breakfast.

The Bull Hotel

Sitting invitingly on the market square of the small Cotswolds town of Fairford, and actually made up of 2 separate pubs, the Bull Hotel has a spacious interior decorated with bold colours and styles that catapult the building into the 21st century, while still managing to retain a sense of timelessness, with an eclectic assortment of antiques, lighting and well-chosen textiles. The Bull is a cosy place above all – as a coaching inn should be – with a large and comfortable bar with open fires, local craft ales and plenty of places in which to loll about, and a spacious restaurant fashioned out of the inn's old stables that has a real sense of occasion, and serves a menu of hearty Mediterranean and modern British dishes along with stone-baked pizzas. Its 21 rooms are arranged over 3 floors and individually furnished to reflect their various shapes and sizes, with window shutters, good-quality linen, flatscreen TVs, wifi and en-suite bathrooms with walk-in showers. All in all, a very comfortable place from which to explore the southern Cotswolds.

GLOUCESTERSHIRE Market Place Fairford GL7 4AA
01285 712535 thebullhotelfairford.co.uk
HOW MUCH? Double rooms £100 a night midweek, £120 a night weekends, including continental breakfast.

The Cricket Inn

Set in the Devon coastal village of Beesands, the Cricket Inn is perched right on the beachfront in a sensational seaside spot. In recent years this unassuming old fishing inn has been reinvented as a light and spacious gastropub serving delicious food, with a handful of comfortable rooms upstairs to collapse into after a pleasant evening. It feels wonderfully remote, with 7 rooms in all, 5 of which have awesome views of Start Bay, which you can actually enjoy without even getting out of bed. There's a seaside-cum-nautical theme throughout, although the rooms follow a more incongruous cricket theme and are named after famous grounds and players. They all come with en-suite baths, complimentary toiletries, flatscreen TVs, tea- and coffee-making facilities and room treats, wifi and extremely comfortable king-size beds, while in the morning their mighty breakfast is a fabulous way to start any day. The welcome is warm and the service excellent – indeed we can't think of many better places for a peaceful foodie break by the sea.

DEVON Beesands Kingsbridge TQ7 2EN 01548 580215
thecricketinn.com
HOW MUCH? Double rooms £90–£120 a night including breakfast.

Hampton Manor

This Gothic manor house – the former home of 19th-century British Prime Minister Robert Peel – has been reinvented as a grand and rather funky destination for food and rooms that does a pretty good job of luring trendy folk from nearby Birmingham out into the countryside. Despite the grandeur of the building, with its chinoiserie, stained glass and sweeping main staircase, they've turned it into a homely sort of place with an excellent restaurant at its heart (which has won a Michelin star and 4 AA rosettes) and 15 very comfortable bedrooms to retire to at the end of the evening. The emphasis is on confident, nothing-is-too-much-trouble service and seasonal, organic food, partly based on ingredients from the hotel's own garden. The common denominator in the rooms is Arts and Crafts style, with bold patterns and a mix of classic and contemporary furniture, big bathrooms with monsoon showers and robes and toiletries. On summer evenings you can relax on the outside terrace and make believe you truly are 'to the manor born'.

WARWICKSHIRE Shadowbrook Lane Hampton-in-Arden
Solihull B92 0EN 01675 446080 hamptonmanor.com
HOW MUCH? Double rooms from £160 a night, not including breakfast.

The Angel at Hetton

Country-chic accommodation and in the Dales

Hetton's Angel Inn is one of the Dales' most celebrated gourmet-dining destinations, and the accommodation is pretty fabulous too – 4 contemporary bedrooms in a cottage conversion adjacent to the inn, and a restored barn across the road which goes for a handsome European country-chic style in its 2 studios and 3 suites. You pay your money, you take your choice – polished beams, an antique Victorian bed and a rustic air in the Rylstone Suite, for example, or a grown-up, white-is-alright designer suite with patio doors that open on to the garden. Attention to detail is spot-on too, from iPod docks in the rooms to fresh milk and lemon in the fridge, while you're just a step away from the Yorkshire Dales' original and perhaps best gastropub, for which as a resident you have a guaranteed reservation.

As a romantic retreat, or for a big gesture or celebration, it's hard to beat the cosy, cossetted Angel experience – as Steve Coogan and Rob Brydon famously found out in the TV series The Trip. The service is great, the food fabulous and you couldn't be in a better or more scenic location. The inn has recently been taken over by Michael and Johanna Wignall – formerly of Gidleigh Park in Devon – so we're expecting great things and expect it to continue to maintain its very high standards of food and service.

Rested and fed, the Dales awaits in all its glory the next day – you're in the heart of a small hamlet, around six miles from Skipton and its castle, and not far from excellent walking country around Grassington.

NORTH YORKSHIRE Hetton Near Skipton BD23 6LT
01756 730263 angelhetton.co.uk
HOW MUCH? Double rooms with breakfast Sun–Thurs £150–£175, Fri and Sat £175–£200.

What's nearby?

MALHAM COVE If you've never been to Malham Cove before, it's almost a shame to give the game away in advance. Better to let you stroll the mile out from the village, alongside a babbling stream, until... there it is, a stupendous, curved limestone cliff, almost 300-feet high.

BOLTON ABBEY Rustic England in a nutshell – the estate village, the romantic ruins of the 12th-century priory and the Cavendish Pavilion for tea and cake.

GRASSINGTON With a cobbled Georgian centre full of handsome stone buildings, there's a strong community vibe here, from farmers' markets to film nights.

Rocksalt Rooms

A boutique B&B bolthole full of personality

There are a lot of things to like about Rocksalt Restaurant and Rooms, not least its enviable location on the South Kent coast. Owned by chef Mark Sargeant, it's a place to enjoy top-notch local and seasonal food, and with 4 boutique bedrooms as well, there's somewhere sleek to lay your head post-dinner. The rooms are just a short walk from the main Rocksalt restaurant – they're comfy, luxurious and rather romantic, decorated in a warehouse-rustic style, with bare brick walls and funky fabrics. Each is individually done, but they all share certain features as standard – antique beds, Egyptian cotton sheets, flatscreen TVs and modern wet rooms. Taking a family break? There's a 2-room option that gives you more space. Continental breakfast is delivered to your door in a hamper, so you can enjoy a lazy breakfast in bed with a zippy coffee from the in-room Nespresso machine – and the 2 front rooms have floor-to-ceiling French windows, which allow you to enjoy views of Folkestone's harbour with your croissants.

The rooms are set right on the harbour above the Smokehouse, Rocksalt's fish-and-chip offshoot, and in addition to the classy chippy, there are a number of old-fashioned whelk and cockles stalls dotted around the cobbled harbour. Fancy strolling along the coast or into the country during your stay? Hampers are available to pre-order – and provide the perfect picnic. Folkestone is also on a roll: the Harbour Arm promenade has been restored and the area as a whole has become known as a bit of an arts hub. Keep in mind also Sargeant's sister places – The Wife of Bath and The Duke of William – both also in Kent and just as delicious.

KENT 4-5 Fishmarket Folkestone CT19 6AA
01303 212070 rocksaltfolkestone.co.uk
HOW MUCH? Double rooms from £85 including continental breakfast.

"Rocksalt is built around seasonality, locality and simplicity, allowing the best produce around the south coast to shine through."

Mark Sargeant, Rocksalt Rooms

What's nearby?

LOWER LEAS COASTAL PARK Ranged across the cliffs above the beach, this is one of the most beautifully landscaped green spaces you'll find on this coast.

THE CLIFFE Based in the excellent White Cliffs hotel, this manages to be at once relaxed and sophisticated, with a beachy dining room lined with local art.

DUNGENESS Simple fishermen's huts reconditioned into artists' studios and even a couple of convivial pubs under the shadow of the brooding power station.

The Sheep on Sheep St

Situated right in the heart of the picturesque Cotswolds town of Stow-on-the-Wold, The Sheep is a clever update of a previous business – basically a restaurant with boutique rooms that has quickly established itself as one of the best places to stay in what is a popular Cotswolds location. Made up of 3 knocked-together, honey-coloured cottages, it has 22 rooms furnished in a classic yet contemporary style that feel both special and cosy at the same time. About half the guest rooms are located in the main building while the others are divided between 2 separate buildings behind. They come with king-size beds, TV and wifi and lots of room treats – tea- and coffee-making facilities, Nespresso machines, mineral water and whatnot. As for the restaurant, it's a large bright space featuring a lovely long bar and a flickering wood-fired pizza oven, which they don't only use to make pizzas but for cooking much of the meat and fish too – everything from a fabulous Wagyu burger to steaks, fish, scallops, salt-and-pepper squid, and, yes, those pizzas, which are pretty good and well-priced.

GLOUCESTERSHIRE Sheep Street Stow-on-the-Wold GL54 1AG 01451 830344 thesheepstow.co.uk **HOW MUCH?** Double rooms £90–£150 a night including breakfast.

The Seafood Restaurant

This is the flagship restaurant of the Rick Stein empire, and as such you would expect it to be pretty good, but we recommend it for what may seem to be 2 rather obvious reasons. First of all it does great-value packages which include at least one meal in the downstairs restaurant, plus as a guest you get priority on booking in the restaurant, which isn't at all an easy place to get into. The other thing of course is the rooms, which are bright and cheerful and have a definite seaside feel. All have lovely bathrooms with luxurious toiletries and towels, and come equipped with milk, tea and coffee and biscuits and a minibar; and some also have their own terraces from which to enjoy the sea views, which are pretty special. Service is excellent too, and breakfast as delicious as you would expect, whether you have the full monty downstairs or a continental option in your room. Dogs are welcome – and they even provide a dog-sitting service if required. All in all, a perfect place for a foodie break by the sea.

CORNWALL Riverside Padstow PL28 8BY 01841 532700 rickstein.com **HOW MUCH?** Double rooms with breakfast £165–£310.

The Swan, Long Melford

Set at the end of Long Melford's long and eminently walkable high street, The Swan is an up-to-date sort of place that fashionably likes to refer to itself as a 'restaurant with rooms', which is just about right – it's less formal than a hotel but definitely a cut above most pubs. Its rooms are comfy and rather stylish – 7 in all, split between 4 rooms in a separate building next door but one and 3 rooms in the main building. They're all a decent size without being enormous, and they either have a spacious shower or seductively-lit old-fashioned bathtubs, or both. Each room is subtly lit and eclectically furnished, with bright eye-catching fabrics and bold colours, Freeview TVs, decent wifi, tea- and coffee-making facilities, still and sparkling water, homemade cookies and a bottle of fresh milk. The restaurant is not an especially cheap place to eat, but the cooking is high quality, with an emphasis on local ingredients. As for the location, there's lots to see within walking distance and in the surrounding area, including the tourist honeypot of Lavenham, 4 miles away.

SUFFOLK Hall Street Long Melford CO10 9JQ
01787 464545 longmelfordswan.co.uk
HOW MUCH? Double rooms £155–185 a night with breakfast ; DB&B £115–132 per person.

Maison Talbooth

Originally this was in fact just a restaurant – Le Talbooth – a fancy place by the river which later acquired this rather agreeable nearby country house, with 12 boutique guest rooms and a pool in the grounds. The long-running restaurant maintains a considerable reputation for high-end dining, and each of the rooms is deliberately different but traditional in style, with excellent beds and large bathrooms, complimentary soft drinks and snacks, satellite TVs and free wifi. There's a homely vibe throughout, with an informal flagstoned reception area and a lounge and terrace looking out over manicured lawns and gardens. Beyond here, things get nice and chilled – maybe some tennis or a plunge in the outdoor heated pool (usable in winter too) and hot tub, or down-time in the pool house with its satellite TV, honesty bar, robes and open fire. There's a spa with various treatments on offer, and when the time comes for dinner you can be whisked off to the original Talbooth restaurant, 2 minutes away in the hotel's courtesy car, for a slap-up dining experience.

ESSEX Stratford Road Dedham Colchester CO7 6HN
01206 322367 milsomhotels.com
HOW MUCH? Double rooms from £235 to £400 including breakfast.

Sibton White Horse

A proper local pub tucked away in rural Suffolk

It was always Neil and Gill Mason's dream to run a country pub, and around 12 years ago they finally managed it with the White Horse, which is a traditional country pub par excellence. The atmosphere couldn't be cosier or the welcome warmer, and not only have they made it into a destination for food, they've done so without alienating the regular drinkers, who still prop up the bar while everyone else tucks in. They also have 5 cosy rooms in a separate block next door so you can linger a little longer after enjoying your dinner. These have been furnished in a contemporary country style and have decent-sized bathrooms, tea- and coffee-making facilities, biscuits, mineral water, Freeview TVs with DVD players and wifi.

Outside, there's a small summer caravan site, and the pub also plays host to the odd beer and music festival and features a BBQ during summer months in the pub garden, where you can admire the well-tended kitchen plot, whose herbs, salad, fruit and veg all finds it way onto the restaurant menu. Neil and Gill are proud that the pub has been awarded 2 AA rosettes, and the menu makes the most of the great produce that Suffolk provides, with classic pub grub at lunchtime and a more refined dinner menu that changes about a quarter of its dishes every week.

The inn makes an excellent base for visiting the nearby Suffolk Coast – the ancient port of Dunwich and the Minsmere RSPB reserve are nearby, Walberswick and Southwold not much further, and there are lots of opportunities for country walks not only to the coast but also to picturesque neighbouring villages – Neil and Gill can supply plenty of suggestions.

SUFFOLK Halesworth Road Sibton IP17 2JJ 01728 660337
www.sibtonwhitehorseinn.co.uk
HOW MUCH? Double rooms from £80 to £110 a night depending on time of year; 2-night minimum stay during Easter–October.

"We like to feel we run a proper, honest, all-round local pub, well tucked away but definitely well worth finding."

Neil Mason, Sibton White Horse

What's nearby?

BLYTHBURGH CHURCH Known as the 'cathedral of the marshes', its tower can be seen from miles away and it has a beamed ceiling decorated with carved angels.

EMMETS. PEASENHALL A village shop like no other, with a delicious range of home-cured ham and bacon (it's the UK's oldest producer) and a cosy tearoom.

RSPB MINSMERE An unusual mix of woodland, heath and marshland that is truly one of the most glorious spots for birdwatching along the entire Suffolk coast.

The Waveney Inn

A contemporary riverside pub with boutique rooms

We like the Waveney Inn but it's a hard place to describe. It's a pub, with a wide-ranging menu of pub food; it also has a collection of boutique-style rooms, all of which are very comfortable, up-to-date and well-equipped; and it's also part of the Waveney River Centre, a camping, glamping and self-catering site that occupies a beautiful, almost secret spot by the river that is home to all sorts of activities. In short there are any number of reasons to come, and it's a fabulous place to enjoy the more untouched southeastern corner of the Broads National Park. First the rooms, of which there are 7 in all – made up of 5 doubles, 1 twin and a family room. Some have views over the river and marshes, and all are spacious and beautifully kitted out, with flatscreen TVs, big comfy beds and large bathrooms with toiletries. Rates include the use of Waveney River Centre's large indoor pool and the foot ferry across the river to the marshes, plus an excellent breakfast in the downstairs pub/restaurant, which the rest of the time serves a high-quality pub grub menu including baguettes and sharing platters and main courses from steaks and burgers to fish and chips, ribs and pasta dishes. You can order anything in small, regular or large portions, and there's an outside terrace overlooking the marshes to enjoy it. Best of all, though, is the location, which is the only destination at the end of the long country lane that leads here. There is a nature trail for kids, bikes, canoes and day boats for hire, and the footpaths through the marshes on the far side of the river are glorious, leading eventually to the watery expanse of Oulton Broad. It's a great place to throw away the car keys and forget the rest of the world for a few days.

NORFOLK Waveney River Centre Burgh St Peter NR34 0BT 01502 677599 waveneyinn.co.uk
HOW MUCH? Double rooms with breakfast from £85 to £115 a night depending on the room and season. Family rooms £100–£135 a night.

"The Broads' best-kept secret – a haven of tranquillity on the banks of the Waveney, with Carlton Marshes on our doorstep."

James Knight, Waveney River Centre

What's nearby?

CARLTON MARSHES Take the ferry across the river to spot marsh harriers and kestrels in this Suffolk Wildlife Trust expanse of reeds, marshy meadows and big skies.

BURGH ST PETER Stroll into the village to see the curious ziggurat-like tower of the parish church and its amazing 14th-century font, decorated with grotesque faces.

OULTON BROAD This broad stretch of open water is Lowestoft's most compelling attraction – hire a boat for the day or take a cruise up the river.

SEASIDE

It's a fact that nowhere in the UK is more than 75 miles from the sea, and the total coastline is around 20,000 miles long. That's a lot of harbourside hotels, sea-view B&Bs and beach hostels, from Cornwall to the Scottish islands and from Pembrokeshire to Scarborough. Whatever you're looking for – a vibrant resort, a clifftop B&B or a cosy pub close to a quiet beach or overlooking a spectacular bay – we've got it covered.

Hemsby Beach, Norfolk

The Beach at Bude

Coastal chic overlooking Bude's coolest beach

If you ask a local to direct you to the coolest bar in Bude, most of them will wave you towards The Beach Bar. For here, killer cocktails – or, by day, simply coffee and cake – are as much a part of the lifestyle as the sandy beach that can be seen from its terrace. Lucky, then, that this cool and contemporary vibe has rubbed off on the New England style rooms also on offer here, where the limed oak furniture, Lloyd Loom chairs and king-size beds all add to the stylish seaside environment. If you are in the mood to socialize, the hotel's buzzing bar is a great place to start – or end – your evening, indeed the hotel does the cool party vibe just perfectly. If you want a quieter space to relax, they also offer the brand-new Club Rooms.

The rooms encompass 'Classic' and 'Classic Plus' – which have walk-in showers and sometimes baths as well, but are rear-facing so there are no views of the sea – to 'Superior' and 'Deluxe', which tend to be larger and have terraces or Juliet balconies and boast sea views. There are also 2 suites, each with 2 bedrooms and 2 bathrooms, and one with a private terrace and kitchen, which are perfect for families or those staying longer.

As for the Beach's bar, this also serves delicious cakes as well as those more-ish cocktails, but it you want a something more substantial, the Beach restaurant does food in keeping with the spirit of the place, with a lunch menu full of hearty small plates – haddock tempura, salt-and-pepper squid, ox-cheek croquettes, sliders – and more cheffy, refined dishes in the evening that could just be the perfect end to a perfect day by the sea.

CORNWALL Summerleaze Crescent Bude EX23 8HL
01288 389800 thebeachatbude.co.uk
HOW MUCH? Double rooms with breakfast £120–£170 per room per night in low season, £175–£250 high season.

"We're proud to have created a relaxing and beautiful space, perfect for romantic weekends, family breaks or simply watching the sun set over the beach."

Will Daniel, The Beach at Bude

What's nearby?

BUDE SEA POOL We love this part-natural, part manmade saltwater swimming pool – a fixture on Bude's main beach since the 1930s.

MORWENSTOW The National Trust tearooms here anchor a lovely circular coastal walk, taking in the views from the so-called Hawker's Hut, built from driftwood.

The Sail Loft

Beachside style, good food and comfortable rooms

A 5-minute stroll from the centre of genteel Southwold, the Sail Loft is sandwiched between the marshes and the dunes – the latest venture of one Jonny Nicholson, who a few years ago revitalised the Bell in sleepy Saxmundham, 15 miles or so inland, and has now turned his attention – and his unpretentious style of cooking – to Southwold. In doing so he's brought a refreshing taste of beach-shack-chic style to the slightly tired offerings of the town, not to mention some pretty decent food based on the best local produce, and a handful of comfortable rooms to boot, some looking back over the marshes, the others gazing out to sea.

You can enjoy breakfast in your room or – better still – in the restaurant downstairs, which has the feel of a funky seaside joint, with rustic furniture, bare floorboards and a crowd that's as mixed as Southwold itself. The food has an emphasis on fresh fish and seafood that perfectly suits the restaurant's duneside location: mussels, scallops, crayfish bisque risotto and all sorts of yummy fish and seafood creations are complemented by more grounded items such as beef Madras, pork belly and an excellent homemade burger.

Overall it's a great beachside place to rest up for a few days if that's what you're after – close enough to Southwold's facilities for convenience but far away enough to feel a little bit remote and rather special, with an almost Mediterranean feel when the weather is co-operating. Sit on the outside terrace on a summer's evening, and squint... you could be among the sandy dunes of southwestern France.

SUFFOLK 53 Ferry Road Southwold IP18 6HQ
01502 725713 sailloftsouthwold.uk
HOW MUCH? Double rooms from £160 a night including breakfast.

"A cosmopolitan beach vibe, local produce and soulful cooking, a comfy bolthole upstairs, the Sail Loft is all about what we enjoy."

Jonny Nicholson, The Sail Loft

What's nearby?

SOUTHWOLD PIER Wonderfully retro, with not a fairground ride in sight. Instead there's decent food, gift shops and (our favourite) the 'Under the Pier Show'.

ADNAMS BREWERY Still based in the centre of Southwold, this iconic brewery runs regular tours – not only to view the brewing process but their gin distillery too.

WALBERSWICK Stroll down to Southwold's harbour and take the foot ferry to Walberswick, with its fishermen's huts, beach and a couple of nice pubs.

The Old Quay House

A whitewashed Victorian building that was once a refuge for seamen, The Old Quay House is now a chic, boutique hotel nudging the River Fowey. Architect-designed, with elegant modern decor, its deluxe rooms are right on the river – sit at the window and all you can hear is the water lapping and boats passing. The food in its Q restaurant is excellent – with just a handful of starters, mains and desserts that changes each night – and the waterside terrace a fantastic place to eat. There are just 13 bedrooms, so this is one seafront hideaway you might want to keep to yourself. As for hotel life, expect an attentive but never intrusive service, and country-house touches like the open fire and a library. The best rooms come with binoculars, while all rooms come with waterproof jackets and … teddy bears – the last, to be put outside the door instead of a Do Not Disturb sign. Note, no under 12s are allowed, but families would in any case be better off at the family-friendly Rosevine near Falmouth, which is owned by the same company.

CORNWALL 28 Fore Street Fowey PL23 1AQ 01726 833302 theoldquayhouse.com
HOW MUCH? Classic rooms from £160 a night B&B, Superior rooms from £205, Deluxe rooms from £300.

Artist Residence Penzance

Smack bang in the middle of Penzance, it would have been all too easy to buy up this Georgian mansion and run a traditional hotel with bragging rights about its top location. Not so for the Artists Residence, where time and effort has gone into a boutique design that really stands out from the crowd, with 9 rooms, individually designed and decorated by Cornish and British artists, and 13 'House' rooms in their signature eclectic style, plus a 3-bedroom cottage, complete with log-burner and copper rolltop bath. All the rooms have bathrooms with eco-friendly toiletries, flatscreen TVs and wifi. Breakfast is served in its brilliant Cornish Barn restaurant, which is also open for lunch and dinner, serving local, seasonal dishes, and meat and fish dishes from the smoker. There is a beer garden with table football, ping-pong and a BBQ, and an indoor bar-lounge with a wood-burner and a focus on local ales. It all adds up to a stunning hotel with a unique design, delicious food and thoroughly laid-back atmosphere – topped off by that location which, yes, they should still brag about!

CORNWALL 20 Chapel Street Penzance TR18 4AW 01736 365664 artistresidence.co.uk
HOW MUCH? Double rooms with breakfast from £100 a night.

St Enodoc Hotel

Set in spacious, beautifully manicured grounds overlooking the Camel Estuary, the St Enodoc is a real delight, with 20 rooms and suites that are bright, modern and cosy, many with far-reaching sea views. There's beach life right on the doorstep, not to mention one of Cornwall's best hotel restaurants – the former domain of Nathan Outlaw and still with a great reputation for good, locally sourced food. The hotel is a relaxed sort of place, with slate floors and bright, contemporary fabrics; modern Cornish paintings adorn the walls and overall the hotel has a calm, almost Mediterranean vibe, with a lovely lounge area with a wood-burning stove. The rooms are bright and stylishly decorated with seaside colours and up-to-date bathrooms with underfloor heating and local toiletry products from St Kitts herbery. Quite a lot have sea and estuary views and they all boast big comfy beds, satellite TV and wifi. The spa offers a range of massages and treatments, plus there's an outdoor pool, gym, games room and tennis court.

CORNWALL Rock PL27 6LA 01208 863394
enodoc-hotel.co.uk
HOW MUCH? Double rooms £170–£200 a night, suites from £295 a night – all with breakfast.

The Old Coastguard

The folk behind this hotel cut their teeth on the excellent Gurnard's Head near Zennor and the 2 places have plenty in common, not least a glorious scenic location and a determinedly laid-back vibe that is infectious. Situated in the picturesque seaside village of Mousehole near Penzance, The Old Coastguard has 14 comfy guest rooms, all but one of which have some sort of view over the sea. Downstairs rows of sofas look seaward, dogs and children get a hearty welcome, and there's often live music in the restaurant alongside Sunday lunch. The rooms are spacious, with big comfy beds equipped with Roberts radios and posh toiletries, good-quality tea and coffee, and lots of books to browse. Some have balconies, and most have baths, but all are that little bit different. Whichever you choose, you'll be so cosy you may not want to leave, but luckily there is plenty to tempt you downstairs, not least the hotel's lovely gardens – which stretch all the way down to the sea – a wood-panelled bar and of course what is a very high-quality restaurant.

CORNWALL The Parade Mousehole Penzance TR19 6PR
01736 731222 oldcoastguardhotel.co.uk
HOW MUCH? Double rooms £140–£245 a night with breakfast, DB&B £215–£300. Family rooms £200–£255.

Saunton Sands Hotel

Kid-friendly luxury and sublime coastal views

As you would expect in a hotel that was recently voted one of the Top 100 family hotels in the UK, Saunton Sands has a relaxed and family-friendly vibe – not to mention-one of the best coastal views in the country, over the vast stretch of Saunton beach and the adjacent dunes. Its spacious guest rooms come in all shapes and sizes – both cosy and deluxe doubles, family rooms and so-called 'Living Suites' and fully fledged apartments. They also have a number of inter-connecting rooms that are ideal for families with older children.

All the rooms have large and comfy beds, Freeview TVs with Sky Sports thrown in, plus tea and coffee, Temple Spa toiletries and wifi. The more contemporary Living Suites have a Bose sound system and a fridge, and offer an early check-in, and parents will be pleased to know they can book the children into the beautifully equipped playroom for up to 2 hours each day and treat themselves to a relaxing massage or beauty treatment at the same time. There's a really lovely new spa, an indoor and outdoor pool, a sauna and gym, tennis and squash courts – and a restaurant that's one of the best in the area, serving a regularly changing, locally sourced seasonal menu. There's also a simpler restaurant, the Terrace Lounge, which serves lunch, afternoon tea and dinner.

But the hotel's greatest asset is perhaps the beach and its dunes, where they also run the Beachside Grill, whose wooden deck is a great place to watch the surf while having lunch with your family or just nursing a drink or snack. Overall it really is family – and seaside – heaven.

DEVON Saunton Near Braunton EX33 1LQ
01271 890212 sauntonsands.com
HOW MUCH? Double rooms from £144 a night for an inland-facing room in low season to £368 a night for a deluxe sea-facing room in high season.

"You can leave the hustle and bustle of modern life behind and escape to pure tranquillity at Saunton Sands."

Peter Brend Jr, Saunton Sands Hotel

What's nearby?

BRAUNTON BURROWS As if the beach wasn't special enough, you can also explore Braunton Burrows behind, where the dunes are up to 30m high.

THE ROCK INN This Georgeham pub is a local institution for its food, which includes fabulous Exmoor steak, mackerel, Lyme Bay scallops and much more.

SQUIRES Fresh as a daisy, it's as if the seafood has been thrown straight off the boat and into the kitchen at this iconic Braunton chippy. Even Rick Stein is a fan.

CRUISING

Scotland's Western Isles are a special place, and there is no better way to explore this magical region than by boat. St Hilda Sea Adventures operates small-ship cruising and wildlife holidays, taking in the beautiful islands, sea lochs and mountains of the Inner and Outer Hebrides. They have 2 cruise ships – St Hilda, a classic 54ft wooden ketch that sleeps 6 in 3 cabins, and the 82ft Seahorse II, built for the Norwegian fjords and small enough to anchor in remote places that larger ships are unable to access. The Seashorse II has a wonderful deck saloon, a boat deck for lounging, a crane for launching tenders and sea kayaks, and sleeps 11 in 7 cabins.

Cruising the Western Isles is a unique experience; you can charter an entire boat if you want, or just pay berth-by-berth. Each boat has its own skipper, and an onboard cook who prepares meals 3 times a day. All linens and towels are supplied and there is plenty of space if you want to bring your own equipment, such as bicycles, canoes, paddleboards and suchlike. Above all there's nothing like being rocked gently to sleep by the waters of the bay or waking up to the sound of water lapping against the hull. Each day is as action-packed or as relaxing as you please. You can fish, swim, dive, set lobster pots and marvel at the golden and sea eagles, dolphins, porpoises, basking sharks, otters and even the occasional minke whale. The small ships' tenders can also take you ashore for cliff walks, or you could just wander along the shore beach-combing and examining the pretty seaside rock pools.

ST HILDA SEA ADVENTURES Oban Argyll PA37 1PX 07745 550988 sthildaseaadventures.co.uk. Cruises run from April to October.

Soar Mill Cove Hotel

A fabulous family-friendly hotel in the South Hams

This South Hams seaside hotel has been owned by the Makepeace family for 3 generations, and the welcome is warm and the service and hospitality genuine and old-fashioned. But there's nothing old-school about the hotel itself; its 22 rooms are well furnished and thoughtfully equipped, with big bathrooms, wifi, books and games, and even binoculars for enjoying the spectacular views (and maybe spotting a dolphin). You can almost hear the waves from your room, and the glorious coastline is just a step away.

Accommodation is available in several options – all with beautiful views across the rolling hills or down to the cove. Some rooms and suites are ideal for families, while those looking for a little more privacy can stay in one of the self-catering retreats. There's an indoor heated saltwater swimming pool, a spa and gym, tennis and pitch-and-putt and a games room with snooker and table tennis. There's also a really good restaurant offering locally caught seafood and fresh Cornish delights, while the newly opened Castaways Café is ideal for younger guests to kick back and relax. But the extra beauty of Soar Mill Cove really lies in its position, just outside Salcombe in a gorgeous part of the South Hams; it's right on one of the most spectacular sections of the South West Coast Path and in a perfect location for great walks throughout this beautiful part of Devon. It's also dog-friendly, so you can bring your pooch along to share the experience.

What else? Well, the nice thing is that if (heaven forbid) anything's amiss, you can talk to the owners themselves – something we think is pretty special these days, rather like the hotel itself.

DEVON Near Salcombe TQ7 3DS 01548 561566
soarmillcove.co.uk
HOW MUCH? Double rooms with breakfast £159–£284 depending on season and sea view; family rooms and suites £209–£389. Self-catering from £950 per week.

"The cove at Soar Mill is such a magical place… I never tire, no matter what the season, of the ever-changing vista."

Keith Makepeace, Soar Mill Cove Hotel

What's nearby?

THE COVE Down in Hope Cove, this is one of our fave Devon beach bars, described by Devon Life as 'the South West's best craft beach bar by a country mile'.

OYSTER SHACK It might take a degree in navigation to find this place, but it's well worth the effort – for its fab oysters, moule frites, fresh crab and lobster.

BIGBURY & BURGH ISLAND Connected to the mainland at low tide, Burgh Island is home to a fabulous 1930s hotel – plus the sandy causeway is a great beach.

The Greenbank Hotel

Charming historic hotel right on Falmouth harbour

On the water's edge at Falmouth harbour, The Greenbank is a crowd-pleaser with class. Originally built in 1640, it's the town's oldest hotel, with uninterrupted views from both rooms and restaurant – perfect for a relaxing coastal break. The location could hardly be better and the best guest rooms make the most of it – not just with sea views and ocean-inspired colour schemes, but comfy king-sized beds, private balconies, decent bathrooms and – in the Florence Suite at least – harbour views from your rolltop bath. It's just fabulous to draw back the curtains for another glistening view of the sea in the morning – though not all rooms have water views, so make sure to ask for one if that's important to you. All rooms do, however, have wifi, flatscreen TVs, tea- and coffee-making facilities and 24-hour room service.

The restaurant looks seawards, anyway, so you can always feast on the views of Falmouth harbour before tucking into sumptuous food from the 2 AA-rosette menu, on which fish and seafood feature highly. The Water's Edge terrace bar has even more waterside appeal, and there's also a hotel pub – The Working Boat – for hearty meals, brunch and Sunday roasts. The Greenbank is only a few footsteps from Falmouth town, so all in all it's the perfect place from which to explore south Cornwall's most historic resort and port. The hotel is dog-friendly too, and also happens to be the only hotel in the Southwest to boast its own quay and private pontoon, so is also perfectly set up for travelling into town by water taxi... or indeed visiting on your own yacht!

CORNWALL Harbourside Falmouth TR11 2SR
01326 312440 greenbank-hotel.co.uk
HOW MUCH? Double rooms with breakfast from £109 a night. Dogs £12.50.

"We like guests to feel like the outside has been brought inside, as though they could step out of bed onto the water's edge."

Ben Young, The Greenbank Hotel

What's nearby?

GYLLYNGVASE BEACH Made for swimming, games and lounging, this is Falmouth's best beach and has a great café too.

FERRY TO ST MAWES Make the short hop to the chic fishing village of St Mawes – for the castle, 2 beautiful sheltered beaches and to browse its handful of artsy boutiques.

HARBOUR LIGHTS This close to the sea you'd expect decent fish and chips, and this chippie has been serving some of the Falmouth's best for many years.

Blue Hayes

Sumptuous boutique suites with panoramic sea views

Nothing is too much trouble at this grand, white aristocratic residence high on a clifftop just outside St Ives. With panoramic sea views and a beautiful position, there's a Mediterranean feel when the sun is shining, especially when you drift out on to the balustraded terrace to view the bay, with its pines and palms and well-tended gardens below. There are just 5 double suites and a smaller single suite – all are very spacious, decorated in cool off-whites and creams, with comfy beds with high quality mattresses and goose-down pillows, tea- and coffee-making facilities and smart TVs. Well-proportioned bathrooms feature body-jet showers and Molton Brown toiletries. Three of the 6 suites have wonderful sea views, and 2 have large private outdoor spaces – a spectacular private balcony in the Master Suite and a huge roof terrace for sunbathing in the Trelyon Suite. Of the 2 that don't overlook the sea, one has French doors leading out on to its own private patio garden. There's wifi throughout and a very convivial bar and dining room, and room-service is available in case you fancy breakfast in bed – which you almost certainly will. From the garden gate you're on the downhill path to the beach and only a short walk from the centre of town, but if you'd rather stay in and make the most of the evening views the hotel also serves light suppers on request (Cornish crab salad, seared tuna, local lobster and the like). It's a very calm, sleek experience all round, with a fabulous location and a personal approach to service, and this private hotel couldn't be better placed for a luxury stay in St Ives.

CORNWALL Trelyon Avenue St Ives TR26 2AD
01736 797129 bluehayes.co.uk
HOW MUCH? From £235 a night for the smallest suite in March or October up to £315 a night for the Master Suite in high summer. All rates include breakfast.

"Breakfasting on our balustraded terrace, overlooking the turquoise sea and white sands, is the ultimate tonic."

Malcolm Herring, Blue Hayes

What's nearby?

PORTHMINSTER BEACH With white sands lapped by azure seas, Porthminster Beach is among Britain's best beaches – and it has an iconic beach café as well.

BARBARA HEPWORTH MUSEUM The monumental sculptures in her former studio were Hepworth's nod to the region that inspired her and so many other artists.

GODREVY BEACH CAFÉ Home to one of Cornwall's most popular surf breaks, this beach also has a very popular café tucked into the sand dunes behind.

Atlantic Hotel

Old-fashioned luxury and a spectacular seaside location

Lots of hotels advertise rooms with sea views, but very few actually offer a panorama of the sea from every room. And what views! The Atlantic Hotel is well named, occupying an enviable location perched on a headland above Fistral, Tolcarne, Lusty Glaze and the other beaches far below. It's a large, full-service hotel, with two pools and a spa, restaurant and bar – and a sense of old-fashioned elegance that is part of its charm. The Beatles filmed their *Magical Mystery Tour* film here in the 1960s, but the hotel has also done a good job of updating itself in recent years, winning a number of awards for its restaurant, rooms and facilities. Each room is different, but all are light, generously proportioned and furnished in a contemporary style, with large beds, big flatscreen TVs, decent-sized bathrooms with toiletries, bathrobes and slippers, and tea- and coffee-making facilities and minibars. Some have their own terraces, while others are in a separate building positioned to take full advantage of the pool facilities.

It's the sea that dominates, not just in the rooms but in the public spaces too. The bar and restaurant – Silks – is a chic venue at any time of day, offering all-day dining from a full menu to light lunches and a fabulous Afternoon Tea. The spa facilities, have all been recently re-furbished, and there's a heated outdoor pool and hot tub which you can enjoy during summer, and the rest of the year a heated indoor pool and hot tub, sauna and steam room, as well as all the treatments you might expect. After your treatment you can stroll through the hotel's gardens and take in those spectacular views all over again.

CORNWALL Dane Road Newquay TR7 1EN
01637 872244 atlantichotelnewquay.co.uk
HOW MUCH? Double rooms with breakfast from £133 a night.

"Panoramic views, sandy beaches and amazing surf... sit back, relax and enjoy North Cornwall's beautiful coastline."

Esther Ledder, Atlantic Hotel

What's nearby?

BLUE REEF AQUARIUM Come face-to-face with marine life via an underwater tunnel that takes you beneath reef sharks, giant turtles, stingrays and pufferfish.

TOLCARNE BEACH People come from all over the country to ride the famous Wedge break at Tolcarne Beach. Grab your bodyboard and give it a try.

LUSTY GLAZE BEACH Tucked into a private cove, this is a place for all sorts of adventure activities, gigs and food and drink at the bang-on-the-beach restaurant.

The Rosevine

The perfect family hotel by the sea

Owned by the same company as the excellent Old Quay House in Fowey, this family-friendly Cornish country house by the sea combines the comforts of a luxury hotel with the freedom of having your own studio or apartment. Set in 2 acres of gardens above the sandy cove of Porthcurnick, the hotel is in a brilliant location for walks along the South West Coast Path as well as for the best bucket-and-spade beach days. There are also water sports galore at Portscatho, a 10-minute walk away, and you can easily hop on a ferry to Falmouth from nearby St Mawes. There is a miniature football pitch and climbing frame, while the upper lawn is scattered with wicker furniture, ideal for sea-gazing or cloud-spotting – indeed on a warm day, with the sea a cobalt blue, you can kid yourself you are in the Med; and when the weather is bad, there is an indoor heated pool, a grown-ups-only lounge and a well-equipped playroom. The hotel's decor is subtle and understated, with soft heritage greys, huge comfy sofas, an open fire and a mix of Lloyd Loom, antique and upcycled furniture, while the shutters in the dining room, looking out over the gardens to the sea, give a French château feel. The apartments are comfy, most have sea views and balconies or terraces, and there is enough space for family time without everyone tripping over each other. You can self-cater or use the restaurant, where the menu features local seasonal produce and also plenty of classics (burgers, steaks, etc) to appeal to less adventurous eaters. Basically it's a brilliant attempt to address the practicalities of family holidays without compromising on luxury or style. Long may it continue!

CORNWALL Portscatho TR2 5EW
01872 580206 rosevine.co.uk
HOW MUCH? Double rooms £139–£219 a night; studios, suites and apartments £149–£379 a night (B&B); self-catering cottage £1463–£2793 a week.

"At the Rosevine we strive to provide an unforgettable informal experience for the whole family in the most perfect surroundings."

Andries Loots, The Rosevine

What's nearby?

ROSELAND PENINSULA The best thing about the Rosevine is its position on the Roseland Peninsula and the beautiful walks along the South West Coast Path.

ST JUST Overlooking the creek, the churchyard in this tiny hamlet was described by John Betjeman as the most beautiful on earth. See if you agree...

THE RISING SUN, ST MAWES It would be a pity to come to the Rosevine and not visit St Mawes, and this pub is a nice place to stop for a pint if you do.

The Grove Cromer

A welcome so warm you won't want to leave

The Grove is the sort of hotel we really like at Cool Places. It's family-run and has been for years; it occupies a lovely historic building, which exudes a lived-in and appealing comfortableness that is hard to find (and even harder to fake) and it is run by enterprising people who are always looking to make the most of their property – and to go the extra mile for their guests. Hence the lush and secluded garden is home to a heated indoor swimming pool along with a handful of cottages and yurts, and their restaurant is as much of a draw for non-residents as it is for hotel guests. Plus this is – in the self-catering cottages at least – a dog-friendly establishment. Rooms range from cosy doubles and twins to a handful of family rooms. Most of the guest rooms are in the main house, but there are also 5 'Orchard Rooms', more contemporary in style, tucked away in a timber-framed building in the garden, a couple of which are perfect for families. The style of all the rooms is simple, understated and homely, with up-to-date furnishings and well-appointed en-suite bathrooms; they all have flatscreen TVs and DVD players and there is wifi throughout.

Finally there's the location, which is wonderful: the hotel occupies secluded grounds set well away from the main road, and the cliffs and beach below are just a short walk away through the woods on the far side of the garden. It's also a short stroll into the busy resort of Cromer in one direction, a slightly longer one to the nearby village of Overstrand, where the sand is lovely, there are crabs and lobsters for sale and there's a good clifftop beach café.

NORFOLK 95 Overstrand Road Cromer NR27 0DJ 01263 512412 thegrovecromer.co.uk
HOW MUCH? Standard double rooms with breakfast £95–£140 a night; Orchard rooms £110–£150; family rooms £130–£208; self-catering cottages £80–£200 a night; yurts from £120 a night.

"It's not hard to run The Grove – the historic buildings, gardens and beautiful landscape force people to take a deep breath, relax and enjoy spending time here."

Chris Graveling, The Grove Cromer

What's nearby?

CLIFFTOP CAFÉ This old donkey shed enjoys the perfect location, perched on the clifftop above Overstrand's lovely beach – the perfect spot for a crab sandwich.

FELBRIGG HALL A charming Jacobean mansion located amid gorgeous and extensive parkland, and including an exquisite walled garden.

THE GUNTON ARMS Enjoy venison cooked on the open fire and gawp at the priceless modern art on the walls – there's nowhere quite like the Gunton Arms.

YHA Boggle Hole

Tucked away in a converted mill outside Robin Hood's Bay in North Yorkshire, this has always been a desirable, family-friendly place to stay, but it's looking even better after a recent renovation. With a welcoming café-bar at its heart, a roaring log-burner and plenty of outdoor seating, there's a hideaway seaside feel that lends itself perfectly to lazy days in one of North Yorkshire's hidden gems. The original mill has 42 beds spread across variously sized rooms, while the timber-framed Crow's Nest has another 40-odd beds in mostly private and family rooms. Some have amazing sea views, while throughout there's a quirky use of reclaimed timbers, upcycled furniture, flotsam and jetsam from the beach, and nooks and crannies hiding all sorts of unusual discoveries. There's all the usual hostel stuff too, including a self-catering kitchen, and just a few steps away is the beach – a perfect place to enjoy a spot of rock-pooling, fossil-hunting, beach-combing or swimming – plus the hostel also lays on regular activities, guided walks, star-gazing events and the like.

NORTH YORKSHIRE Mill Beck Whitby YO22 4UQ 0345 371 9504 yha.org.uk
HOW MUCH? Dorm beds from £15 a night, private rooms from £25, family rooms from £29.

Falmouth Lodge

Occupying an Edwardian half-timbered terraced house in Falmouth, within easy reach of the town centre and just a street away from the pearly sands of Gyllyngvase beach, this budget option is a mainstay of life in this historic Cornwall port town throughout the year. Judi, the owner, is a true traveller with a knack of making things homely. There is a comfy living room and open fire in winter, an Aga (where you can cook your dinner) and outdoor spaces back and front so you can make the most of sunny days. There are 6 rooms in all – 3 can be rented as dorms or family rooms, 2 are doubles or twins, and there's also an attic room (with a sea view), which is the one for anyone who is after a bit more privacy, as it has its own bathroom. In short, we reckon this is one of the UK's best seaside places to stay on a budget– a great place for groups of friends or families, or for anyone travelling alone who wants to meet other people, and a genuinely perfect location for surfers, beach bums and coastal path walkers alike!

CORNWALL 9 Gyllyngvase Terrace Falmouth TR11 4DL 01326 319996 falmouthbackpackers.co.uk
HOW MUCH? £19–£35 per person a night, including breakfast.

Cohort Hostel

Danny and Lee Strickland took over what was a rather tired old building in 2015 and have turned it into something much more in tune with the cool St Ives vibe – a clean and contemporary hostel, right in the centre of town, with 7 mixed dorms and 2 female-only dorms furnished with custom-built 'pod beds' with a privacy curtain, plug socket, light, USB port and lockable, under-bed storage, plus 3 private rooms. It's won a couple of awards since it opened and is a very sociable place to stay, with a very comfy lounge and bar, a private courtyard with table football and a set of hot outdoor showers for surfers, a TV and movie room, a fully-equipped kitchen for self-caterers – and free superfast wifi throughout. There's also plenty of storage space for bikes, surfboards and other luggage. The location is great too, bang in the centre of St Ives, and walking distance from pubs, restaurants, the bus and train stations and the beach, making it a fabulous place to stay if you're visiting St Ives on a budget.

CORNWALL The Stennack St Ives TR26 1FF
01736 791664 stayatcohort.co.uk
HOW MUCH? Dorm beds from £22 a night; double rooms from £48, triples £70.

Deepdale Backpackers

Just off the main road, in the heart of Burnham Deepdale, this wonderful campsite-cum-hostel has for years been at the heart of this North Norfolk coastal village – and not just because of the diversity and excellence of its accommodation but also for the shops and cafés of Dalegate Market next door and the regular music sessions, summer festivals and other activities and events throughout the year. If you want to explore this part of the North Norfolk Coast on a budget, there's no better place than Deepdale, which is both a campsite and a hostel. There are around 85 camping pitches and the backpackers hostel has both beds in dormitories and private en-suite rooms. There's a well-equipped kitchen, a dining area and lounge, and laundry and drying facilities too. There are also diversions a-plenty in and around Burnham Deepdale. Hire a bike or slip on your walking boots to follow the nearby coastal path or just mess around in the marshes before dinner at one of the 2 excellent pubs in the village. You won't want to leave.

NORFOLK Deepdale Farm Burnham Deepdale PE31 8DD
01485 210256 deepdalebackpackers.co.uk
HOW MUCH? Dorm beds from £12, double rooms from £30, twins from £30, family rooms from £60.

Budock Vean Hotel

A beautifully situated hotel, spa and resort

Set on a splendid private estate above the lovely Helford river, this is not simply a traditional country house hotel. It is also a perfect choice for families – both nuclear and multi-generational. We love the way you can choose between sitting by an open fire, in the conservatory or an outdoor terrace, and the variety of public spaces (several lounges, cocktail bar, snooker room) mean that there is plenty of room for everyone, even on a wet day. We also adore the huge pool, which is another great place to while away a wet afternoon; it has an open fire and sauna, as well as a little terrace with a hot tub. There is a small spa, with seasonal spa treatments, beautiful gardens leading down to the hotel's foreshore, where boat trips and guided kayak adventures set out, and, finally, a lovely 9-hole golf-course that is free for guests.

As for the rooms, most of them have been updated in a contemporary country-house style, with lush new bathrooms and walk-in showers. Breakfasts are generous and traditional, with hot dishes cooked to order, and lunch and dinner can be either a formal occasion in the restaurant or a more casual affair in the bar. There is also a children's tea daily at 5.30pm. In short, this is a hotel with facilities galore that enjoys a special South Cornwall location not far from Falmouth, at the end of the scenic estuary of the Helford River. It's a good place for both romantic couples and families, and it also has a number of self-catering cottages in the grounds – 4 occupying what were once the estate's outbuildings, and 3 contemporary purpose-built houses – all of which enjoy full use of the hotel's facilities and are dog-friendly.

CORNWALL Mawnan Smith Falmouth TR11 5LG
01326 252100 budockvean.co.uk
HOW MUCH? Standard double rooms with breakfast £73–£118 a night, Superior rooms £86–£131, Signature rooms £99–£146. Stay 5 nights or more and the prices drop by 15%.

"Minutes from the coast path… escape the rat race and discover our little oasis by the Helford River."

Martin Barlow, Budock Vean Hotel

What's nearby?

HELFORD RIVER CRUISES From the hotel, these take you along the Helford River and into the creeks, including Frenchman's Creek (of Daphne du Maurier fame) to spot herons, egrets and cormorants.

GLENDURGAN GARDEN This sub-tropical garden tumbles down to an idyllic beach. Get lost in the maze and let the kids get dizzy on The Giant's Stride.

FERRYBOAT INN Just down the road from the hotel, this is a brilliant and historic waterside village pub that has great views of the scenic Helford River.

Greystones

A stylish B&B with stunning views

Not all B&Bs are created equal, a fact you are quickly reminded of when you arrive at this beautifully situated grand old house on a hill above the bay in Oban. The warmness of the welcome and spaciousness of the rooms are only exceeded by the stunning nature of the views – right across to Mull and the smaller isle of Kerrera.

Run with style and panache by well-travelled ex-architects Suzanne and Mark McPhillips, this former maternity hospital is about as comfortable as could be, with a great location right in the centre of town and just a short walk from the waterfront. It's their second B&B venture, and there's a stylishness to the rooms that perhaps you don't expect in a building of this nature, with contemporary furniture, soft, muted tones and modern art, along with flatscreen TVs and DVD players, wifi, high-quality bed linen, tea- and coffee-making facilities and (a nice thought) glasses and a corkscrew so you can enjoy a glass of wine while getting used to those views. There's a sitting room and library downstairs, and Suzanne and Mark cook up a fabulous breakfast in their turreted dining room every morning – not only a superb cooked Full Scottish and good quality smoked salmon, but also delicious and unusual alternatives like smoked haddock frittata.

As for Oban, it's a busy town with plenty to draw you, from the bizarre colosseum of McCaig's Tower to some of the best fish and seafood restaurants on the west coast. For many travellers, it's also the main jumping-off point for ferries to the various islands of the Hebrides.

ARGYLL 1 Dalriach Road Oban PA34 5EQ 01631 358653
greystonesoban.co.uk
HOW MUCH? Double rooms £110–£185 a night, including breakfast.

"Greystones is the perfect place to relax – just sit and watch the boats against a backdrop of the isle of Kerrara and the mountains of Mull."

Suzanne McPhillips, Greystones

What's nearby?

MCCAIG'S TOWER This mock-colosseum is one of Scotland's largest follies, and a masterpiece of Victorian philanthropy – plus the views from the top are superb.

EE-USK Oban is seafood capital of Scotland, and this is the place to find out why, serving creamy oysters, giant langoustines and their signature grand platters.

ISLE OF KERRERA Get off the tourist trail by visiting Kerrera, which despite being visible from Oban's harbour is beautifully unspoiled and quiet.

Manor Town House

Home comforts with super style and views to die for

If you're looking for a B&B room with a view over the beautiful Pembrokeshire coast, then look no further. The lovely Manor Town House, overlooking the sea in Fishguard, provides a warm welcome and fabulous views in what is one of the best places to stay in the area. The affable owners, Helen and Chris, have a distinguished fan club – Bill Bryson declared their B&B 'lovely' and Nick Crane reckoned it to have the UK's 'best breakfast view', not to mention the 'best breakfast'. And Bill and Nick are not far wrong. Along with the inspiring views, Manor Town House has 6 lovely guest rooms, 4 of which have sea views – and 2 of these have beds perfectly positioned for watching both sunrise and sunset over the sea. All rooms are en-suite (3 have showers, 3 baths) and all are individually decorated with flair and style, with well-chosen antique furniture and super-comfy beds (Chris, or maybe it's Helen, has even counted the number of springs to ensure you have a good night's sleep!). You can also expect all the other comforts you get in most high-end establishments, such as TV & DVD, dressing gowns, luxury toiletries, bottled water, Nespresso machines and more.

Downstairs there is a room stuffed full of DVDs and books, a licensed honesty bar, and a couple of cosy rooms with log fires that are adorned with work by local painters and photographers. They have good wifi, and the B&B's breakfasts have won awards for the best use of local produce, so you'll be well fed too. In short no stone has been left unturned at the Manor Town House, which is as close to the perfect contemporary seaside B&B as it's possible to get. We think you'll love it.

PEMBROKESHIRE 11 Main Street Fishguard SA65 9HG
01348 873260 manortownhouse.com
HOW MUCH? Doubles rooms with breakfast £95–£115.

"First-time visitors can't believe how much of a hidden secret our place is; our regulars hope it stays that way. We love to make them all feel at home and to treat our no-rules B&B like their own home."

Helen and Chris, Manor Town House

What's nearby?

PEMBROKESHIRE COAST PATH Fishguard sits right on the 186-mile length of this coastal footpath and offers tempting hikes in both directions.

CARN INGLI Most Pembrokeshire visitors head for the beach but Carn Ingli is also worth a visit, with magnificent views from its 346m summit.

STRUMBLE HEAD A wild and scenic spot, with a dramatically sited lighthouse and lots of places to spot dolphins, seals and seabirds.

Number One St Luke's

Definitely not your average Blackpool B&B – when Mark and Claire Smith first opened Number One in a regular house in a residential street in a quiet part of South Shore, the boutique stylings and all-round gorgeousness stuck out like a sore thumb. Roll on a few years and there are a fair few contemporary accommodation choices now, but Number One still keeps its nose in front – it was Visit Britain's 'B&B of the Year' a decade ago, and there's a personal service here that's very appealing if you're tired of bland hotels. The house style is glam-boutique rather than understated – it is Blackpool, after all – and you've got the lot in each of 3 individually styled rooms, from whirlpool baths to wifi, while there's a hot tub outside in the garden. For an intimate Blackpool romantic retreat we reckon you could hardly do better. There are also more rooms (and sea views) at their bigger seaside hotel, Number One South Beach. Lastly, if like Claire you have an electric car, you can also charge it overnight at their own electric car-charging point.

LANCASHIRE 1 St Luke's Road Blackpool FY4 2EL
01253 343901 numberoneblackpool.com
HOW MUCH? Double rooms with breakfast – midweek £120, weekends £125.

The Old Rectory

If there were proof that things in Hastings were on the up, it's this 18th-century rectory on the edge of the Old Town, which has been tastefully dolled up as a luxurious boutique hotel, with 8 quirkily decorated guest rooms that charm and indulge at the same time. The rooms vary from the relatively simple Rock-a-Nore to the fancier All Saints and Crown, but all come with tea- and coffee-making facilities, fresh milk and mineral water, Freeview TVs with DVD players, bathrobes, Egyptian cotton sheets and well-appointed bathrooms – many with baths – stocked with the hotel's own brand of toiletries. There's also a suite with space for 4 – perfect for friends, 2 couples or a family. Breakfasts are locally sourced and delicious – homebaked bread, kippers from the Old Town fishmonger, eggs from a nearby farm – plus they make their own sausages and bacon. There are two chic lounges and an honesty bar, a lovely walled garden with patio and pond, and a recently added treatment rooms and sauna for a spot of proper pampering!

EAST SUSSEX Harold Road Hastings TN35 5ND
01424 422410 theoldrectoryhastings.co.uk
HOW MUCH? Double rooms with breakfast from £110 to £165 a night.

The Cavalaire

Brilliantly run by its friendly, down-to-earth owners Derek Jermey and Garry Clarke, The Cavalaire manages the rare feat of being both stylish and refreshingly unpretentious – a bit like Brighton itself. Situated in the heart of funky Kemptown, its 10 rooms are comfortable and contemporary, with good, recently refurbished bathrooms kitted out with powerful showers and good-quality toiletries, tea- and coffee-making facilities with real milk and biscuits, Freeview TVs and digital radios. Even if you don't treat yourself to one of the 4-posters, you'll find your bed made with high-end linen and loaded with colourful cushions. The breakfast, too, served in the bright and tasteful dining room, is first class, with lots of locally sourced ingredients, pancakes as an option, as well as a fab veggie alternative, and good coffee. Basically, though, there's no secret to the Cavalaire's success, which is mostly down to owners who are prepared to go the extra mile for their guests and whose eye for detail is impeccable.

EAST SUSSEX 34 Upper Rock Gardens Brighton
BN2 1QF 01273 696899 brighton.cavalaire.co.uk
HOW MUCH? Double rooms with breakfast from
£95–£250.

Driftwood Beach House

Run by affable hosts Jez and Michelle Hills, this seaside B&B is right across the road from Seasalter Beach, with its breathtaking views across Whitstable's bay in one direction and the marshes and surrounding countryside in the other. It has a cool, shabby chic decor partially inspired by the owners' travels, and 3 double rooms – the soothing Moroccan Room, the Chess Room and the Spa Room – all with comfy beds, en-suite bathrooms, smart TVs and ultra-fast wifi. Each room also has its own private decked area – the Chess Room boasts, yes, a giant terrace chess set; the Spa Room has its own sunken outdoor hot tub; while the Moroccan features a shaded decking area. It's a short walk to the excellent Sportsman gastropub, a well-known place beloved of food critics that is very handy for a spot of dinner – if you can get a table! But you may prefer to head off in the other direction, to the more varied delights of Whitstable itself – after all, those oysters won't eat themselves!

KENT 230 Faversham Road Seasalter CT5 4BL
01227 638291 whitstablebedandbreakfast.co.uk
HOW MUCH? Double rooms £85–£130 –
including breakfast.

Pebble House B&B

Five-star B&B luxury in a stunning seaside location

Escaping Londoners Simon and Andrea Copper rebuilt this beautiful Mevagissey B&B in 2011–12, and you can immediately see why they bothered – it enjoys stunning 180-degree views from its clifftop perch at the top of the village. But they didn't just rebuild it. They have taken Pebble House to a new level, transforming this landmark 1930s building into a proper boutique B&B that makes the most of what is by any standards a unique location.

They have just 4 luxury guest rooms, all of which have sea views and floor-to-ceiling windows, and 3 of which have Juliet balconies. Bathrooms are well equipped, uniquely decorated and stocked with Molton Brown goodies – and there's a front terrace to drink in those views while you sit and watch the fishing boats bobbing about in the bay. Simon and Andrea take care to look after the other details too, and have a washing room for muddy walking boots and a drying room for wet beach clothes. Breakfast is an award-winning affair, enhanced by Andrea's homemade granola and soda bread as well as the sea views from the light, bright breakfast room. It's all beautifully done, and uniquely 'Everything is for Sale', so if you especially like your bed, or the reclaimed mirror on the wall of your room – it's yours! You can rent Pebble House on an exclusive-use, self-catering basis (and bring your kids), but otherwise it's an adults-only B&B, and fully licensed, so makes a perfect romantic hideaway, handy for the South West Coast Path for extraordinary walks and for any number of other attractions in what is a beautiful part of Cornwall. But, as Simon and Andrea are such great hosts, you may not want to leave.

CORNWALL Polkirt Hill Mevagissey PL26 6UX
01726 844466 pebblehousecornwall.co.uk
HOW MUCH? Sea view double rooms with breakfast from £170 a night, suites from £190. Exclusive use £2196–4596 a week.

"We wanted to create an exceptional experience for everyone when we rebuilt Pebble House, with its stunning sea views, and we hope we have achieved that."

Andrea and Simon, Pebble House B&B

What's nearby?

EDEN PROJECT It hardly needs an introduction, but if you're in the area a visit to the domes and biospheres of the Eden Project is a must.

LOST GARDENS OF HELIGAN Re-discovered in the 1990s, the famous gardens here have been painstakingly restored to their former glory.

VAULT BEACH Located lust beyond Gorran Haven, this crescent of fine shingle and sand is a much quieter affair than many Cornish beaches, and all the better for it.

Achmelvich Beach Hostel

The legendary white sands of Achmelvich Beach are often compared to those of the Caribbean – and they are just yards from your bed at this wonderfully sited remote Scottish hostel. What was once an old school building has been converted into a 22-bed, dog-friendly place to stay, with a compact self-catering kitchen and a larger dining area. It's a simple base but also one that has all you need for a comfortable stay, especially as you're going to be spending most of your time outdoors. The rooms vary in size and include dormitory accommodation, private rooms and one family room. The hostel is set above its own crescent of white sand, while the local area is a wonderful place to explore the coastline and find even more secluded beaches, or to head out on bracing hill walks. In the summer, group hikes are organised by local rangers and watersports enthusiasts can enjoy canoeing, kayaking and windsurfing nearby.

Rick Stein's Café Rooms

These rooms in the heart of Padstow are the budget alternative of the many Stein accommodation offerings in town, but as you would expect it's still pretty comfy, with 3 cosy rooms above Rick Stein's excellent café. The style is quirkily chic, with brass bedsteads, distressed old wardrobes, fireplaces and shuttered windows that overall create just the right vibe for a short break by the sea. But it's not all antiques: each room has a flatscreen TV, wifi, tea- and coffee-making facilities, complimentary mineral water and biscuits and lovely en-suite bathrooms that come with Molton Brown toiletries and bathrobes. One of the rooms has a 4-poster, a couple are dog-friendly and the location is great too, right in Padstow's buzzy centre. Breakfast is as excellent as you would expect, served of course downstairs in the café, and you get the usual priority booking on all Stein restaurants, so if you want you can spend the money you have saved on your accommodation on a slap-up meal at the flagship Seafood Restaurant, just a few minutes' walk away.

HIGHLANDS Recharn Lairg Sutherland IV27 4JB 01571 844480 hostellingscotland.org.uk
HOW MUCH? Dorm beds from £19 a night, private rooms from £45 a night.

CORNWALL Middle Street Padstow PL28 8AP 01841 532700 www.rickstein.com/stay/rick-steins-cafe
HOW MUCH? Double rooms with breakfast from £125 a night.

YHA Brighton

The flagship YHA Brighton is basically a spruced-up central Brighton hotel that offers funky accommodation on a budget in a location that many of the pricier chains would kill for. Housed in a rather fine Regency building with handsome public spaces, it's a minute's walk from Brighton Pier and has 24-hour access, so there's no danger of missing out on the seaside action. As a budget base, it hits all the right notes – you can still pay by the bed in good-quality dormitories (mostly in 4- and 6-bed rooms, all of them en-suite), and there's a good café and bar, open to all, a well-equipped self-catering kitchen and a bike store. But if you're prepared to pay more, it also has lots of en-suite double rooms that are far more hotel than hostel, some of which even a rolltop bath and a sea view. It's very much in the vanguard of new British hostelling – value for money, whichever type of room you choose, but a genuinely stylish choice for travellers, backpackers, Brighton weekenders and budget-conscious families.

> **EAST SUSSEX** Old Steine Brighton BN1 1NH
> 0845 371 9176 yha.org.uk
> **HOW MUCH?** Dorm beds from £14.50 a night, private rooms from £25, family rooms from £35.

Seven

Londoners looking for a quick and easy weekend break by the sea might not until recently have considered Southend-on-Sea. Which is a pity because it's really easy to reach from the capital, and walking or riding the mile or so length of its famously long pier is a rite-of-passage for lovers of UK seaside towns. Now, with the arrival of Seven, Southend's first properly posh boutique hotel, there's somewhere special to stay too. Situated among the resort's elegant Regency terraces, it does a pretty good job of injecting a bit of glamour into the town, with 37 guest rooms, around half of which have sea views, decorated in cool pastel shades alongside dark wood and brass and fancy custom-made headboards; bathrooms have walk-in showers and underfloor heating. Don't miss the restaurant, whose thoroughly British menu is thoroughly delicious, highlighting local ingredients like oysters, cockles, excellent salt-aged lamb and shorthorn beef, cooked in its charcoal oven. Outside, the lights of Southend shine that little bit brighter now Seven is in town.

> **ESSEX** 7 Clifton Terrace Southend-on-Sea SS1 1DT
> 01702 900010 thesevenhotel.co.uk
> **HOW MUCH?** Double rooms from £100 a night, not including breakfast (£10).

The Pier at Harwich

A stylish hotel that evokes Harwich's maritime spirit

Harwich isn't perhaps the obvious location for a boutique hotel and a fancyish restaurant, but that's one of the things we like about this place, which is part of the excellent, Essex-based Milsoms group of hotels. They recently spent a large sum of money revamping this wonderful old building, right on the harbour in Harwich, and have turned it into a boutique hotel with an all-day dining restaurant that is as chic and stylish a place to stay as you'll find anywhere on the East Coast. Perhaps the best thing about the renovation is the way it references Harwich's seafaring past, with both its bar and restaurant and 14 upstairs bedrooms designed to make the most of the stunning sunsets and glorious harbour views. All the bedrooms are equipped with flatscreen satellite TVs, complimentary soft drinks and aromatherapy toiletries, and there's wifi throughout. There's a restaurant on the first floor that opens out on to the building's elegant period wrought-iron balcony and serves fish and seafood (among other things) fresh from the harbour, while downstairs the NAVYÄRD bar is a stripped-back and cool space with estuary views from every table, a good choice of ales and cocktails and a bar menu inspired by the town's Scandinavian roots – open sandwiches, sharing platters and great oysters.

We love it when any old building is brought up-to-date and given a bit of overdue love and care; when it's done this well, and with this much respect to its location, we love it even more. In short, The Pier is a great stop-off for an early ferry, but why stop there? At less than 2 hours from London, it's the perfect weekend escape.

ESSEX The Quay Harwich CO12 3HH
01255 241212 milsomhotels.com
HOW MUCH? Double rooms with breakfast £120–£140 a night. Mayflower suite from £200 a night.

"No one realises how much there is to do and see in Harwich – a museum around every corner, great seafood landed in the harbour and spectacular sunsets along the river."

Sue Bunting, The Pier at Harwich

What's nearby?

SEAL-WATCHING Try one of the regular 2-hour round-trips to see the seals in Hamford Water, an area of reedy creeks, mudflats and marshes a short way down the coast.

HARBOUR FERRIES A network of foot ferries criss-cross Harwich's amazing natural harbour, linking you with the docks at Felixstowe and the Shotley Peninsula.

A HOUSE FOR ESSEX Overlooking the Stour estuary, this is artist Grayson Perry's shrine to his home county; you can walk around the outside or rent it as a holiday let.

Barford Beach House, Cornwall

COASTAL COTTAGES

Five words to gladden your heart – Holiday Cottage By The Sea. Wake up with an ocean view, stroll on the beach and enjoy all the fun of the seaside in your coastal home-from-home. We say 'cottage' – but we also mean romantic clifftop hideaways, fancy sea-view apartments and family beachside villas. They're yours for the weekend or the week – all you need to bring is a bucket and spade!

Barford Beach House

The ultimate luxury holiday home by the sea

Barford Beach House was created by Ken and Illona Aylmer as their ultimate luxury seaside beach house. Every room has been designed to make the most of the awesome sea views, with fairytale features and quirky design touches throughout, and it's perfect for a family gathering or a party weekend with a group of friends. Part of the Tregulland & Co portfolio of luxury Cornish holiday properties, the building sleeps up to 16 guests in 6 en-suite bedrooms, with views of breaking surf and access to a secluded private beach at Wanson Mouth. It's also just a short walk from Widemouth Bay, with access to pubs and cafés as well as miles of beautiful sandy beaches and surf spots. With so much glass, the house is full of light, and a balcony runs across the entire first floor, allowing you to enjoy those sea views to the fullest. The interior design shows a splash of fun and a 'rough-luxe' feel – smoked oak flooring, polished brass and silver bateau baths, a 10-foot long 18th-century Persian oak dining table, Moroccan bed throws and vibrant art. There's even an abandoned fishing boat installed in the grounds of the house. On still evenings the outdoor wood-burner will keep you toasty as you lounge on the large outdoor sofas – just what you need before jumping into the hot tub or sauna. As well as a dramatic copper-clad kitchen/dining/sitting room, the house has possibly the largest master suite we've ever seen, with its own cocktail bar, terrace and huge brass bath. A cinema and playroom for younger guests is well kitted-out with DVDs, games and books, while for adults there is 'The Bunker', a secret underground bar with an awesome sound system, pool table, retro arcade-games and classic pinball machine. Basically your ultimate luxury Cornwall holiday home by the sea.

CORNWALL Wanson Mouth Poundstock EX23 0DF
01566 770880 tregullandandco.co.uk
HOW MUCH? Rates start at £3000 for 3 nights (low season) or £6000 for a week, increasing to £8000 a week in high season.

"Building Barford has been a real labour of love... and we're overjoyed with the result."

Ken and Illona Aylmer, Barford Beach House

What's nearby?

WIDEMOUTH BAY One of north Cornwall's most beautiful beaches, with great sand and lots of rockpools to explore at low tide. Surf too if you're so inclined.

BUDE Seaside town with a fabulous mix of traditional shops and cool surf hangouts. Don't miss Granny Wobbly's Fudge Pantry, or brilliant family-friendly Summerleaze beach.

Pentire Penthouse

This circular apartment overlooks Newquay's iconic Fistral Beach, possibly the best surfing beach in the UK, and is a sophisticated, thoughtfully designed property full of mid-century retro furniture and cool design touches that make it ideal for families or groups of friends who fancy a spot of designer luxury. This huge duplex apartment sleeps 8 in 4 en-suite double bedrooms, with 2 extra beds available on request. The bedrooms are top-notch – super-king-size beds, 400-thread-count Egyptian cotton bedding, down surround pillows and feather duvets – and the enormous master suite has not only great sea views from your bed but also a private balcony, bathroom and large sitting area. It's even more stunning when you venture up the glass staircase to the enormous open-plan kitchen/living/dining room with wraparound glass walls. But the best thing of all is the huge roof terrace, from which you can enjoy awe-inspiring sunsets from the comfort of your own 8-person hot tub. Now that's what we call spoiling yourselves!

CORNWALL 1 Esplanade Road Newquay
TR7 1PY 01566 770880 tregullandandco.co.uk
HOW MUCH? 4-night midweek breaks from £1207; 7 nights from £1907 (low season) to £4000 (high season).

Flying Boat Cottages

A collection of 12 New England-style beach homes, kitted out to suit the most discerning of guests, the Flying Boat Cottages are a picture-perfect place to dip your toes into Scilly island life. There is direct access to the beach – lovely if you want an early morning dip or sunset stroll – and facilities on site are second to none, with a handsomely designed spa featuring both indoor and outdoor pools, tennis courts, a jacuzzi and gym. There's also a decent bar and bistro, and bike hire if you fancy pottering around the island under your own steam. Inside, these are not so much cottages as glam 5-star beach hideaways, each sleeping from 6 to 10 people and boasting a cool island vibe – contemporary colours and decor, underfloor heating, open-plan living and big windows with the all-important ocean views. There is also wifi throughout and widescreen satellite TVs. You get ferried from quay to cottage for the full upmarket celeb experience, so don't stint on the packing – you're going to need to look good in these surroundings.

ISLES OF SCILLY Tresco TR24 0QQ
01720 422849 tresco.co.uk
HOW MUCH? Cottages cost £1600 to £6000 a week, depending on season..

Buddha Beach House

There aren't too many places in Britain where you can squint and pretend you're in the Caribbean. But on a sunny day this beautiful coastal property is one of them. Not only that: the South West Coast Path passes right by; there's a sandy beach within a few metres, and you're a shortish drive from many of south Cornwall's major attractions. There are 2 houses, the larger of which is Buddha Beach House, which has 4 bedrooms, a massive living area, a games room with table football and pool table, Wii and satellite TV and a sea-facing terrace with a hot tub. Even on inclement days you can fire up the wood-burner, gaze out at the sea and fancy from your cosy vantage point that hurricane season has started. There's also the smaller On The Rocks down below. Both properties have a housekeeper to unpack any shopping ordered in advance and generally make everything nice, and you can also hire a private chef for a special occasion, or even just if you're arriving late. A lovely place to stay – in a beautiful and accessible part of Cornwall.

CORNWALL Whitsand Bay Torpoint 01460 30609
beachhouse-cornwall.co.uk
HOW MUCH? Buddha Beach House £1295–£4295 per week. On The Rocks from £595 per week.

Caerfai Farm Cottages

An organic, family-run dairy farm that has won awards a-plenty for its eco-initiatives, Caerfai Farm is one of the original pioneers of the low-carbon life, manifest in the landmark wind turbine you pass on your way down the lane to get there. As well as a wonderful coastal campsite, they have a group of holiday cottages, which enjoy equally spectacular views over the Pembrokeshire coast – 4 in all, each sleeping between 2 and 6 people. All the cottages are well-equipped with essentials but they also have wood-burning stoves – a cosy extra on this stunningly beautiful but admittedly rather exposed stretch of the coast. There is also a fantastic little farm shop that's open from mid May until the end of August and sells outstanding local produce, including matured Caerfai Cheddar and Caerphilly cheese produced on the farm, along with excellent croissants for breakfast. What's more, you're just an easy walk from St Davids and the coastal path – and Pembrokeshire's splendid beaches.

PEMBROKESHIRE Caerfai Farm St Davids SA62 6QT
01437 720548 caerfaifarm.co.uk
HOW MUCH? Cottages £255–£340 a week. Short breaks and long weekends available out of season.

Stone's Throw Cottage

Charming terraced cottage in the heart of Mundesley

Contemporary style, and an attention to those little details that make you feel not merely welcome but instantly at home, has made something really special out of this Victorian terraced cottage, situated on the Northeast Norfolk coast, just yards from an award-winning blue flag beach.

The wood-burner in the living room and a sun-trap patio ensure that the cottage is comfortable year-round, and little touches, such as milk chilling in the fridge and a Bluetooth speaker, are both thoughtful and practical: put your favourite playlist on, light a fire, pour a glass of wine or make a pot of tea... and forget about unpacking until tomorrow. Stone's Throw has 3 bedrooms (comfortably sleeping 5 in 2 doubles and a single) and a well-equipped stone-flagged kitchen/dining room with a washing machine, microwave and a Nespresso machine. The lounge has a glass-fronted wood-burning stove (complete with a basket of logs) and is a wonderful place to curl up on a chilly evening. It is also very child-friendly (travel cot, high chair, games, puzzles, DVDs, even baby cutlery and a baby bath), with the beach and an unusually imaginative playground (with a real boat to play in) a couple of minutes' walk away, not to mention a fab mini-golf course!

As for Mundesley, it's a charming, traditional seaside village, split between a quiet inland quarter and a slightly busier seafront stretch, with a handful of shops, cafés and pubs which serve food if you don't feel like cooking, and an excellent beach café down on the extensive sandy beach. A beautiful place to stay in a special part of Norfolk.

NORFOLK 24 Victoria Road Mundesley NR11 8JG
07786 374088 stonesthrowmundesley.co.uk
HOW MUCH? £105 a night April–October, minimum 3-night stay; £85 a night November–March, minimum 2-night stay. During school summer holidays and at Christmas a week's stay costs £750.

"This beautiful part of Norfolk has it all - quiet sandy beaches, amazing coastal and country walks, stunning historic houses and gardens and huge array of family attractions."

Kate Barker, Stone's Throw Cottage

What's nearby?

CROMER Why not walk the Norfolk Coast Path up to Cromer, where there's a decent beach, a pier, excellent fish and chips – and of course delicious crabs!

EAST RUSTON VICARAGE GARDEN This magical garden – home of the horticultural correspondent of the Eastern Daily Press – surpasses all expectations.

HAPPISBURGH Visit Happisburgh's iconic lighthouse and medieval church before having a drink at a cosy pub once frequented by Arthur Conan Doyle.

PASSIONATE ABOUT...

THE SEA

Based in the small village of Staithes, North Yorkshire, Sean and Tricia Hutchinson of Real Staithes are the best local guides you could wish for, running exciting, low-impact, sustainable tours from their home in this almost absurdly atmospheric old fishing village on the North York Moors coast, not far from Whitby. Sean is a fisherman through-and-through, and these aren't any old tours, but rather immersive experiences with a family that is deeply rooted in its community. Never happier than when at sea, Sean will take you out in his boat to fish for pollock, mackerel and lobster, afterwards teaching you how to prepare it before cooking and eating it on the beach. Sean and Tricia also offer foraging trips for edible seaweeds, uncovering fossils and rare stones, even learning how to make your own natural paints from foraged materials, along with whale-spotting and bird-watching expeditions at sea. Tricia makes sure that everyone is fed and watered, cooking up the fish you've caught or providing warming homemade soup at the end of the day.

Finally, if you've not been to Staithes before, you'll love it – the young James (later Captain) Cook had his first job here (as a shop assistant, oddly, not a seaman), and the cobbles, alleys and cottages are pretty much as they were in the 18th century. There's a great pub on the harbour too – perfect for discussing the day's mackerel catch and the one that got away...

REAL STAITHES White House Church Street Staithes North Yorkshire 01947 840278 realstaithes.com

Marine Point

Right above the harbour in the popular tourist hotspot of Mevagissey, Marine Point is a spacious apartment that makes a convenient base for exploring the town and its many nearby attractions, or it could be just a chilled-out place in which to sit on your balcony and watch the fishing boats coming and going. Either way, it's a great antidote to folksy Mevagissey, a luxurious space decorated in contemporary style, with leather sofas, oak woodwork, limestone tiling and Cornish artwork, complemented by superfast wifi and smart TVs. There are 3 bedrooms, all with luxurious mattresses, TVs and iPod docking stations, and one has an en-suite shower-room. Mevagissey is one of Cornwall's most attractive fishing ports, with lots of backstreets to explore, and there are good beaches nearby at Portmellon, Gorran Haven and Hemick. Marine Point is also a great place to return to after a day beach-lounging and swimming, before sauntering down to enjoy the town in the quiet of the early evening, when all the day-trippers have gone home.

CORNWALL 7 Nare Court Polkirt Hill Mevagissey PL26 6UX 07770 834268 harbour2horizon.co.uk
HOW MUCH? From £533 to £1461 a week.

The Warrens

Situated right at the foot of the dunes at glorious Camber Sands, The Warrens couldn't enjoy a better location, bang on the beach and just a few minutes' drive from the historic and very appealing town of Rye. It's a lovely white clapboard house typical of this part of Kent and Sussex (you're right on the border), and can sleep up 10 people in its 5 bedrooms. All accommodation is on one floor so it's perfect for those with limited mobility; there is a shared bathroom with rolltop bath and a further 2 wet rooms; and the well-equipped kitchen boasts a cooker, giant fridge, microwave, dishwasher, washing machine and a large dining table. Outside, a lovely garden faces south and has a BBQ and lots of garden furniture, although you may find that you spend most of your outdoors hours on the beach. Among other facilities, there''s wifi, digital TV and a DVD player, parking for up to 4 cars and dogs are permitted. Be sure to check out their sister glamping site, Original Hut Co, also in East Sussex.

EAST SUSSEX First Avenue Sea Road Camber TN31 7RR
01580 830932 camberaccommodation.co.uk
HOW MUCH? From £900 to £1600 a week, short breaks £650–£1100.

No.1 Wavecrest

With a prime location right on the beach in Whitstable, just a short stagger from the Old Neptune pub, No. 1 Wavecrest is the ideal place from which to enjoy the town's multiple attractions. You're right at the heart of things here, but away from the traffic, with scintillating views across the estuary. And it's a lovely house, full of light, beautifully furnished and very welcoming, with 3 bedrooms – 2 doubles and a twin. The master bedroom has an en-suite shower room and a balcony just about big enough for you all to enjoy a cocktail in the evening and take in the celebrated Whitstable sunsets. The bay window in the comfortable living room looks out over the water – which is just a few steps from your front door – while the side view takes in the action on the conveniently situated public tennis courts next door. There's also a smart TV and DVD player in the living room, and a well-equipped next door kitchen, with table and chairs. It's hard to imagine a better spot from which to appreciate Whitstable's many charms.

KENT 1 Wavecrest Whitstable CT5 1EH
01227 281800 whitstableholidayhomes.co.uk/no1-wavecrest
HOW MUCH? From £850 to £1600 a week.

Solomon's Island

There's a pretty good chance you won't have stayed in a holiday cottage quite like Solomon's Island. Nine miles up the coast from Land's End, it's not actually on an island but instead is a remote cottage with commanding views over one of Cornwall's wildest stretches of coastline. It's also an entirely off-grid destination, with power provided by an array of solar panels and water from the cottage's own borehole. Inside, all is welcoming and cosy, with 3 bedrooms – one double, one twin and a large room for kids with 3 single beds. Downstairs there's a sitting room with a wood-burning stove, a dining room with a Rayburn stove, and a kitchen beyond with a conventional hob, microwave and fridge. You can stroll to Chûn Quoit and on up to Chûn Castle over Woongumpus Common, or walk down to one of Cornwall's furthest-flung beaches at Portheras Cove. Or maybe just sit in the garden and enjoy the tranquillity of this stunning location. The perfect place for green-minded families or groups looking for an isolated bolthole.

CORNWALL Morvah Penzance TR19 7TT 07958 340288
solomonsisland.co.uk
HOW MUCH? From £410 a week off-season to £790 a week during peak season.

Halzephron House

A unique seaside spot overlooking the ocean

Perched atop a headland on a relatively untouched stretch of the Cornwall coast, Halzephron House enjoys a blessed location, surrounded by National Trust-owned land and with sea views that seem to pan out almost infinitely in all directions. It's a secluded sanctuary from where you can really immerse yourself in the wow-factor of Cornwall without the crowds, and without having to get in a car to visit places. The Southwest Coast Path runs around the edge of the gardens, and there's an award-winning pub a 5-minute walk away. Not only that, for fans of the TV series there are 2 *Poldark* locations nearby. In part it's a B&B, with one lovely en-suite bedroom that makes the most of the sea views and has its own private deck and entrance. But it also has a number of self-catering options –a cottage whose stylish interior featured in *Country Living* magazine a few years ago and which can comfortably sleep 6 people; a cosy dog-friendly romantic cabin for 2 people with its own garden, wood-burner, double bedroom and bathroom with a double-ended bath; and the well-named Observatory, which has views of the sea from every room, a large lawned garden with its own wildflower meadow, a firepit and an outdoor cooking area. As a walking holiday cottage, it can't really be beaten, since you can set off right from the front door.

Finally there's a relaxation and wellness strand to Halzephron House, with individual yoga sessions and treatments from reflexology to holistic massage available on request. They also host regular weddings, plus there are all sorts of activities available on your doorstep, from surfing to sea-fishing trips to just pottering about on the Helford River.

CORNWALL Gunwalloe Helston TR12 7QD
07899 925816 halzephronhouse.co.uk
HOW MUCH? Cottage £700–£2000 a week Observatory £850–£950, Cabin £750–£850, Tower suite £130 a night.

"Sharing our oceanside 'secret garden' with stargazers and nature lovers is hugely rewarding."

Lucy Thorp, Halzephron House

What's nearby?

CHURCH COVE At the end of the lane from Halzephron House, you may recognise this beautiful beach from the TV series Poldark. We just know it's a great beach, and much quieter than other local options.

GUNWALLOE BEACH The golden sands at this National Trust beach are backed by marshes and overlooked by a tiny medieval church.

HALZEPHRON INN This historic inn is a popular coastal pitstop, with a rustic interior full of smuggling lore and serving great food in hearty portions.

COUNTRYSIDE

Staying in the UK countryside doesn't have to
be all chintz, country pine and floral china.
We've picked some of our favourite Cool Places
for a thoroughly lazy weekend, walking holiday
or family getaway – we're talking country house
hotels, stately homes, boutique mansions,
gracious farmhouses and upmarket B&Bs
where you can enjoy the best of the beautiful
British countryside.

The Horn of Plenty, Devon

Abbots Lodge

Just one fabulous suite deep in the country

Situated on the edge of the pretty village of Wigmore, overlooking a lush valley on the Herefordshire/Shropshire border, Abbots Lodge is unlike most other B&Bs. For a start, it's only got one bedroom, which is more like a small apartment, if we're honest – a lovely, large and bright beamed room that opens on to its own shady patio and boasts a dining and sitting area with log-burning stove, a small kitchen and large en-suite shower. It's beautifully done – some of the furniture has been made by hand and all the woodwork is lovely – with a comfy yet contemporary feel. You can come and go as you please via your own private entrance, and owners John and Janet put a lot of effort into making your stay as memorable as possible, serving an excellent breakfast every morning at your own dining table, and cooking up delicious meals in the evening to those who want them (Janet was a professional chef in another life).

The location is gorgeous, with views across the wooded valley; you're a short walk from the ruins of Wigmore Castle by way of a direct footpath, and there is a brilliant pub in the village – The Oak – which serves excellent food. You could just spend your time pottering around on the various walks and cycle routes from Wigmore, finishing up with a glass of wine on the terrace and a couple of choices from Janet's excellent seasonal menu. But if you want to get into your car, Ludlow is just a short drive away and the location is perfect for exploring what is a really beautiful and arguably relatively unknown part of the country.

HEREFORDSHIRE Wigmore HR6 9UD
01568 770036 abbotslodgebandb.co.uk
HOW MUCH? Double room with breakfast £105 a night, less 10% for stays of 4 nights or more.

"Our guests often comment on how lovely it is to stay somewhere so peaceful and spacious."
Janet Morris, Abbots Lodge

What's nearby?

WIGMORE CASTLE One of the area's many castles, this is a particularly evocative ruin, and was a former stronghold of the notorious Mortimers. Fabulous views and you walk there direct from Abbots Lodge.

THE OAK, WIGMORE Chef Rory Bunting has helped to make this popular gastropub in his home village one of the best places to eat in the area. A very nice place to have on your doorstep.

The Slate Shed

A boutique B&B in the glorious Snowdonia National Park

The folks behind the glamping, camping and cottages at Graig Wen also run a lovely boutique B&B, housed in what was once a Victorian slate-cutting mill. There are 5 guest rooms, all of them dog-friendly and decorated in a bright, contemporary style and equipped with flatscreen TVs, free wifi, posh toiletries, lovely Welsh wool blankets and bathrobes. You are welcomed with chocolates and a drink, and you can soak up the fabulous views over the Mawddach Estuary during your stay (rooms Bran or Miri Mawr have the best views). Breakfasts are yummy, too, with everything sourced from local farms or friends and family – and you can opt to have a breakfast hamper delivered to your room if you're feeling lazy. Meanwhile, everyone is welcome to enjoy the spacious communal Caban area with its equally stunning views, honesty bar, books, maps and games.

There is tons to do in the local area, from hiring a bike and cycling to the local pub to hitting the nearby beaches, just 5 minutes away. Tackle Cader Idris, the spectacular mountain right at the back of Graig Wen, or explore a stack of challenging mountain-bike trails at nearby Coed-y-Brenin, around 5 miles north of Dolgellau. From your room, you can walk directly through the surrounding 45 acres of wild woodland and meadows to the edge of the Mawddach Estuary and Mawddach Trail. Plus Harlech Castle, Portmeirion and the Ffestiniog steam railway are within easy reach. It's also a fabulous place just to stay put and do a bit of star-gazing, with some seriously dark skies in this part of the Snowdonia National Park.

GWYNEDD Graig Wen Arthog Near Dolgellau LL39 1YP 01341 250482 slateshed.co.uk

HOW MUCH? B&B rooms £90–£130 a night. They take children over the age of 10 but all the rooms are either doubles or twins, so the self-catering cottages are best for young families.

"The best thing about staying here is waking up to the breathtaking views of the Mawddach Estuary and mountains."

Sarah Heyworth, The Slate Shed

What's nearby?

CREGENNAN LAKES Walk up Arthog 's waterfalls to these wild upland lakes to enjoy the views across the estuary and Barmouth's iconic bridge.

CADER IDRIS Choose your route to the peak (893m) of South Snowdonia's most popular and beautiful mountain.

COED Y BRENIN 9000 acres of forest, pristine rivers, waterfalls and wild swimming spots, and also the UK's largest mountain-bike centre. with trails for riders of all abilities.

Magazine Wood

With its wonderful North Norfolk location, this charming country B&B already has a lot going for it, but what makes this property really stand out from the crowd is that it also offers the things we love about a boutique hotel, such as privacy and a high level of service. Just a few miles from the coast, this award-winning bolthole is somewhere you can really switch off, with 3 completely self-contained luxurious suites (2 in a separate barn in the garden), stylishly decorated with soothing colours, tasteful fabrics and super-comfy beds. There's a fridge stocked with essentials, a sofa and dining table, binoculars for bird-watching, Netflix, plus your own iPad to cater for all your needs, including ordering breakfast. For the technophobes among you, just pick up the phone – owners Jonathan and Pip are always on hand. Fancy a spa treatment? They've got you covered: you can be pampered in the comfort of your own room. Or just grab a glass of wine, sit out on the terrace and enjoy the sunset – they're pretty spectacular around here.

NORFOLK Peddars Way Sedgeford PE36 5LW
01485 750740 magazinewood.co.uk
HOW MUCH? Double rooms with breakfast from £115 a night.

Lord Crewe Arms

This inn on the Durham/Northumberland border is an extraordinary building with an extraordinary history – a 12th-century abbot's lodgings that dominates the impeccably preserved village of Blanchland. Inside the main building, it's all stone corridors, soaring ceilings, heraldic shields, hidden nooks and majestic fireplaces. There are guest rooms in the old abbot's residence and the restored miners' cottages that flank the adjacent cobbled square, and while no 2 are the same, you can count on a certain updated country-chic style, and all feature king-sized beds, bathrobes, aromatherapy toiletries and carefully selected art and furniture. Colours throughout are earthy and muted, just like the peaceful surroundings, where the loudest sound you'll hear in the morning is the birdsong. Breakfast is a sophisticated and restful start to the day, with home-baked bread, locally smoked salmon or the full fry-up to set you up. Drinking in the medieval Crypt Bar and eating in the Bishop's Dining Room is as atmospheric as it sounds – and the food is delicious.

NORTHUMBERLAND The Square Blanchland DH8 9SP
01434 677100 lordcrewearmsblanchland.co.uk
HOW MUCH? Double rooms with breakfast £140–£160 a night.

Costislost

Just outside Wadebridge, this is about as tranquil a North Cornwall retreat as you could imagine, with 4 spacious rooms looking out on to the rolling countryside beyond. Proprietors Nick and Jane have a track record in the hospitality business, and it shows in every detail of this boutique B&B. The rooms are impeccably furnished, with an eclectic mix of antiques and contemporary items. Wooden floors are spread with kilims, you sleep in large wrought-iron 4-poster beds and there are stylish easy chairs from which to admire the glorious views. Breakfast is a sumptuous affair, with a help-yourself buffet and hot dishes on demand, all based on an array of fantastic local produce, including Jane's own granola, while the house itself is decorated with work by local artists, all of it for sale. Jane runs healthy cookery courses and they also offer yoga sessions and complementary therapies (massages, reiki). All in all, we can't think of a better – or healthier! – place from which to enjoy this part of Cornwall.

CORNWALL Washaway Wadebridge PL30 3AP
01208 840031 costislosthouse.co.uk
HOW MUCH? Double rooms £130–£140 a night, including breakfast.

Crossways Farm

In the middle of the Suffolk countryside, this 14th-century farmhouse would be an enticing place to stay whoever was running it. But as luck would have it, it's the home of Yalda Davis, who has turned part of this lovely old building into as welcoming a B&B as you could wish for, with 2 guest rooms available on an exclusive-use basis. There is a separate entrance, a spacious bathroom and a sitting room with a wood-burning stove. Breakfast is delicious and locally sourced, including eggs from Yalda's own chickens, and environmentalists will be pleased to know that the property's power is in part provided by the solar panels at the bottom of the garden. In summer you can enjoy your own private garden, complete with hammocks, table and chairs; there is a rowing boat for exploring the small lake, and Yalda is always happy to introduce the various animals who share the grounds with you. As Yalda says, Crossways Farm is more than just a place to stay. We're lucky she has decided to share it with us.

SUFFOLK Brettenham Road Hitcham IP7 7NT
01449 740325 crosswaysfarm.co.uk
HOW MUCH? From £150 a night for 2 people, £190 for 3 people, less 10% for stays of 5 nights or more.

Stow House

An exceptional B&B in the heart of the Yorkshire Dales

A boutique B&B in the heart of the Yorkshire Dales, Stow House occupies an artily (and artfully) renovated Victorian vicarage with magnificent views from every room. The excellent breakfast served here is freshly cooked to order, with homemade bread and granola alongside sausages and bacon supplied by the local butcher, and they can also make packed lunches or an evening meal for larger groups. Should you fancy a drink there's an honesty bar, or the powerful cocktails mixed by your hosts, Sarah and Phil, come highly recommended. Sarah, meanwhile, cannot help enough while you're settling in, or if you need advice on the local area: Aysgarth Falls are just a short stroll away, and there are plenty of more challenging local walks as well as country pubs and National Trust sights to visit. Wensleydale cheese is made nearby, and the surrounding countryside will be familiar to fans of the TV series *All Creatures Great and Small*.

The 7 exceptionally comfortable rooms are all different, but each is light and airy, with unique modern artwork and a well-specified bathroom, most of which have large baths. Our own favourites are the 2 bright modern spaces on the top floor – Shotgun Clare and Cowboy Balance – with wood beams and big velux windows cut into the eaves. The living room, snug/library and dining room downstairs all have wood-burners. Dogs are welcome in most rooms, and on fine days they can join the owners' pets in the extensive gardens.

NORTH YORKSHIRE Aysgarth Leyburn DL8 3SR
01969 663635 stowhouse.co.uk
HOW MUCH? Double rooms from £110 to £175 a night, including breakfast.

"Built as a vicarage for the Reverend Stow in 1876, the house has wonderful views, every luxury and an eclectic art collection."

Phil and Sarah, Stow House

What's nearby?

AYSGARTH FALLS The backdrop for Kevin Costner swashing his buckle in a Robin Hood romp, these wide and picturesque falls are unsurprisingly one of the Dales' most popular attractions.

BOLTON CASTLE For a snapshot of noble medieval life, seek out Bolton Castle, whose halls, kitchens and dungeons are decked out as if still inhabited.

THE GEORGE INN, HUBBERHOLME If you need just one reason to visit this historic Dales pub, consider this... it has won the British Pie Awards 3 years running.

The Castle Hotel

The perfect country bolthole

Once you get to the top of the main street of the tiny town of Bishop's Castle, which is where you'll find The Castle Hotel, you will feel like you've really got away from it all. There are glorious views over the surrounding countryside, which is beckoning and accessible, and the hotel makes a very comfortable place to stay for aspirant walkers and cyclists, and is very family-friendly.

The Castle has been here since the early 18th century – owners Henry and Rebecca claim Clive of India was once the landlord – and it's just our sort of place: comfy rather than posh, with 13 large and cosy rooms with flatscreen TVs, tea and coffee-making facilities and wifi throughout. There's a very good restaurant downstairs serving a menu featuring lots of local produce and a veggie option or 2 and a pleasant bar that is well used by locals and makes a point of serving proper brews from the local area, including the town's two micro-breweries. The hotel also has a lovely, almost Mediterranean-style garden that overlooks the Shropshire Hills from its high perch behind the main building, and is perfect for enjoying an early evening glass of wine in its covered arbours.

Finally, the Castle is one of the most dog-friendly hotels that we know of – not only encouraging you to bring your pet but also providing a 'Dog Welcome Box' in your room which includes a feeding mat, food bowl, towel, lead, treats and even poo bags. Plus your hound might like to play with the owners' friendly dachshund Millie. In short, we reckon The Castle is about as friendly and relaxing a place to stay in the countryside as you'll find.

SHROPSHIRE Bishop's Castle SY9 5BN
01588 638403 thecastlehotelbishopscastle.co.uk
HOW MUCH? Double rooms with breakfast £110–£155 a night.

"Come and share Bishop's Castle with us – a quirky border town with a thriving spirit for art, music and alternative living amid ancient and unspoiled countryside."

Henry and Rebecca, The Castle Hotel

What's nearby?

STOKESAY CASTLE Quite simply England's best-preserved fortified manor house, with an amazing beamed hall and a tower with spectacular views.

THREE TUNS Brilliant and atmospheric old pub and brewery right in the mdidle of Bishop's Castle. You can drink, eat and then take one of its brewery tours.

LONG MYND Around 7 miles long, the almost other-worldly landscape of this high, steep plateau is rightly the focus of many a local walk and footpath.

Huntingtower Lodge

A contemporary B&B with exquisite views

Perfectly poised for anyone wanting to explore the western Highlands, Huntingtower Lodge is a contemporary B&B with a really cosy atmosphere and an adults-only policy that makes it a perfect place to simply relax and unwind. Guests are met with tea and homemade cakes, something that pretty much encapsulates the welcoming feel of the place under the helm of Peter and Tina Moss. Peter is a Mountain Leader with extensive knowledge of the area as well as recommendations for local restaurants and attractions – ideal for those who want a heads-up over breakfast about trails to follow or places to visit.

That is, of course, if you manage to drag yourselves from the comforts of the accommodation. The 5 rooms are all individually designed, from the modern stylings of the Studio to the sumptuous romance of the Waterfall Suite, and they all share a large, comfortable lounge on the ground floor and staggering views across the loch to the Ardgour Hills and the hamlet of Stronchreggan on the far shore. It's an ever-changing picture that forms a superbly scenic backdrop to your stay. Downstairs, the sofas provide somewhere to sit and flick through a selection of maps, guide books and novels, while DVDs and games can help with a night in if the weather turns bad. A garage for secure bike storage and with space for drying clothes means that when you do get out you're well catered for, and the number of local footpaths and trails means you won't need to go far to find something to do. The location is breathtaking and the B&B provides accommodation to match.

HIGHLANDS Druimarbin Fort William PH33 6RP
01397 700079 huntingtowerlodge.com
HOW MUCH? Double rooms with breakfast from £105 a night – less 5% for stays of 3 or more nights; 2-night minimum.

"Huntingtower Lodge is the perfect place to enjoy spectacular loch views, abundant wildlife and the unspoiled landscapes and scenery of Lochaber."

Peter and Tina Moss, Huntingtower Lodge

What's nearby?

CLACHAIG INN Unlike the Campbells, this ancient pub welcomes tourists and walkers, who come to tackle the local peaks and appreciate the jaw-dropping scenery.

CRANNOG The Crannog is the stuff of Highland legend, a seafood oasis right on the shores of Loch Linnhe where the marine delights are as impressive as the Highland scenery.

JACOBITE STEAM TRAIN The 84-mile round-trip from Fort William ot Mallaig and back has been described as 'the best railway journey in the world. Give it a try.

Old Downton Lodge

A beautiful hotel in a great, off-the-beaten-track location

Nestled in the rolling green South Shropshire hills, Old Downton Lodge has been here so long it almost feels part of the landscape, a mixture of timbered medieval and Georgian houses, barns and outbuildings that have been ingeniously converted to host a very comfortable rural bolthole – and with a restaurant that was recently voted one of the best 100 places to eat in the UK, atmospherically housed in the lodge's grand Norman hall. The restaurant is certainly top-notch, with 3 AA rosettes and a Michelin listing, but there are also 9 very comfy guest rooms – plus a bridal suite in a separate building – to tumble into at the end of the evening, grouped around a herb- and flower-filled courtyard. There is a deliciously comfy sitting room fashioned out of the old stable, with a wood-burner and a bar squeezed into a corner, and a mighty timbered roof that echoes the look and feel of the guest rooms themselves. These are as different from each other as you might expect, and as well as the high-timbered ceilings many have stone walls and flagstoned floors covered with Turkish rugs. Most of the bathrooms have been recently refurbished and all the rooms have comfortable beds, including 3 4-posters, and well-chosen bits and pieces of furniture – along with wifi, homemade biccies, complimentary mineral water and all the stuff you would expect in a place of this standard. As for the location, it couldn''t be better, with any number of suggested circular walks to do in the surrounding countryside (for which they will provide a picnic if ordered in advance). There are a couple of electric car-charging points too. So just throw away those keys, charge up your car, and... relax!

SHROPSHIRE Downton on the Rock Ludlow SY8 2HU 01568 771826 olddowntonlodge.com
HOW MUCH? Double rooms £155–£345 a night, including breakfast.

"A home-from-home, but better – with friendly staff and a relaxed atmosphere."

Willem and Pippa Vlok, Old Downton Lodge

What's nearby?

LUDLOW CASTLE This ruined castle and popular market town is worth a visit at any time of year, especially when it hosts the town's annual food festival.

DOWNTON GORGE A beautiful area of natural woodland in a limestone ravine formed by the fast-flowing Teme river. Gorgeous walking.

MORTIMER FOREST These ancient hunting grounds on the border of Herefordshire and Shropshire are popular with walkers, cyclists and horsey folk.

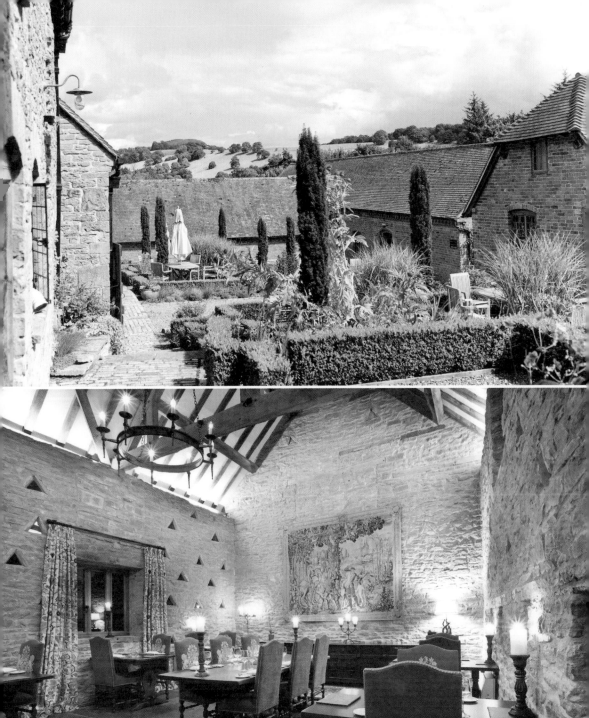

We've got to say that Alison O'Neill – aka the 'Barefoot Shepherdess' – is one of our favourite people in Cumbria. Not only is she a real live shepherdess – she runs a small sheep farm in the Cumbrian part of the Yorkshire Dales, in a beautiful spot overlooking the lush rolling fells of the Howgill Fells. She also takes people out on guided walks and wild swims that truly bring the local landscape alive, whether in the immediate locality of her beloved Howgills – where she is originally from – or on the fells of the nearby Lake District.

Alison is not by any means an ordinary sheep farmer. Dressed in the distinctive tweeds and skirts she markets as a sideline, she also runs walks on the Scottish island of Harris and buys handwoven bolts of tweed directly from the weavers there. She's full of stories about the area she grew up in and will take you to an array of gorgeous places you wouldn't otherwise have known about, including some fabulous spots for wild swimming. Not only that, but true to her name she always conducts at least part of her walks barefoot, so she can feel the Cumbrian turf and soil beneath her feet. Why not take off your shoes and join her?

Shacklabank Farm Firbank Sedburgh Cumbria LA10 5EL
01539 620134 shepherdess.co.uk

Brooks Country House

Shabby-chic country living on a Herefordshire estate

Once at the heart of a 1000-acre Herefordshire estate a few miles north of Ross-on-Wye, this funky 22-bedroom Georgian manor is the perfect place to spend a few days away from whichever big city you live in, not only for its relaxed country weekend feel but also for the facilities, which include a heated outdoor swimming pool, games room, sauna and small gym – goodies that weren't lost on the likes of Led Zeppelin, Oasis and Jamiroquai, who holed up at previous incarnations of the hotel while recording nearby.

The latest version has been refurbished throughout, with contemporary wallpaper, chandeliers and high-end vispring beds with goose down pillows and duvets, but it retains a shabby-chic, rock-star vibe – Brooks' schtick is 'affordable luxury', and it's deliberately not posh, designed to evoke the cool country pad of your beatnik cousin rather than the aristo hangouts of the huntin', shootin' and fishin' brigade. Half of the rooms are in the main house and vary from regular doubles to larger rooms with king-size or super-king-size 4-posters that showcase the best of the views over the sumptuous grounds. They all feature antique furniture and a hospitality tray of goodies on arrival, and bathrooms are generously sized with rolltop baths and power showers. The rest of the rooms are in an old coach house and a stable block. As in all good country house hotels, there is a restaurant on-site – fashioned out of the former library, so you don't have to leave if you don't want to. You can also wash your dinner down with the hotel's very own dry white wine, produced at the estate's Pengethley vineyard.

HEREFORDSHIRE Pengethley Park Near Ross-on-Wye HR9 6LL 01989 730211 brookscountryhouse.com
HOW MUCH? Double rooms with breakfast £100–£140 a night.

"We love Herefordshire, with its amazing produce, endless country views and rural beauty – and Ross-on-Wye offers a great selection of indy stores for retail therapy."

Carla Brooks, Brooks Country House

What's nearby?

ROSS-ON-WYE Perched above the River Wye, this a lovely old town has a tangle of narrow streets and a folksy vibe in tune with the surrounding countryside.

THE RED LION A decent pub in the neighbouring village of Peterstow that serves real ales and hearty pub grub to a loyal crowd of regulars. Good Sunday roasts too.

ROTHERWAS CHAPEL This tiny Catholic chapel was originally medieval but has a stunning interior restored by the Victorian architect Pugin.

Crestow House

What could be better than escaping for the weekend to a luxurious and intimate retreat in the Cotswolds? Crestow House offers guests just that. Set on the edge of Stow-on-the-Wold, this beautifully restored Victorian manor house is an oasis of tranquillity – with a home-away-from-home atmosphere, stylish comfortable surroundings and top-notch service. The property was designed by world-renowned architect Sir Edwin Lutyens and retains plenty of original features, but combines them with furniture created by local craftsmen and accessories from around the world. Each of the 7 boutique bedrooms are individually decorated, and come with all the mod cons needed to ensure a comfortable stay. When you're not relaxing there, make the most of the manicured grounds or take a dip in the outdoor pool; after a game of croquet, chill with a book in the library, or browse their ever-changing collection of art. There's lots to do nearby (this is the Cotswolds, after all) but we'll be honest: lazing around at Crestow is pretty good too.

GLOUCESTERSHIRE Fosseway Stow-on-the-Wold
GL54 1JX 01451 831709 crestow.co.uk
HOW MUCH? Double rooms with breakfast from
£180 a night.

Howard's House Hotel

From the idyllic hamlet location to the relaxed country-style decor in a Grade II-listed house, Howard's House is perhaps the perfect Wiltshire country retreat. A 17th-century house built of honeyed stone and set in beautiful gardens, it's not so much a hotel as a comfortable and informal place to loaf before an open fire in the lounge or dawdle over breakfast in lovely gardens. There are 10 rooms in all, each one different, but all with tea- and coffee-making facilities, flatscreen TVs, ultra-comfy beds and en-suite bathrooms with both bath and shower and luxury toiletries. Seclusion is the key word, accompanied by warmth and comfort, and the in-house restaurant completes the picture, serving great Modern British cuisine with local ingredients that include fruit and veg from the hotel garden. The centre of Salisbury is just 15 minutes' drive away and a network of good walks in the lovely Nadder Valley is right on your doorstep. Overall this is an ideal country hideaway for walkers and foodies alike.

WILTSHIRE Teffont Evias Salisbury SP3 5RJ 01722
716392 howardshousehotel.co.uk
HOW MUCH? Double rooms with breakfast
£190–£225 a night.

The Farmhouse at Redcoats

In the hamlet of Redcoats Green, Hertfordshire, this family-owned hotel has recently been restored to its role as a place to escape to for a weekend or short break in the countryside. It's good to see it back in business: parts of the building date back to the 15th century and the owners have rebuilt the neighbouring barn, adding a cool bar and wedding venue along with 15 additional guest rooms. All the rooms have tea- and coffee-making facilities, complimentary mineral water, TVs and super-fast wifi, and the barn rooms are all air-conditioned. The rest of the hotel revolves around the old bar at the centre of the old farmhouse, and the restaurant which looks out on to the hotel's well-tended gardens – meaning you don't have to do much once you're here other than stride off across the fields in your wellies. They serve a moderately priced and extremely delicious contemporary British menu based around seasonal and local ingredients; Norfolk seafood, local game and pork, Hereford steaks and a trio of roasts on Sundays.

HERTFORDSHIRE Redcoats Green Hitchin SG4 7JR
01438 729500 farmhouseatredcoats.co.uk
HOW MUCH? Double rooms with breakfast from
£95 to £160 a night.

The Montagu Arms

Part of the same group that owns the nearby Careys Manor, the Montagu Arms is a bit of a favourite of ours, partly because it ticks all the boxes we look for in a good country hotel. It's in a fabulous location, right in the heart of the New Forest; it occupies a nice old building with lovely gardens; and it has an excellent restaurant, so if you're feeling lazy, you don't have to stray very far in search of sustenance. In fact, the nice thing about the Montagu Arms is that you can leave your car keys in your pocket while you're here, venturing out into the forest on long walks and cycle rides during the day – the 2-mile walk along the river to Buckler's Hard is a popular one – and collapsing into the arms of the hotel in the evening, where you can enjoy the great food and service on offer. The rooms are good sizes and are all very comfortable – traditional but not fussy in style; a couple have 4-posters, and all have flatscreen TVs and spacious en-suite bathrooms with bathrobes and toiletries. A lovely country bolthole in an excellent location.

HAMPSHIRE Beaulieu New Forest Hampshire SO42 7ZL
01590 612324 montaguarmshotel.co.uk
HOW MUCH? Double rooms with breakfast from
£189 a night.

Alkham Court Farmhouse

One of Kent's most luxurious boutique farmhouse B&Bs

There's nothing like staying on a farm, but it's simply a fact that not all farmhouse B&Bs are created equal – indeed you'd be hard pushed to find a B&B anywhere, of any description, that comes up to the high standards of Alkham Court Farmhouse, one of our favourite B&Bs in this part of the world and winners of the award for 'Best B&B in England' in 2018. Owners Wendy Burrows and her husband Neil, genuinely enjoy sharing the delights of their Kentish farmhouse with other people. There's a personal welcome on arrival, together with a slice of homemade cake, which you can enjoy in the garden or next to the wood-burner indoors, depending on the season. Wendy is always keen to share her favourite walks and cycle rides and tell you about nearby attractions. There's a sauna and hot tub in the barn, and they serve legendary, award-winning breakfasts and provide optional packed lunches and evening snacks.

There are just 4 guest rooms, each individually furnished but all equipped with high-quality bed linen, bathrobes and slippers, tea- and coffee-making facilities, a Nespresso machine, still and sparkling mineral water, Freeview TV and a DVD player, digital radio and mini fridge, and – a nice touch, this – fresh flowers on arrival. On the ground floor, the Garden room has a country feel, and can be joined with the next door Wisteria room to make a comfortable family suite. Also on the ground floor, the spacious Pheasant room is more contemporary, with a generously proportioned walk-in shower. A cosy hideaway upstairs is the Badger room, also with a super-king-size bed and a large en-suite shower, plus a sofa to loll about on.. If only all B&Bs were like this!

KENT Alkham Court Meggett Lane South Alkham CT15 7DG 01303 892056 alkhamcourt.co.uk
HOW MUCH? Double rooms with breakfast £140–£170 a night.

"We try to make sure that everyone is relaxed and feels welcome from their arrival to the end of their stay."

Wendy and Neil, Alkham Court Farmhouse

What's nearby?

DOVER CASTLE With perhaps more to see than any other castle in England, its position is iconic, its history – from medieval times to WWII – fascinating.

SMOKEHOUSE This modern chippy does splendid standard cod or haddock but also more exotic choices – bream or skate cheeks with chips, anyone?

WHITE CLIFFS OF DOVER The National Trust have made sure everyone can see the bluebirds, with a wheelchair-accessible clifftop path and lots of dog-friendly routes.

The Oaksmere

It's always nice when someone comes along and rescues a tired old hotel, and that's exactly what happened when local businessman Fraser Duffin came upon this Suffolk country house a few years ago, and which is now a welcoming boutique country house hotel. There's a cosy, flagstoned bar, which doubles as the village's main watering hole, and a really good, very stylish-looking restaurant that serves a menu that is local, British and mainly meaty, using beef from the next door farm, local game and pork from Blythburgh. As for the rooms, they are all different, with big windows and high ceilings in the Victorian wing and cosy beams in the Tudor part of the building – plus 4 rooms in the old coachhouse. They're all pretty contemporary, with bespoke headboards, Nespresso machines, biccies and mineral water, minibar and satellite TV, and bathrooms with rainfall showers and whirlpool baths. It's a country house escape not far from London that doesn't stand on ceremony – jump in the car on a Friday night... and flop!

SUFFOLK Rectory Road Brome Eye IP23 8AJ
01379 873940 theoaksmere.com
HOW MUCH? Double rooms with breakfast £109–£129 a night, suites £179–£209.

Manor House

Sarah Copley's Tinkersley Cottage was one of our favourite Derbyshire B&Bs, so we were sad when she decided to up sticks and move but delighted that she decided not only to stay in Derbyshire but also open another B&B – the Manor House just outside Matlock, on the edge of the Peak District National Park, roughly between Ashbourne and Bakewell. It's a cosy, authentic sort of place that picks up where she left off with 3 beautiful bedrooms, all with en-suite bathrooms, in a Grade II-listed greystone Georgian manor house in the centre of Brassington, an attractive village in the southern Peaks. There is wifi, breakfasts are sumptuous, and on arrival you're served with tea and cake. All in all it's a beautiful place from which to explore this part of Derbyshire and the Peak District, and you're just a short drive from the county's grandest stately home, Chatsworth House, and only 20 minutes' from Sarah's lovely shop – Vintage Living – in the village of Baslow, where B&B guests are entitled to a discount off everything.

DERBYSHIRE Brassington Matlock DE4 4HJ
01629 540792 themanorhousebrassington.co.uk
HOW MUCH? Double rooms with breakfast £85–£95 a night.

Another Place, The Lake

If you're going to the trouble of updating a country hotel in the Lake District you need to do it right, so kudos to Another Place, The Lake, handsomely sited on the shores of Ullswater. It's stylish yet unstuffy, and really family-friendly – and its romantic lake views and great restaurant make it a proper adults' retreat too. Rooms are split between the original Georgian house and a new wing. If you want a 4-poster bed and an original feature or two, then the main house is for you. Other rooms and suites are more contemporary, with anything from a lakeview balcony to a star-gazing beanbag under a bathroom skylight. The indoor pool is a beauty, and there's a sauna, spa and outdoor hot tub. The Living Space is a Scandi-style bar/restaurant with a family-friendly menu and lakeview terrace, while the main restaurant is a more grown-up affair, with a charcoal grill doing glorious things to steaks, chicken, lamb and fish. But if we had to plump for our favourite meal, it's the buffet breakfast, which does everything thoughtfully and brilliantly, just like the hotel.

CUMBRIA Watermillock Penrith CA11 0LP
01768 486442 another.place
HOW MUCH? Double rooms from £170 per night, family suites from £285, breakfast included.

Rectory Manor

Tucked away in a Suffolk village, arriving at Rectory Manor is a bit like attending an old-fashioned country house party – Tom the efficient butler and Honey the dog are here to greet you, and there's the chance to take the weight off your feet in the book-lined lounge, where a fire burns in the grate and you're tempted to either tinkle at the grand piano or help yourself to a drink from the well-stocked honesty bar. There are 3 rooms in the main house, classic in style yet with contemporary touches – one has a wall-length mural of Venice's Bridge of Sighs – and 4 more in a converted stable block. All are generous sizes, and come with decanters of gin and whisky for a nightcap. Tom is always on hand if you need anything, and like the best country houses there is a pool and tennis court in the garden while occasionally the owner Frank pops up to talk you through the history of the building and his family (they all seem to have been adventurers and spies). All rather appropriate while playing a spot of croquet on the lawn.

SUFFOLK Great Waldingfield Near Lavenham CO10 0TL
01787 372428 rectorymanorhotel.co.uk
HOW MUCH? Double rooms from £95 to £135 a night. Breakfast £12 per person.

Millgate House

A lavish B&B in a stunning Georgian townhouse

It's a pretty safe bet you won't have stayed in a B&B quite like this one before. Richmond's Millgate House is quite simply extraordinary – a Georgian townhouse of lavish, theatrical elegance sitting above a magical, sheltered walled garden with views down to the River Swale and its waterfalls. It's won almost every award going, with visitors charmed and amazed in equal measure by a house that is positively stuffed with antiques and art.

There are eye-opening curios and wonderfully ornate pieces at every turn, and while all 3 main rooms are lovely in their way, the 2 overlooking the garden (one twin, one double) certainly have the finest aspect – and we particularly like being able to step out of a free-standing Edwardian bath on to a Turkish rug, in front of a cast-iron fireplace. Meanwhile, in the glorious garden-view dining room, a splendid breakfast on polished mahogany tables is right up our street.

There's also a romantic self-contained (and self-catering) garden apartment, available by the night, with an en-suite double bedroom, living room and open fire, while the stylishly converted Coach House at the foot of the gardens has another 5 en-suite bedrooms plus full kitchen (available for whole-house lets only). The owners Austin and Tim have been here 37 years and have made Millgate House and its fabulous garden a place very much in their own image – charming, discreet and hugely likeable. Trust us, you won't want to leave.

NORTH YORKSHIRE 3 Millgate Richmond DL10 4JN
01748 823571 millgatehouse.com
HOW MUCH? Superking, Twin and Garden Apartment
£165 a night; king double £145; standard doubles £125.

"We have spent almost 50 years in Richmond, building up our house and garden – a lifetime's work – into what we think is the best guesthouse in the land!"

Austin Lynch, Millgate House

What's nearby?

RICHMOND CASTLE The ultimate castle for family visits – what right-thinking child isn't going to love the idea of encamped armies, medieval knights and poleaxe competitions?

REETH Swaledale's main village is a handsome place with old inns and shops skirting the edges of a grassy square – popular with walkers on overnight stops.

THE BOWES MUSEUM A short drive into County Durham is rewarded by a gloriously out-of-place French château, with lavish collections of art.

Swallow Barn

Owner Penny Reynolds calls Swallow Barn a luxury B&B and she isn't joking: 2 beautifully decorated guest rooms boast country-chic decor, wifi, Nespresso coffee machines, satellite TV and Bluetooth speakers. The en-suite wet-rooms come with lovely Cowshed toiletries and each room has its own private outside space, with sun-loungers, a firepit, garden games and exquisite views. A continental breakfast is delivered to your door each morning so you can enjoy a lazy breakfast in bed or – if the weather is cooperating – outside in the wildflower meadows. The location, too, can hardly be bettered – deep in the English countryside yet just a mile outside Frome, which is home to a very cool vibe, lots of great indie shops and a decent array of places to eat. Walkers can access the long-distance Macmillan Way footpath by simply strolling through the back garden, and you're also only a short drive from the lovely Georgian city of Bath. Take it from us, when the time comes to leave you'll be thinking of moving down here yourself.

SOMERSET The Cross Buckland Dinham Frome BA11 2QS 07967 003261 swallowbarnfrome.com
HOW MUCH? Double rooms with breakfast £120 a night – 2-night minimum stay.

YHA Snowdon Pen-y-Pass

If you want to stay near Snowdon and want to conquer the mountain, there's perhaps no better place than this historic hostel, which nestles beneath the mountain itself in a unique position that has lent it an impressive mountaineering history: George Mallory himself stayed here in the 1920s when training for Everest. Newly renovated, it's one of the jewels in the YHA's crown and a great hostel for walkers, with an array of facilities that make returning from a hard day on the mountain a pleasure. There are 27 rooms, divided between multi-bedded dormitories and private rooms with en-suite bathrooms.
There's a decent café and bar, a self-catering kitchen and some snug social areas in which to rest your weary bones. There's no phone signal, mind, but you probably don't care about that if you're the kind of person who has fetched up here. The real bonus is that you can walk out of the hostel and right up Snowdon itself, and climbers should know that the National Mountain Centre at Plas-y-Brenin is also nearby.

GWYNEDD Nantgwynant Caernarfon LL55 4NY
0345 371 9534 yha.org.uk
HOW MUCH? Dormitory beds from £15 a night, private rooms from £35, family rooms from £30.

The Painswick

Midway between Stroud and Gloucester, this magnificent manor is now a stylish and luxurious country house hotel, nestled into one of the Cotswolds' most delightful small towns, with individually designed bedrooms that are airy, contemporary and spacious, and excellently equipped with ultra-comfy beds and bathrooms with powerful modern showers, posh bath products and fluffy robes – some have free-standing baths too. The restaurant serves a modern menu that is well priced and imaginative – not least the breakfasts, where you can opt for a 'Full Elvis' with waffles, banana, peanut butter ice cream and crispy bacon alongside the classic Full English. All of this is in excellent counterpoint to the hotel's treatment rooms, which offer massages, facials and everything else in-between. If we're honest, it's difficult to leave what is a very comfortable place to do not very much at all, but if you do manage to drag yourself away, Painswick itself is worth a stroll, and the property has impressive views down the Slad Valley, which has ample opportunities for country walks.

GLOUCESTERSHIRE Kemps Lane Painswick GL6 6YB
01452 813688 thepainswick.co.uk
HOW MUCH? Double rooms with breakfast
from £169.

Hotel Endsleigh

Quite literally situated on the border between Devon and Cornwall, in the glorious Tamar Valley, this fairytale hotel is the country cousin of the excellent Tresanton in Cornwall, both of which are owned by the renowned hotelier Olga Polizzi. Occupying a former hunting lodge, the hotel boasts 100 picture-perfect acres of formal gardens, streams, woodlands, follies and grottoes. The 18 rooms and suites are artfully decorated, with a stylish mix of old and new, wooden floors, painted wallpapers, rolltop baths and book-lined shelves. Touches of modern luxury include walk-in showers and big comfortable beds. There's also a suite in the former gatekeeper's lodge with a private garden and wood-burning stove. Some of the rooms are dog-friendly and have particularly beautiful views over the grounds, with the result that you will want to get out and explore. It's a lovely place to return to after a hard's day's yomping through the woods, with a cosy lounge and a restaurant that serves good, well-priced and unpretentious food.

DEVON Milton Abbot PL19 0PQ 01822 870000
hotelendsleigh.com
HOW MUCH? Double rooms £190–£330 a night,
suites/Lodge £325–£400. All including breakfast.

The Horn of Plenty

Boutique rooms and high-end food with views

Almost bang on the Devon–Cornwall border, high above the Tamar Valley, the Horn of Plenty looks like the house of your richest friend – and if you don't have a pal like that, then you still get to stay in this rather splendid country manor house, enjoying its impeccable service and attention to detail (although you will have to pay...).

Built in 1866, it was the former crib of a local mine-owner, later converted into a restaurant in the 1960s, when its then owner became the first British woman to be awarded a Michelin star. It's now been a hotel for 30 years, and the individually designed guest rooms have more than kept pace with the times. They are spacious and well-equipped, with high-quality beds, sleek bathrooms with all the luxuries you would expect, and sweeping views – most of the rooms have balconies. Rooms in the main house retain their high ceilings, large windows and original fireplaces; some of those in the coach house conversions have a country feel while others are lovely, generously proportioned contemporary spaces. A number of the coach house rooms are also dog-friendly and there are 5 acres of grounds for walkies. The food, too, is bang up-to-date and is the other star attraction at the Horn of Plenty. Expect well-executed and perfectly formed lunch and dinner menus that are full of delicious, original choices, from local wood pigeon and wild rabbit to Brixham mackerel and Dartmoor lamb – at decent prices, too, for country-house living; the 5-course £70 tasting menu gets you the chef's best seasonal effort, rounded off with tasty Devonshire cheeses.

DEVON Gulworthy Tavistock PL19 8JD
01822 832528 thehornofplenty.co.uk
HOW MUCH? Double rooms with breakfast £130–£275 a night, including dinner £210–£355.

"This is a great place from which to explore the West Country: the Coast, Dartmoor, Tamar Valley and numerous stately homes and gardens are within a short drive."

Julie Lievers, Horn of Plenty

What's nearby?

POSTBRIDGE This tiny hamlet is home to the largest of Dartmoor's medieval 'clapper bridges' – slabs of granite supported by, er, slabs of granite basically.

BURRATOR RESERVOIR The largest stretch of open water on Dartmoor, surrounded by thick woods, footpaths and lots of wildlife.

COTEHELE A 14th-century house with gardens, watermill and woodland, accessible via an excellent riverside walk from Calstock.

Calcot Manor

With around 200 acres of prime Cotswolds countryside and 35 guest rooms filled with all manner of luxury items, Calcot Manor is a stunning place to stay, but the nice thing is you don't have to be on your best behaviour to enjoy it, plus they positively encourage families. The rooms themselves are spacious and very well equipped, with ultra-comfy beds, satellite TV, fruit and snacks in your room and bathrooms with powerful modern showers, fluffy bathrobes and Aromatherapy toiletries. There are 12 adult-only bedrooms are located in the main building, and the remainder – including family rooms – can be found in the grounds. The hotel also has a spa, a great indoor pool, gym, steam room and sauna, while the kids can enjoy the Playzone or The Mez, which has Xboxes, PlayStations and suchlike. There's also an outdoor pool, bikes, horseriding, an excellent restaurant and – a nice touch – a proper in-house pub, The Gumstool, which is cosy and comfy and serves a hearty gastropub menu, so you never need leave the womblike confines of Calcot Manor at all.

GLOUCESTERSHIRE Near Tetbury GL8 8YJ
01666 890391 calcot.co
HOW MUCH? Double rooms with breakfast from £199 a night.

Applegarth Villa

Hot tub suites? Count us in at Applegarth Villa, which is a glam 5-star Lake District retreat in Windermere village. The building is a bit of a gem, one of those lovely Arts and Crafts mansions built by Victorian gents hankering after a country villa. As a hotel it's seriously stylish, with 15 individually fashioned rooms that go for bold colours, designer furniture, sumptuous fabrics and super-smart bathrooms with underfloor heating. They start at 'deluxe' and go up to 'ultimate luxury' which in the case of the top 2 suites means lavish spaces with the choice of either an enormous spa bath and private terrace or an 8-foot-wide circular bed in front of 2 panoramic bay windows. There are also 7 hot-tub suites in the coachhouse with private terraces and far-reaching views. – 2 of which are dog-friendly. The conservatory restaurant has the same outlook, so breakfast is a joy on a sunny day, and there's no need to go elsewhere for dinner – it's good value and the food artfully presented, best preceded by a drink in the handsome bar.

CUMBRIA College Road, Windermere LA23 1BU
01539 443206 lakesapplegarth.co.uk
HOW MUCH? Double rooms £140–£320, hot-tub suites from £425–£475 – all including breakfast.

Park Farm House

Looking for somewhere intimate with great facilities deep in the English countryside? This pint-sized boutique B&B ticks just about every box. Situated just outside the pretty Somerset village of Lullington, it's the sort of place that's easy to settle into but hard to leave. With just 2 en-suite bedrooms, it punches far above its weight in terms of facilities, with a large open-air swimming pool, tennis court and croquet – and, of course, a million-and-one walks in the bucolic countryside around. A late 19th-century Arts and Crafts house, the guest rooms are lovely, and owner Katherine serves afternoon tea every day. Breakfasts are hearty affairs that set you up for the day. It's a romantic retreat for couples – children are welcomed, but only if they are over 12. Frome is a short bike ride away (there are bikes for hire on-site) and has a good monthly market, great shops, pubs and restaurants, and the sort of vibe you would expect in a town that is regularly voted the most attractive place to live in Britain. Like we said, not many boxes remain unticked at this enticing B&B.

SOMERSET Lullington Frome BA11 2PF
01373 831402 parkfarm-house.co.uk
HOW MUCH? Double rooms £95–£115 a night including breakfast.

Careys Manor Hotel

You couldn't get much more central to the New Forest than by staying in this hotel in the heart of the national park. The elder sister of the excellent Montagu Arms in nearby Beaulieu, Careys Manor is right on the doorstep of the walks, cycle rides and wildlife that make this part of the country so special. It's a well-established old place, with 77 rooms that are spacious and well-equipped and have large bathrooms, bathrobes and toiletries, wifi and flatscreen TVs. Some have double doors opening out on to the hotel's gardens while others, located in the original manor house, are quirkier and more individual, and feature 4-poster beds. There is also a self-catering cottage in the grounds sleeping up to 7 people. All guests have full access to the lovely large indoor swimming pool and gym, and can pay a bit extra to enjoy the full array of spa facilities, including the sauna, steam room and hydrotherapy pool. Finally there's the elegant Cambium restaurant, which sets itself up as the best place to eat for miles around, and actually isn't very far off.

HAMPSHIRE Brockenhurst SO42 7RH 01590 623551
careysmanor.com
HOW MUCH? Double rooms with breakfast from £169 a night.

Tickton Grange

A beautiful family-owned country house and restaurant

When the Whymant family came to Tickton Grange over 30 years ago, it was dilapidated and unloved in the extreme. Now it's one of Yorkshire's finest country house hotels, collecting award after award for its accommodation, food and highly personal service. The family story is writ large across the hotel – successful Northamptonshire shoemakers who moved back to the place they used to come on holiday, and who have subsequently renovated every inch of the building using local craftsmen and artisans. There are 21 guest rooms spread across various buildings: apart from the main house, lodgings are also in the renovated stables and pump room, servants' quarters and workers' cottages. Family members grew up in these rooms and played in the gardens, so the sense of pride here is palpable. As you might imagine, no room is the same, but expect country-house chic and plenty of welcoming touches – handmade chocolates and fresh flowers among them. Nothing's too much trouble, and service comes with a broad smile from staff who have been with the family for years.

Then there's the restaurant, Hide, a great place for dinner that has gathered plenty of its own garlands too. Its chef David Nowell, if not quite part of the furniture at the hotel, has been here a while and is a stalwart of the regional dining scene, producing what we reckon is astonishingly good food at less than astonishing prices, using fantastic local produce. With Beverley and Bridlington on the doorstep too, this is surely the perfect getaway for a weekend in East Yorkshire.

EAST YORKSHIRE Tickton Beverley HU17 9SH
01964 543666 ticktongrange.co.uk
HOW MUCH? Double rooms £130–£155, suites £200.

"A family home with touches of luxury at every turn, in an unsung region of rugged coastlines and rolling wolds."

Helen Whymant, Tickton Grange

What's nearby?

BEVERLEY MINSTER One of Europe's finest Gothic churches, with the canopied tomb of the Percys and extraordinary minstrel carvings among many highlights.

BRIDLINGTON Not as full-on as Scarborough or as genteel as Filey, but there's nothing like a day on the beach at Brid or a stroll around its Georgian Old Town.

WILBERFORCE HOUSE Pop into Hull to visit one of East Yorkshire''s most fascinating museums – the home of abolitionist prime minister William Wilberforce.

YHA Black Sail

A remote hostel amid the Lake District's highest peaks

Generations of walkers have made a grateful beeline for Ennerdale's majestically sited Black Sail stone 'hut', a former shepherd's bothy that serves as one of the UK's most renowned youth hostels. High up in the western fells – a good couple of hours' walk from anywhere, and 6 miles from the nearest car park on Ennerdale Water – this is more hikers' refuge than backpackers' hostel, offering basic but very welcome accommodation in the middle of what is by any standards dramatic walking country.

There are 3 bare bunkrooms (with a total of 16 beds) and you have to step outside to find the shower and toilet, but the always-open lounge is a real haven for passing hikers who often call in for a cuppa on their way up or down the mountains. The fire is lit most days, and, come the evening, guests hunker down over a communal meal cooked by hostel staff, as boots, clothes and anything else that got soaked that day gently dry by the stove. Ennerdale is also 'Dark Sky' country, so bring binoculars for a spot of unrivalled star-gazing from right outside your mountain bunkroom.

Note – this is a walk-to-only hostel, either up the valley from Ennerdale Water or (shorter but tougher) over the tops from Honister Pass. Be aware that there are no electric sockets (so no recharging) and only a limited mobile signal. It's also available for exclusive hire – just in case you want a truly out-of-the-way feel to your private party!

CUMBRIA Ennerdale CA23 3AX 0345 371 9680 yha.org.uk
HOW MUCH? Dormitory beds from £21.50, private rooms from £51.50. Available for exclusive hire from Autumn half term to the Easter holidays. No credit cards on site – cash or cheque only.

"The location is magical and the atmosphere special. If you love the grandeur of the Lake District, you should try Black Sail at least once."

Lucy Duszczak, YHA

What's nearby?

GREAT GABLE There may be higher mountains in the Lakes but is there a more handsome one? Fittingly, it's Great Gable's profile that features in the Park's logo.

BUTTERMERE One of the region's most dramatic lakes, Buttermere is ringed by high peaks. Walk the 4 miles all the way round in a relatively easy 2 hours or so.

KIRKSTILE INN The beer garden here has a terrific view of Melbreak, an hour's climb from the inn. Head inside for superior bar meals and a own-brew beers.

Split Farthing Hall

Everyone's got an opinion on how and where to de-stress, but sometimes the hunt for a 'cure' can in itself get those fight-or-flight hormones pumping. Not so at Split Farthing Hall, a family home in the middle of the North Yorkshire countryside that focuses on nothing else but how to re-balance your life in an atmosphere designed to feel a million miles away from your daily cares. Run by Andrea and Dr Claire Maguire (an unusual stepmother and stepdaughter combo), it offers wellbeing retreats for women that take in yoga, healthy eating, life coaching and meditation. It's about activities and workshops rather than pointless pampering, but the accommodation is very comfortable and all 8 bedrooms are nicely furnished with en-suite bathrooms. There are 2 cosy sitting rooms plus a library, hot tub and sauna, and the grounds in summer are lovely, with plenty of outdoor seating and places to roam. Nothing is too much trouble, though it's not a luxury hotel – just a serious alternative to merely getting away from it all for a while.

NORTH YORKSHIRE Bagby Thirsk YO7 2AF
01845 591272 rawhorizons.co.uk
HOW MUCH? 2-night retreats from £345 per person.

Lakeside Hotel

Windermere's finest lakeside hideaway sits at the southern end of England's largest lake. It's a highly polished, family-owned affair to which people return year after year – and who can blame them? This is a special hotel, and not just because of its spankingly good location; there's an old-world elegance to the place, from the rooms to the lake-view conservatory and well-tended gardens, but you get contemporary style too, including a spa and indoor pool. The rooms range from ordinary doubles with woodland views to 'Ultimate Lakeview' rooms, which have patio doors opening on to terraces or gardens overlooking the water. There are also spacious family rooms that can accommodate 2 adults and up to 3 children, and a series of 'Country House' rooms in a separate wing that look away from the lake to the fells and woodland behind. Eat in the brasserie and bar or the more formal Lakeview restaurant – both are pretty good value, serving fabulous local beef and Herdwick lamb cooked on a charcoal BBQ.

CUMBRIA Lakeside Newby Bridge LA12 8AT
01539 530001 lakesidehotel.co.uk
HOW MUCH? Double rooms from £189 a night, including breakfast.

The Duke William

Located in the heart of the Kentish countryside, just 15 minutes east of Canterbury and close to the quaint village of Wingham, the Duke William is a perfect country getaway. Owned by Mark Sargeant, former head chef at Claridges, it has 4 comfortable rooms named after some of his culinary heroes (the likes of Ramsay and Floyd) and is decorated in calming shades of grey with flashes of colour on cushions and prints. Rooms have en-suite shower rooms and king-size beds plus a helpful welcome pack with info on local walks and attractions. Stay in Stein and make the most of the sun terrace and spectacular views out to rolling fields. The pub is a lovely spot for a drink or two, but food is the thing here, and you can either feast on homemade bar snacks – scotch eggs, sausage rolls, mussel popcorn – or, if you fancy something more substantial, peruse a main menu featuring hearty dishes such as Cumberland sausage toad-in-the-hole or pork belly with peas, broad beans and black pudding, and enjoy it in the light and airy conservatory, the restaurant or the pub itself.

KENT The Street Ickham Canterbury CT3 1QP
01227 721308 thedukewilliamickham.com
HOW MUCH? Double rooms from £80 including breakfast.

YHA The Sill, Hadrian's Wall

YHA has bagged a real beauty with this hostel, located at Northumberland National Park's stunning landscape discovery centre, known as The Sill. Inspired by the nearby Great Whin Sill, the building reflects the landscape with its dry stone walls, glass and timber – renewable energy is used throughout and you can even walk on the green roof. There are 86 beds across 26 rooms, 18 en-suite, including 8 private twin rooms and 2 with disabled access. This makes it pretty adaptable – great for couples, families or Hadrian's Wall walkers alike. There's a light-filled reception and café at the centre, and a panoramic terrace, and the hostel offers meals and also a self-catering kitchen plus all the other usual facilities, including decent wifi. You can get a drink next door at excellent Twice Brewed Inn, and some of the finest Roman sites are just a short walk away, while the Hadrian's Wall bus stops nearby. Above all, though, it's real Dark Skies country out here, with zillions of stars visible to the naked eye. As good as hostelling gets.

NORTHUMBERLAND Military Road Bardon Mill
NE47 7AN 0345 260 2702 yha.org.uk
HOW MUCH? Dormitory beds from £21 per person, private rooms from £49 a night.

Ty Mamgu, Ceredigion

COTTAGES FOR COUPLES

Trust us, we know – it's not hard finding a holiday cottage, but it can be a struggle finding one just the right size for two. Who wants to pay extra for unused bedrooms and space you don't need? So here are some of the our favourite cottages for couples – bijou, romantic boltholes, where you can hunker down and enjoy a relaxing holiday à deux.

Cider Mill Cottage

Former cider mill and delightful country retreat for two

Just a few miles northwest of Worcester, on the edge of the Malvern Hills, this old beamed cider mill offers snug and cosy accommodation for two. Situated down a bumpy farm lane, about a mile from the main road, the cottage is quite literally well off the beaten track and feels gloriously isolated, enjoying stupendous views over the surrounding countryside. It's been beautifully converted and has a well-arranged open-plan living area with a wood-burning stove, and a contemporary kitchen ingeniously built around the original mill wheel (of the old cider press). The kitchen is warmed by an Aga so you can really live out your country living fantasies – you are, after all, not far from the home of The Archers!

Upstairs, there's a master bedroom with an antique double bed, along with a bright single room and a well-equipped modern bathroom, with more vintage pieces of furniture throughout. A welcome basket is provided on arrival, full of garden produce and homemade goodies, and Catherine, the owner, lives in the nearby main house and is always on hand to advise on the best country walks or which pubs serve the best food – and she'll also let you use their lovely swimming pool if you ask nicely. At the very least you should take a stroll through her gorgeous garden and make the most of the view – the nearby Teme Valley is a hidden gem, boasting quintessentially English countryside that is typical of this part of Worcestershire. There are also lots of walks right from the doorstep. You might start off thinking about this as a quiet weekend escape, but there's plenty to do and a full week suddenly seems rather an attractive option.

WORCESTERSHIRE Ayngstree Clifton-upon-Teme WR6 6DS 07590 073084 cidermill-cottage.co.uk
HOW MUCH? From £460 a week; short breaks and weekends from £257.

"The Teme Valley is peaceful, beautiful, and tempts you to explore its hidden gems all year round."

Catherine Prindezis, Cider Mill Cottage

What's nearby?

MALVERN HILLS Designated an AONB, the high hills, thick woods and historic forts and castles of the Malvern Hills are as scenic a part of England as you'll find.

ELGAR'S BIRTHPLACE The hills of Worcestershire seem made for the music of Elgar, and he was born in nearby Broadheath, where his house is open to the public.

WITLEY COURT This English Heritage ruined mansion is a magical place, with fabulous gardens and an amazing (restored) Baroque church.

Ty Mamgu

Based on a working organic farm in a beautiful part of Wales, Ty Mamgu is a romantic, self-catering cottage for 2 set in a peaceful garden. It's very much a place for privacy and seclusion, with few distractions apart from the amazing stars at night, which you can view from the cottage's private deck, or the stunning rural views that you can enjoy during the day. There is no internet and water is from a natural spring, and we'd recommend you leave your car keys in the drawer and make the most either of the property itself, which is furnished in a funky, cottagey style with a retro kitchen and wood-burning stove, or the glorious countryside which surrounds it. A games barn provides rainy day entertainment, with table tennis, darts and pool, and the farm's own shop is stocked with all manner of holiday treats from the local area. No surprise, then, that *Conde Nast Traveller* reckoned Ty Mamgu one of the UK's 'best spring hideaways', and we can't really disagree. There's even a piano for cosy nights in – and we think there's a good chance you'll be having a few of those.

CEREDIGION Llandysul SA44 4SR 01865 594349
sheepskinlife.com
HOW MUCH? Prices range from £350 to £455 for 3 nights to £590–760 for 7 nights.

Mill Stream Loft

This stunning first floor studio apartment, situated in the heart of rural south Somerset, fits the bill perfectly for a romantic weekend away. It's very peaceful and rural, yet extremely easy to get to, and is furnished as a bright, stylish and comfy retreat that, frankly, you won't want to leave. Located just a mile south of Ilminster, it sits in the grounds of the house of local couple Karen and Richard, above their collection of classic cars. It's furnished with contemporary flair but is very cosy too, with an open-plan living area, and, tucked away around a corner, a comfortable king-size bed and en-suite shower. It's warm in winter, cool in summer, has a balcony, wifi, TV and DVD player and parking. The kitchen is well equipped so you can eat in or make the short mile or so walk to the nearby village pub, The New Inn, where they serve good food and local brews. There are plenty of other nice walks in the area around, plus it's a 5-minute stroll into Ilminster, with its handsome market square and shops and restaurants. All in all just the thing for a sneaky countryside break.

SOMERSET Oxenford Dowlish Wake Ilminster TA19 0PP
07753 748480 facebook.com/millstreamloft
HOW MUCH? Prices from £350 to £760 a week; short breaks available for £245 to £530.

Lower Polnish

A traditional Scottish blackhouse, this open-plan, one-bed house on the 3500-acre Ardnish peninsula is as remote as can be. Don't let its location put you off, though – this far-off hideaway, with no internet or phone reception, is not that hard to get to, and in any case is well worth the journey. You have to leave your car in the parking space and walk the last 300m, through some woods and across a babbling burn. The house is newly renovated and is spread across a single level; it's lovely and light, and a stone's throw from the sea. There's a wood-burning stove and a sitting room and glazed conservatory. Sit in here with a hot brew or a glass of wine and take in the views. If you are tempted out, the peninsula is a walker's paradise and the only neighbours seals and white-tailed sea eagles. After a day out discovering the area, you'll look forward to getting back to the comfort of the cottage. A piece of advice? Make sure you check out the dark skies on a clear evening – there's probably nowhere better for star-spotting.

ARGYLL Lochailort Ardnish Peninsula
ardnish.org
HOW MUCH? From £500 to £650 a week.

Symonds Yat Rock Lodge

Open-plan, contemporary and comfortable, these dog-friendly lodges are the ideal place for seeing the Wye Valley, and come with a very warm welcome from owners Darren and Claire. Each lodge has a spacious living and dining area, a king-size mezzanine bedroom and fully fitted kitchen, a deluxe shower room with a view and outside space with sensational scenery. Claire's artwork adorns the walls, an array of re-purposed furniture decorates the spaces and there's a wood-burner in the lounge for comfy evenings after bracing walks (you can walk straight into the Forest Of Dean from your front door). There's also a communal garden where you can light up a BBQ and enjoy the stunning views – and you should feel free to use the herbs that the family grow or pick fruit from the trees. There are plenty of restaurants and pubs in the area – the New Inn is the closest, less than a mile's stroll through the forest, and serves great steaks and pub food; the Saracen's Head, overlooking the Wye, is a lovely walk via Symonds Yat Rock viewpoint and also serves good food.

GLOUCESTERSHIRE Hillersland Coleford GL16 7NY
01594 836191 rocklodge.co.uk
HOW MUCH? Short breaks £160–£250, 7 days £360–£650.

Dannah Cottages

Two romantic Peak District cottages

Run by Joan Slack of the lovely nearby Dannah Farm, along with her daughter-in-law Helen, Dannah Cottages is made up of 2 supremely relaxing and rather romantic places to stay – the invitingly named Honeysuckle Cottage and Heather Cottage, stunning one-bedroom stone cottages situated just outside Ashbourne, and in the perfect location for enjoying the southern Peak District. The 2 beamed properties have been lovingly restored and have a spruce, up-to-date feel. Each has a bedroom with an enormous contemporary 4-poster bed, fashioned from reclaimed beams, and an en-suite bathroom with double bath and double-shower cube. Downstairs they have bright, modern kitchens with microwave, dishwasher, washer-dryer and TV, and oak-beamed sitting rooms with large flatscreen TVs and squashy leather sofas. Each cottage also has a terrace with Canadian spa hot tubs that are just waiting for you to jump in. Heather Cottage also boasts the 'Den', which you can use as a changing room for the hot tub and is also equipped with bean bags, magazines and indoor and outdoor games, and the 'Snug', which has a fully tiled wet room for those using the hot tub. Honeysuckle Cottage has a newly minted and very luxurious barrel-shaped sauna.

Above all, though, the cottages are both memorable for the little luxuries around every corner, from wine chilling in the fridge to fresh flowers and luxurious toiletries, all of which make them a perfect romantic hideaway for two., They are also extremely well placed as walking holiday cottages, but if you wanted to spend the odd day at home then... well... we wouldn't blame you.

DERBYSHIRE 1 & 2 Townend Main Street Kirk Ireton Ashbourne DE6 3JP 07973 314725 dannahcottages.co.uk
HOW MUCH? 3-night weekend stays or 4-night midweek stays £495–£750; 7 nights £990–£1350. Breakfast is available too – and included in the price – if you don't mind the short drive to nearby Dannah Farm.

"Two stunning, romantic and intimate cottages with private hot tubs in an idyllic rural setting."

Joan and Helen, Dannah Cottages

What's nearby?

KEDLESTON HALL Keira Knightley and Ralph Fiennes romped through this spectacular Robert Adam mansion during The Duchess... and now you can too!

LEA GARDENS The season is short here but we urge you to blaze a trail to this wonderful hidden garden, which has more colour than a Hockney palette.

SUDBURY HALL Used as a backdrop for a TV adaptation of Pride and Prejudice, this magnificent 17th-century country house has extraordinary features.

Sett Cottage

A cosy little hideaway on the edge of the village of Hayfield in the High Peak area of Derbyshire, Sett Cottage is a pet-friendly cottage for 2 (or at a pinch for 4) – lovely and snug with a log burner and a master bedroom with a king-sized bed and impressive free-standing copper bath. It is an old quarry worker's home so beware – the steps up to the front door and stairs inside are quite steep…mind your head! This is great walking country – in fact, in April 1932, Hayfield was the location of the famous mass trespass on to Kinder Scout by The Ramblers Association to get walkers' more rights of way, so it's got something of a historic hiking pedigree. You might also recognise it as the location for the second series of the BBC's *The Village Walks*, and trails nearby include the Pennine Way, Kinder Scout and the Sett Valley Trail – a 2-mile route for cyclists. For those who don't want to roam too far, the village has galleries to browse, lovely riverside strolls and several restaurants and pubs.

DERBYSHIRE Hayfield SK22 2HS 01865 594349
sheepskinlife.com
HOW MUCH? £785–£865 a week.

Holyrood Cottage

Tucked away by Edinburgh's Holyrood Park, this little cottage makes an ideal romantic city ecsape. Less than a 10-minute walk from the city centre, it's furnished in a crisp, contemporary style, with whitewashed bricks, tongue-and-groove woodwork, polished wooden floors and window shutters. Yet it is as cosy as you like, with a wood-burner and unlimited logs. It has a high-ceilinged open-plan living space, divided between a lounge with a sofa and chaise longue and a bedroom with a super-king-size bed, high-quality linen, cushions and a throw. There's a separate kitchen with a table for 2 and everything you might need, while a wee bathroom sports a bath with a power shower and a set of luxury toiletries; there are bathrobes and slippers too for that real home-from-home feeling. Perhaps nicest of all, is the bright conservatory that leads out to a small patio garden, plus you can use the local gym and pool for just £5 per person. A terrific place to come back to at the end of a day's sightseeing.

EDINBURGH Spring Gardens EH8 8HX
07786 262682 holyroodcottage.co.uk
HOW MUCH? From £470 a week in winter to £805 a week. Short breaks £280–£330.

The Gate House

Small but perfectly formed, the Gate House is a near neighbour of Dover Castle and offers a unique opportunity to stay in a miniature neo-Gothic castle. With turrets, beams and a canopied bed, where better for a retro romantic break? Dating from around 1850 and Grade II-listed, the vintage cottage sleeps 2 confortably. Downstairs there's a living/dining room with a gas wood-burner and a sofa bed, plus a fully equipped kitchen. Upstairs is the master bedroom with a romantic canopied bed, along with a dressing room in the turret and good-sized bathroom. Outside there's a small enclosed garden with a patio area and outdoor furniture. As well as being the ideal spot for visiting the castle, the Gate House is close to Dover's amenities, with a pub and shops within half a mile, and there's plenty of free parking nearby. As well as Dover itself, local attractions include the medieval Cinque Port town of Sandwich and of course walks along those famous White Cliffs.

Bryn Cottage

Just when you thought the Stein empire had it all covered, they open up this serviced one-bedroom cottage in the heart of town, where couples can enjoy a romantic stay with views over Padstow's estuary and meals (including breakfast) at the nearby St Petroc's hotel – though they will also deliver a continental breakfast if you prefer. The cottage is basically as self-catering as you need or want it to be. Facilities include a well-equipped kitchen (complete with tea, coffee and other basics), a large living room, a very comfy bedroom with open fire and a luxurious bathroom with a free-standing bath and rainfall shower and Molton Brown toiletries. There is private parking nearby – which is a real bonus in Padstow – plus as with all the Stein places you get priority booking at the group's restaurants. There's also wifi, a laundry service and a secluded courtyard garden in which you can relax on a sunlounger. In short, it's got everything you would expect in a decent hotel and perhaps a little bit more.. but you are the only guest!

KENT Victoria Park Dover CT16 1QX
01304 614419 michellescottages.co.uk
HOW MUCH? Full weeks £375–£600, short breaks £260–£450.

CORNWALL Hill St Padstow PL28 8EB
01841 532700 rickstein.com/stay/bryn-cottage
HOW MUCH? From £765 for 3 nights.

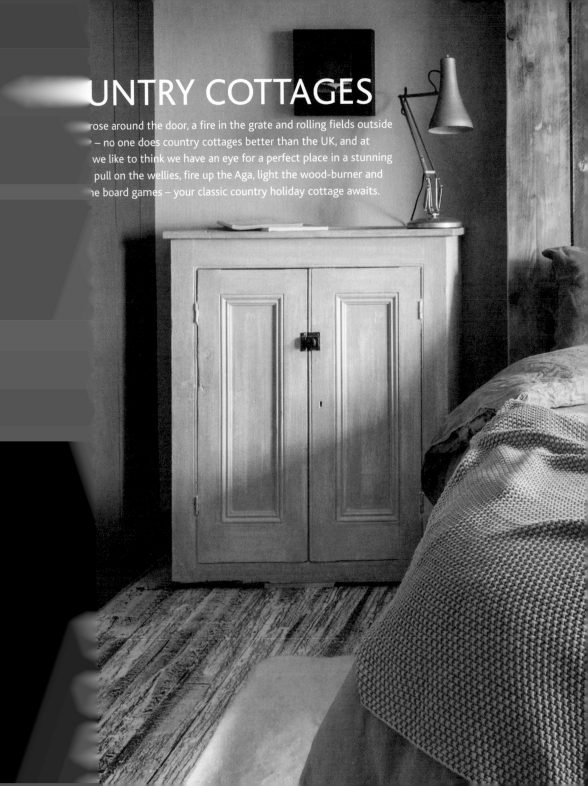

UNTRY COTTAGES

rose around the door, a fire in the grate and rolling fields outside – no one does country cottages better than the UK, and at we like to think we have an eye for a perfect place in a stunning pull on the wellies, fire up the Aga, light the wood-burner and he board games – your classic country holiday cottage awaits.

Godney Arts House, Somerset

Treberfedd Farm

Eco-friendly self-catering in a special part of Wales

With views over the Cambrian Mountains yet just a short drive from the lovely beaches of Cardigan Bay, the enticing cottages and stylish eco-cabins of this working organic farm occupy a special spot, with a night-time darkness that makes it perfect for star-gazing. It has 4 pin-neat cottages sleeping anything between 5 and 8 people, and 2 eco-cabins in a flower-filled meadow for luxurious glamping. The cottages range from a lovely 4-bedroom farmhouse to a couple of converted barns and a picture-perfect thatched cottage. Each has rustic charm in abundance but also a fully fitted kitchen, underfloor heating and all the mod cons you could possibly need, including decent wifi. The cottages all take dogs, as does 1 of the 2 eco-cabins – unique octagonal creations with large windows all the way round. These are more spacious than you might think, with an open-plan kitchen and a super king-size bed that makes the most of the panoramic views, plus fold-down bunk beds for the kids. The unique design of the cabins not only blends into the landscape, but also serves a practical purpose, with insulation provided by grass on the roof and sheep's wool in the walls, while no fewer than 16 Scots Pine trees hold up the roof. Underfloor heating powered by the farm's wind turbine and solar panels helps to keep the place warm year round. They have a playground for children, and you can also follow a farm trail through the meadows and woods. They've been breeding cattle, sheep and chickens here for hundreds of years, and in that respect nothing much has changed on the farm. We're lucky that current incumbents Jack and Eleanor decided to let the rest of us in on the secret!

CEREDIGION Treberfedd Lampeter SA48 7NW 01570 470672 treberfedd.co.uk

HOW MUCH? Cottages from £352 to £1050 a week. Cabins £350–£810 in summer. Short breaks from £199 all year round, minimum 2-night stay.

"There is nothing humdrum about Treberfedd Farm, the far-reaching views and eclectic choice of accommodation make you feel a world away from it all."

Eleanor and Jack, Treberfedd Farm

What's nearby?

DOLPHINS A boat trip out of the harbour from Cardigan Bay Marine Wildlife Centre may see you encounter scores of bottlenose dolphins.

HARBOURMASTER, ABEREARON This waterfront hotel restaurant set new standards when it opened and is still one of the flag-bearers of the Welsh food scene.

NEW QUAY Once home to Dylan Thomas, this charming fishing harbour has a handful of shops, a nice variety of pubs and some cracking seaside restaurants.

Henfaes Isaf

A traditional Welsh farmhouse on the edge of Snowdonia

Situated in a picturesque and peaceful spot in the Upper Dee Valley Area of Outstanding Natural Beauty, this traditional Welsh farmhouse was named one of the '50 Coolest Cottages in the UK' in a recent feature, and we would have to agree. Dating back several centuries, it has been lovingly restored, and with 3 cosy bedrooms is the ideal place for a family holiday or a break with friends. The original beamed ceilings and an oak-panelled wall remain intact, while sympathetic features have been added, including hand-carved details, a stained-glass window made from salvaged glass, and another window created from a cartwheel found on the property. Inside is an array of antique and handmade furniture, and a homely lounge featuring an inglenook fireplace, with logs supplied. The well-appointed kitchen features country-style cabinets built by the current owner's father, while an adjoining former barn has been incorporated into the main house, adding a stylish dining room with handmade Welsh dresser and a light and airy triple bedroom upstairs. What was once a stable hayloft now houses a children's playroom.

There are plenty of scenic walks and cycle routes nearby, many of which can be taken from the door of the cottage. Those seeking a bit more adventure can drive 10 miles to Snowdonia or discover the nearby activity centres of Bala and Llangollen. All in all, this is an idyllic spot to spend some time, whether it be exploring the area or relaxing in the large gardens and enjoying the birdsong and dark starry skies at night.

DENBIGHSHIRE Henfaes Isaf Cynwyd LL21 0NF 07773 294275 facebook.com/henfaesisaf
HOW MUCH? From £490 to £1185 a week; short breaks £370 to £809.

"Come and enjoy the tranquillity of this wonderful farmhouse in the unspoiled Berwyn Mountains, a gem of a cottage that has a special place in our hearts."

Moyra, Ian and Janna, Henfaes Isaf

What's nearby?

LLANGOLLEN STEAM RAILWAY Join the railway at nearby Corwen for a scenic ride along the valley to Llangollen, and its numerous attractions and activities.

TEGID WAY The cottage sits on the Tegid Way, which follows the upper Dee Valley to beautiful Bala Lake, offering stunning views of the Aran Ridge and Snowdonia.

TYDDYN LLAN This fabulous Michelin-starred restaurant is the ideal venue for a big night out, with properly old-school gastronomy and service.

Fingals Apart

Quirky apartments in a gorgeous Devon location

Whether you're looking for a romantic haven or an idyllic family retreat, you've really hit the jackpot with this collection of luxury self-catering cottage apartments, tucked into a quiet Devon valley near the River Dart. Set in the grounds of the owners' Queen Anne manor farmhouse, the accommodation has a quintessentially eccentric English feel and can host anyone from couples to groups of 12 in beautifully peaceful surroundings. A 19th-century mill house conversion, it retains many of its period features and splits into 2 separate apartments, each with a rustic, homely feel. There are also 4 other architect-designed self-catering spaces, namely an oak-framed Barn, the smaller Wisteria Suite, a separate house, Barberry Brook, and the beach-house-style Folly, which has 2 storeys and features a bedroom with doors opening on to a babbling brook. They are all beautifully furnished, filled with oriental carpets, antiques, quirky *objets d'art* and original paintings by local artists. Each has a sense of light and brightness, with balconies, big windows, sitting rooms and private patios overlooking the gardens, a stream and the Devon hills. Dogs are welcome everywhere. If it isn't already clear that this is a one-of-a-kind experience, the facilities seal it. There's a grass tennis court, croquet lawn and table-tennis terrace, gym and exercise space, dedicated games room with a snooker table, a dovecote, and even a piano for anyone so inclined. Best of all, though, is the indoor pool, housed in a conservatory full of exotic plants and opening out on to a balcony over the stream and the patio in the summer, while a sauna has large window looking over the stream. Drag yourself away and you're just a mile from Dittisham, a beautiful village on the Dart.

DEVON Coombe Manor Farm Dittisham Dartmouth TQ6 0JA 01803 722398 fingalsapart.co.uk
HOW MUCH? From £345 for a short break off season.

"Fingals is family-friendly, child-friendly, dog-friendly ….and, well, just plain friendly!"

Sheila Johnston, Fingals Apart

What's nearby?

DARTMOUTH CASTLE This fortress has been guarding the mouth of the River Dart for 600 years. Taking the ferry from Dartmouth Quay is the best way to arrive.

DITTISHAM Nestled on the banks of the river among rolling green hills and wooded valleys, Dittisham is the most picturesque of the Dart estuary's villages.

GREENWAY Accessible from Dittisham by boat, Agatha Christie's former holiday home is stacked full of memorabilia and has wild and romantic gardens.

The Little Barn

There's a feeling of being away from it all that you only get from being on an island, but The Little Barn takes it to the next level. It's an appealing holiday cottage equipped with everything you could possibly need for an island holiday – it's homely, light and spacious, with lots of room for the kids to run riot. There's a large open-plan kitchen-diner, fast wifi, a sitting room with FreeSat TV and DVD player and a spacious deck looking towards St Catherine's Down – a local landmark and the southernmost point of the island. Upstairs it sleeps 2–4 people in a double and a twin bedroom. For cosy evenings, there's underfloor heating, powered by a ground-source heat pump. The owners live in the nearby Main Barn, which shares the property's gardens, meadows and ponds, where you can wander at will. The sea is just a mile away, and there are numerous countryside walks, while the night skies are perfect for star-gazing (there's a telescope for guests' use). Perfect, in fact, for an island adventure.

ISLE OF WIGHT Dungewood Lane Shorwell Newport PO30 3LJ 01983 551322 wightbarn.co.uk
HOW MUCH? From £442 to £1236 a week.

Laggan

Peter is a lucky man. He inherited 3000 acres or so of the remote Ardnish peninsula on the west coast of Scotland, along with a house from which to enjoy it. Unsurprisingly, it's as remote a spot as you'll find in the British Isles – and, as Peter says himself, it's not for everyone: you can only get here by boat, and even then only when the tides allow; it has no electricity, limited mobile reception and of course no broadband; and you're a half-day's walk from your nearest neighbour. But if that's what you're looking for, it may be just the thing. There are 2 comfortable bedrooms; no electricity simply means that you have to use oil lamps for light (there is a fridge and cooker, and heat and hot water is provided by a wood-burning stove); you obviously have to be organised about provisions but the boat is there for your use and it's only a 10-minute journey across to the mainland. Ardnish itself is populated mainly by deer, who roam a landscape made up of bare hills, forest and pure white-sand beaches. A long day's walk without seeing a soul before returning to your cosy cottage is sometimes just what the soul needs.

ARGYLL PH38 4NA 01889 500727
ardnish.org
HOW MUCH? From £900 a week.

Fforest Fields

You couldn't get closer to the heart of rural Wales than by staying at this delightful family farm, situated just a few miles outside Builth Wells in the midst of the green rolling hills of Powys. There is a selection of very comfy lakeside yurts and also a beautiful old farmhouse that sleeps 5 comfortably in a double, twin and a single; it has a wood-burner with all wood supplied and a modern kitchen. Reached by a winding rough track, it feels properly away from it all, with nothing but birdsong to disturb the peace. There is wonderful walking through woods and out on to open moorland direct from the cottage, a couple of lakes for fishing, swimming and paddling, and a small beach and a jetty with kayaks if you want to get out on the water. And that's before you've ventured into the countryside beyond, which is glorious: you can go mountain-biking at nearby Aberwesyn or maybe even catch the renowned World Bog-Snorkelling Championships just outside Lanwrytd Wells – a truly Welsh institution if ever there was one.

POWYS Hundred House Builth Wells LD1 5RT
01982 570406 fforestfields.co.uk
HOW MUCH? From £450 to £850 a week.

East View Farm

There's a sense of peace at East View Farm that makes it hard to believe you're only a dozen miles from Norwich. But the Pond family's 2 holiday cottages are the epitome of rural tranquillity, in the heart of the Norfolk Broads National Park, one of them sleeping 2 people, the other 6. Their own wind turbine provides much of their power – indeed they strive to be as self-sufficient as possible, recycling pretty much everything and installing low-energy alternatives in the well-equipped cottages. It's a delightful place to stay. The gardens are lovely and the roads around are mostly super-peaceful rural lanes ideal for cycling. You're also a short distance from the boating mecca of Wroxham, where you can hire boats and canoes to explore the river and the Broads (nearby Wroxham Barns has a good restaurant, shops and stuff for kids). Jane is a mine of information on the area, and as an added bonus you might be lucky enough to ride on the fabulous miniature railway that her husband and his train-mad mates have installed in the garden – a wondrous sight in its own right.

NORFOLK Stone Lane Ashmanhaugh NR12 8YW
01603 782225 eastviewfarm.co.uk
HOW MUCH? Short breaks £295–£455, weekly breaks £395–£650.

The Olde House

Beautifully furnished Cornwall cottages of all sizes

In a beautiful part of North Cornwall, a hop, skip and a jump from trendy Padstow, Penpont Farm has been in the Hawkey family for 3 generations, and remains at heart a 550-acre mixed working farm. It's a beautiful spot, supporting a diverse array of bird and other wildlife, and we're lucky that back in the 1970s the family decided to open it up to everyone, converting a series of stone and slate barns into no fewer than 32 holiday cottages, ranging in size from one to 5 bedrooms. All are tastefully furnished either in a bright contemporary or more traditional cottage style, with well-equipped kitchens and modern bathrooms.

Over the years the family has added various facilities, and there's now an indoor swimming pool, sauna, steam room and jacuzzi, a games room, outdoor play area, tennis courts and a farm trail, so even if the sun doesn't shine, there is always something to do. Not only that, they are environmentally friendly, powering the properties with a series of solar panels and a recently added biomass boiler, and making the effort with other small touches – there's even a charging point for electric cars.

An on-site store has things you can borrow – beach stuff, games, wellies and so on – as well as buy, so you don't technically need to go anywhere while you're here. But you would be crazy to visit this part of Cornwall and not go to the beach (and there are plenty nearby), not to mention chi-chi Rock or foodie Padstow, 2 towns popularised by John Betjeman and Rick Stein respectively.

CORNWALL Chapel Amble Wadebridge PL27 6EN
01208 813219 theoldehouse.co.uk
HOW MUCH? 1-bed cottages from £505 a week; 2-bed cottages from £525; 3-bed cottages from £555; 4-bed cottages from £620; 5-bed cottages from £1300.

"We feel very fortunate to do what we do – farming the Cornish countryside and sharing the experience with our guests."

Jaime Hawkey, The Olde House

What's nearby?

DAYMER BAY Further down the estuary from Wadebridge and Rock, this is a very sheltered beach that's great for swimming, and there's not a surf dude in sight.

ROCK This coastal fishing village is these days the epitome of modern Cornwall – with a busy tourist vibe, and a great beach, golf course and peaceful church.

TREBARWITH STRAND This long National Trust-owned sandy beach is one of north Cornwall's best – good for rock-pooling, surfing and swimming.

Laverstock Farm

Picture this: a long sweeping driveway leading to a grand farmhouse and a group of homely self-catering cottages. Sounds appealing doesn't it? Located on a working farm in the heart of rural West Dorset, Laverstock Farm offers uninterrupted views out over picturesque countryside and a choice of 6 cottages and 2 shepherd's huts. Just a 15-minute drive from the lively market town of Bridport, it's a lovely spot to take a break – 4-bed Lambrook Cottage is newly renovated, complete with log burner, whilst one-bedroom Gardener's benefits from a private terrace and use of the apple orchard. They also have 2 shepherd's huts, tucked away with their own outside kitchen with a firepit. There may not be any electricity, but you won't be completely in the dark – 4 rechargeable lanterns are provided. Inside, the huts are cosy, decorated in calming Farrow & Ball shades, and there are far-reaching scenic views and roaming animals, a large vegetable garden, children's play area and games room with table tennis and darts.

DORSET Laverstock Bridport DT6 5PE
01308 867866 laverstockfarm.co.uk
HOW MUCH? Cottages and Shepherds Huts
£90–£220 a night.

Tilbury Farm

Nestled within 45 acres of farmland, with breathtaking views over the Blackdown and Quantock Hills, these holiday cottages are the perfect escape for jaded city-dwellers craving a bit of peace and quiet in the country. There are 3 cottages (2 sleep 2, the other 11), each fitted out to high standards, with open-plan living rooms and double bedrooms, flatscreen TVs, DVDs and wifi, and to get your holiday off to the best of starts, both come with fridges stocked with breakfast goodies and your newspaper of choice. They also have a couple of shepherds' huts if you want to get really cosy: set in a huge field of their own, they're super-private, and a third, larger one is on the way. The farm itself has impeccable eco-credentials, with a biomass boiler, solar energy and water from its own bore-hole – plus pigs, sheep and horses, although these are more for fun than agriculture. There is a great country pub (The Rising Sun) a short walk away and the nearest village – Bishops Lydeard – is a short drive away, and has a good farm shop and butchers. Really, the perfect place for wistful, countryside-craving folk.

SOMERSET Bagborough Taunton TA4 3DY
07585 973924 tilburyfarm.co.uk
HOW MUCH? Both cottages cost £460–£645 a week,
shepherds huts from £160 a night, 3 nights £350.

Poltarrow Farm

Owned and run by the Nancarrow family, Poltarrow Farm has been welcoming guests for over 30 years, both on a B&B basis in the farmhouse or in 6 holiday cottages, dotted around the farm's 45 acres. It's a gloriously self-contained rural retreat, with fields and meadows, woodland, a fishing lake and duck pond; there's a decent-sized indoor pool, a sports barn and a soft-play barn for smaller guests, who are also encouraged to help feed the animals each morning. The cottages are beautifully furnished and range from one to 3 bedrooms; all have spacious living rooms, stylish bathrooms, modern fitted kitchens and tastefully decorated bedrooms with big beds, wifi, heating and open fires. A welcome pack containing treats and essentials is provided on arrival and the family is always on hand to offer advice on what to see and do in the region. The farm is conveniently close to the sea but is also a short distance from some of Cornwall's other major attractions. There's even a nice pub, the Polgooth Inn, within easy walking distance.

CORNWALL St Mewan St Austell PL26 7DR
01726 67111 poltarrow.co.uk
HOW MUCH? Cottages £450–£2025 a week.

Little White Alice

When you come to Cornwall you don't have to stay bang on the beach. Yes, the coastline is stunning, but away from the crowds Cornwall's countryside is infused with the sort of tranquillity that you find at Little White Alice, an eco-friendly cluster of holiday cottages set in 29 acres of its own grounds. There are 4 cottages: 2 timber-clad 'Eco Arks', a more conventional converted stone barn and a one-bed apartment. Each comes with a log-burner, TV and wifi and handwoven textiles and headboards. The wild spa invites you to relax into this natural environment, with its wood-fired hot tub and sauna, a cold-bucket shower and a sanctuary room for treatments. There's also a kitchen garden and lots of wildlife to spot in their 12 -acre nature reserve. They keep their own sheep, pigs, chicken, alpacas, goats and bees, and aim to be self-sufficient in every way. Not only that, they have an arts-and-crafts studio where you can learn everything from basket-making to feltwork. All in all, it's a fabulous playground for families and kids to immerse themselves in nature and creativity.

CORNWALL Carnmenellis TR16 6PL 01209 861000
littlewhitealice.co.uk
HOW MUCH? From £365 to £1492 a week.

Godney Arts House

Old and new fuse seamlessly in this super-stylish cottage

Godney Arts House is super stylish – an 18th-century Georgian farmhouse tucked away in the heart of Somerset that's been lovingly restored and renovated by owners Jane and Simon. It's the kind of place where you walk from room to room thinking you'd like to take every piece of furniture home with you – and you can, in fact, do exactly that, for a price of course. It's a relaxing countryside retreat with views to the Mendip Hills, where tradition and quirkiness blend together flawlessly.

On the ground floor there's a fully equipped farmhouse kitchen, a dining room with copper table, a living room complete with wood-burner, and flagstone floors throughout. Simon's hugely varied artworks adorn the walls of the house, adding a special touch. Upstairs, the 3 en-suite bedrooms are characterful and spacious; one has a rolltop bath to luxuriate in and they're all decorated with an eclectic mixture of items that have been collected over the years. Wherever you lay your head, you'll be greeted by French linen bedding. The added bonus? Electricity and heating are generated by solar panels, helping to make your stay eco-friendly. The cottage is in a rather remote spot, with no light pollution, though it's not so isolated that there isn't a great local pub 2 minutes' walk away. Tranquillity reigns, enveloping you in a warm hug, and there's a small south-facing garden for you to enjoy it in. The care and attention to detail taken at Godney Arts House is outstanding – old and new fuse together with ease, making it a truly unique place to stay.

SOMERSET Thornreed Studio Lower Godney BA5 1RZ
07980 000329 godneyartshouse.co.uk
HOW MUCH? 7 nights from £950, short breaks from £595. Minimum 3-night stay at weekends.

"Our concept is simple – to offer an alternative to the bland, and to share our passions in art, design and interiors."

Jane and Simon, Godney Arts House

What's nearby?

GLASTONBURY TOR Steeped in history and legend, there's nothing like a walk up Glastonbury Tor to blow away the cobwebs.

WESTHAY MOOR NATURE RESERVE The lakes and reedbeds here host thousands of wintering birds and are well known for spectacular starling murmurations.

ROGER WILKINS CIDER FARM A working farm where you can sample and buy traditional ciders, cheese and pickles, and enjoy a generous Ploughman's lunch.

Cruckbarn

A spectacular country bolthole for couples or families

It's not every day you get the chance to sleep in someone's 'Grand Design', but that is exactly what Cruckbarn is – a self-realised labour of love built recently by architect John Williams and his friend David on a secluded plot of land high above the Herefordshire village of Wigmore, with spectacular views over the county. John and his partner Janet also own the excellent Abbots Lodge B&B down the road, so they know a thing or two about hospitality, setting up Cruckbarn to provide a delectable country escape that's perfect for couples looking for a secluded bolthole and easy access to the Great Outdoors.

An oak-framed, barn-like structure with a vaulted roof (formed by the 'cruck' frame), it's above all an enticingly cosy place, with a log-burner fuelled by a plentiful supply of logs from the woods outside. There is a well-equipped kitchen and on the mezzanine 2 bedrooms – one with a king-size bed, another with a double bed and a single. The building has wifi, but not much of a phone signal, a Bluetooth music system and a vinyl record deck for those, ahem... of a certain age. But – deliberately – there is no TV. Cruckbarn is also as eco-friendly as you like: natural materials have been used throughout – the beams are fashioned from oak sourced from the nearby forest – and the building has been clad with more timber, reclaimed slates and breathable, old-fashioned lime. It also boasts underfloor heating and hot water provided by a ground-source heat pump. There are acres of nearby woodland to explore, access to a firepit, hammock, woodland swing and kite – which even novices should be able to fly up here – not to mention the ruins of an ancient castle within walking distance.

HEREFORDSHIRE Wigmore Leominster HR6 9UG 01568 770036 cruckbarn.co.uk

HOW MUCH? From £795 a week in low season to £1195 a week in high season. Midweek stays and long weekends £475–£675.

"Cruckbarn has been our 'Grand Design', a really personal project – and it's a true pleasure to hear how much our guests love to stay there."

John Williams, Cruckbarn

What's nearby?

RIVERSIDE INN, AYMESTREY There's a great pub close to Cruckbarn, The Oak in Wigmore (see p.180), but you might also try the timbered Riverside Inn a few miles south in Aymestrey, where the food is also good.

BERRINGTON HALL Just the other side of Leominster, this Georgian house has amazing interiors and was Capability Brown's final major project.

CROFT CASTLE/FISHPOOL VALLEY A National Trust Norman castle, wonderful parkland and the amazing, literally 'picturesque' Fishpool Valley.

Green Farm Kent

A self-catering barn conversion, spa and yoga retreat

Situated deep in the Kent countryside, there's nowhere else quite like Green Farm, a self-contained and very comfortable barn conversion surrounded by 12,500 acres of ancient woodland and pasture, and with a unique spa and wellbeing retreat attached. There are, of course, the obvious attractions of hiking and cycling in its private woodlands, not to mention getting to know the animals on the farm, but what really sets Green Farm apart is its spa, which offers the chance to really unwind in these beautiful surroundings. The facilities are excellent, with a sauna and 2-person outdoor hot tubs and treatment rooms offering everything from deep tissue and hot stone massages to detox wraps and pre- and post-natal treatments.

The self-catering accommodation is lovely, in a refurbished 19th-century barn that includes 2 double bedrooms with super-king-size beds and 2 triple bedrooms, all with en-suite bathrooms and a spacious living room with a large flatscreen TV, DVD player and music system – and there's also extra capacity in the converted cow shed next door, which has a double bedroom and its own kitchen and living room.

Owners MaryAnn and Martin also like to emphasis the retreats and spa stays they organise. The ethos? To provide all you would expect from a 5-star hotel in a homely setting with super-personal service. Guests spend a night or 2 in one of the bedrooms of their characterful 15th century home and can lounge about in fluffy robes or don a pair of wellies and explore the grounds. You can luxuriate on a spa package or enjoy a food and yoga or pilates retreat – each well-organised with classes and talks, seasonal meals and use of the spa.

KENT Church Lane Shadoxhurst TN26 1LT 01233 733997
greenfarmkent.co.uk
HOW MUCH? From £1200 to £2750 a week.

"A country retreat, with spa, yoga and self-catering barn accommodation, offering rural peace and charm just a hop from London."

Maryann and Martin, Green Farm Kent

What's nearby?

SISSINGHURST Vita Sackville-West's renowned garden needs no introduction, and there's lots more to see at this National Trust property.

BIDDENDEN VINEYARDS Grapes flourish on the sunny, south-facing slopes here, and you can do guided tours, stopping afterwards for a tipple at the shop and café.

KING'S HEAD, SHADOXHURST It's a 5-minute walk to Green Farm's local, which serves classic pub food and has been twice voted Shepherd Neame 'Pub of the Year'.

As an antidote to the 'nature deficit disorder' said to be affecting children in Britain, the experience at Bosinver Farm Cottages couldn't be more effective, throwing you and your family firmly into the Great Outdoors without preamble. Owner Pat Smith, a former school teacher and active grandma, believes passionately in the importance of outdoor play and connecting children to nature, and for her there is nothing more inspiring than seeing city kids come to Bosinver and thrive on its old-fashioned outdoor adventures. It's an undeniable fact that most kids will put down their phones and iPads if there is a tree to climb or a lake to swim in — and for parents, too, Bosinver offers a taste of how family holidays were in years gone by.

There are no fewer than 20 cottages at Bosinver, spread across 35 acres of wildflower meadows, woodlands and gardens. There are plush farmhouses, converted barns and stables, picture-perfect thatched cottages and even a stylish eco-house with bells and whistles galore. Many are dog-friendly and they all have every family holiday convenience, while there is also a heated indoor pool, gym, play barn and games room. Not that you'll be spending a lot of time indoors if Pat can help it. There are outdoor play areas, woodland and lakes to explore, and you can follow Farmer Dave to feed the animals and collect eggs from the hens, look out for wildlife on woodland trails, ride ponies, light campfires, hunt bugs and build dens. It's truly a paradise for young children. And if the kids are happy, the parents are too, right?

BOSINVER FARM COTTAGES Trelowth St Austell Cornwall PL26 7DT 01726 72128 bosinver.co.uk. From £412 for 3 nights (off-peak) to £3800 a week (peak season).

Leskernick Cottage

A fabulous off-grid Cornish cottage

Bang in the middle of Bodmin Moor, Leskernick is as wild and remote a place to stay as you could find in England. With 7 acres of its own, but also surrounded by hundreds more of open moorland, its location is more reminiscent of the furthest-flung corners of Scotland than Cornwall.

Accessed via a track (4-wheel drives only) that leads for about a mile-and-a-half to a shallow valley, the cottage was built in the 17th century and is now Grade II-listed. It was originally a single-storey mineworker's residence but has been extended over the years, with an extra floor that makes the most of the wonderful views across the moor, and it now comfortably sleeps 6 people in 3 bedrooms. There's an Aga that supplies hot water and wood-burners (with a generous supply of wood) to keep things cosy, along with oil-fired central heating. On the ground floor, there's a kitchen, utility room, family bathroom and a spacious bedroom with an en-suite wet room as well as a comfy living room with stairs to the two 1st-floor bedrooms. There's also a fabulous dining room with bi-fold doors that open onto a terrace. It feels off-grid, and strictly speaking it is, although electricity provided by a generator in an outbuilding (not 24hr) fires up all the mod cons you might need, including a dishwasher, washing machine, TV and DVD. There is an erratic mobile signal and very basic wifi (weather permitting), but you don't come to the middle of Bodmin Moor to watch movies – despite being just 15 minutes from the A30.

Quite the perfect escape, then, for those who want to get away from it all – but not too far.

CORNWALL Near Altarnun Bodmin Moor PL15 7TJ
07818 407060 leskernick.com
HOW MUCH? From £595 to £850 a week, depending on season.

"We've had songwriters, yogis, stargazers, honeymooners, families and teenagers, and they have all loved escaping 21st-century living at Leskernick Cottage."

Katie Warnes, Leskernick Cottage

What's nearby?

BROWN WILLY At 420m, this is Cornwall's highest peak and can be walked to in an hour across the moor. The views from its 2 cairns are spectacular.

CAMEL TRAIL The former rail line from Bodmin is now one of Cornwall's easiest walks and cycle routes – and a great way to reach the coast from the moor.

STRIPPLE STONES Only 15 stones remain from this neolithic circle, but it's still a super-evocative spot, positioned originally (they say) to witness the spring equinox.

Heath Farm

Luxury cottages in 70 acres of Cotswolds countryside

For many people a cottage in the Cotswolds represents the quintessential English rural idyll, and Heath Farm Cottages don't disappoint. Breathtaking views of rolling countryside, meadows, a lake and woodlands teeming with wildlife are key to the experience; inside, honeyed Cotswold stone exposed walls, oak beams, terracotta, slate floors or hardwood floors and large open fireplaces (logs provided) make for a cosy and welcoming stay. The 5 cottages, each named after a type of nut (plenty of which grow in the grounds) are extremely comfortable and well equipped, with wifi, TV/DVD, modern kitchens and luxury bathrooms, and range from the top floor of what was formerly the barn (sleeping 4) to 2-bed options facing a paved courtyard. They all have open fires and everything you need is provided, from towels and toilet rolls to salt and herbs, with starter amounts of sugar, tea and coffee. There is real attention to detail in these properties, with bespoke furniture made from the farm's own trees and iron fittings created by a local blacksmith. There's also plenty to do: a model aircraft and kite-flying strip and games shed packed full of equipment (most bat & ball games, giant Jenga, boules, archery), lots of footpaths for country walks, cycling, golf or maybe just a game of croquet on the lawn.

Above all the location is perfect: Heath Farm used to be a 370-acre working farm but the Barbour family (who still live in the adjoining house) sold most of their herd years ago – though they do still keep a few sheep, chickens and pigs to keep the larder stocked. They can also advise on where to visit (or where to find the best wild plums or herbs if you fancy a bit of foraging).

OXFORDSHIRE Swerford Chipping Norton OX7 4BN 01608 683270 heathfarm.com

HOW MUCH? From £414 to £664 a week, depending on season, for the 2-person cottages; £429 to £962 for the 2-4 person cottages.

"In the middle of nowhere, at the edge of everything…"

Mon Barbour, Heath Farm

What's nearby?

ROLLRIGHT STONES They say these stones cannot be counted, but it's fun to walk around the neolithic stone circle and have a go. Try with a partner and you won't come up with the same number – just a taste of the atmospheric spookiness of this under-visited monument.

HOOK NORTON BREWERY A pint of 'Hooky' is the local tipple around here, and you could do worse than visit the brewery on one of their 2-hour tours.

CHASTELETON HOUSE An almost perfect Jacobean mansion that's full of early 17th-century treasures but is perhaps best known as the home of croquet.

East Cambusmoon Farm

Luxury eco-friendly accommodation in a National Park

An environmentally aware self-catering oasis set just back from the banks of Loch Lomond, East Cambusmoon Farm is a 5-acre smallholding handily tucked into the heart of the Loch Lomond and Trossachs National Park – a beautiful location with stunning scenery and plenty of activities on hand nearby. The savvy couple who run the cottages – Deborah and Steve Macken – have experience in renewables and have learned lessons from their success in fashioning their own home on clean and green lines. The result is spectacular, with 2 very different cottages joined at the hip to share their magical green touch.

The 2-bedroom Old Dairy is the original property and the 4-bedroom Curlew Cottage the young upstart, with larch cladding and white render. With underfloor heating and wood-burning stoves you're guaranteed to be warm and cosy. The hosts offer free top-ups of the log basket too. Both cottages are open, airy spaces bathed in light and bringing the beautiful surrounding countryside inside. It works so well and is such a cosy hideaway that even if the weather is damp you won't mind too much. Neat touches include some welcome (homemade and local) provisions, free wifi and a trampoline in the barn that helps keep wee ones happy when it rains. All brilliant and compelling proof that a low-carbon footprint and a responsible attitude to the environment doesn't mean sacrificing comfort or style. You can rent the cottages individually, for couples or for families, or together they can accommodate up to 14 people in some style, with 4 bathrooms, an en-suite loo, plenty of patio space, and toys, games and books for young children.

LOCH LOMOND Gartocharn West Dunbartonshire G83 8RZ 07905 093997 lochlomondholidaycottage.com
HOW MUCH? Old Dairy: 2 or 3 nights from £300, 7 nights from £600; Curlew Cottage: 2 or 3 nights from £450, 7 nights from £900.

"Our award-winning cottages provide the ideal base for Loch Lomond and its surroundings whether you're a large group or a romantic couple."

Deborah Macken, East Cambusmoon Farm

What's nearby?

LOCH LOMOND Britain's largest loch is a sparkling beauty, framed by brooding mountains and peppered with forested islands, and offering everything from nature cruises to SUPs, kayaking and waterskiing.

STIRLING CASTLE Could there be a better position for a castle than this? The view, if nothing else, from Stirling's magnificent fortress will take your breath away.

GLENGOYNE DISTILLERY They claim to have Scotland's 'slowest' stills, which produce a complex whisky that you can taste on one of their regular tours.

Portland House, Derbyshire

PARTIES, GROUPS & GATHERINGS

Family reunion, special occasion or house party? You're going to want a bigger venue, and a normal holiday cottage probably won't cut it. Communal dining, space for the kids, multiple bathrooms, gardens and grounds, maybe even a games or cinema room – that's the sort of large self-catering property you need and we have just the thing, from old mills and castles to country mansions and converted farm cottages and stables.

Fawcett Mill

Perfect for large gatherings and the nearby Howgill Fells

There's nowhere quite like the Cumbrian Lakes or Yorkshire Dales if you're considering a big family get-together or a milestone birthday or anniversary celebration – and there aren't many better venues for a gathering than Fawcett Mill, which is handily located on the borders of both regions, just north of the rolling Howgill Hills. It's a beautiful location by any standards: tucked away in its own peaceful valley, above a stream and nearby waterfall, it feels miles from anywhere, although you're only a couple of miles off the M6 motorway.

A solid late-18th-century large limestone cottage, it's cosily furnished in an appropriately country style, with a large living room and a lovely Victorian range and dining room with oak beams and a wood-burning stove. It has 2 kitchens – a small one with an electric oven, fridge, washing machine, microwave and dishwasher, and an additional one with Rayburn oven and hob next to the dining area. There's also a sauna and a downstairs bathroom. There are 3 double bedrooms on the first floor, 2 of which have 4-posters, and one of which has an en-suite, plus a 4th twin room. Above here, on the second floor, are 3 further bedrooms, and with 2 double futon sofa beds in the upstairs lounge, Fawcett Mill can comfortably sleep 20 people.

The garden has seating and a stone-built BBQ – and the Raisbeck stream at the bottom leads to any number of country walks; the Coast-to-Coast Path also passes through the village. Or you could just decide to stay home and buy some beef or lamb from nearby Raisgill Hall Farm and warm yourself in front of the range. After a long day's hike through the Howgill Fells, it's pure heaven.

CUMBRIA Gaisgill Orton Near Penrith CA10 3UB
0800 443377 fawcettmill.info
HOW MUCH? Weekly rates £1695–£1995, short breaks £1295 for up to 4 nights. Christmas/New Year breaks £3795–£3995 a week.

"I couldn't bring myself to sell Fawcett Mill so decided to share it so that others could enjoy its idyllic country location."

Chris Smith, Fawcett Mill

What's nearby?

ORTON FARMERS MARKET Held in the heart of the village every 2nd Saturday of each month, this is a fab market and a great source of high-quality local produce.

TEBAY SERVICES The UK's first family-owned motorway services is a legend in these parts, with a farm shop, artisan butchers and bakers and a brilliant restaurant.

KENNEDY'S CHOCOLATES Orton has its own chocolatier, no less – and you can see their lovely chocs being made in the local shop, or enjoy a coffee in their café.

Aikwood Tower

A spectacular castle in the Scottish Borders

Just 40 miles south of Edinburgh, this Scottish Borders bolthole is a stunning place to stay – a 16th-century fortified tower sited on a hill amid some spectacular scenery. It has historic charm in abundance, and bags of character, though you also get all the bells and whistles as far as a luxurious stay is concerned. Five large and very comfortable bedrooms, classy en-suite bathrooms (some with standalone baths), a fully fitted kitchen with an Aga, and a large bespoke oak dining table ('Aikwood' means oak) mean plenty of space for large groups, family parties and gatherings. Evenings can be spent around the log fire in the glorious Great Hall, maybe a game of table tennis in the lower hall, or quiet time in the library and study. There is always someone around if you need them, with outside caterers available if you don't fancy cooking (there is a second kitchen on site), as well as the chance to try various activities – clay-pigeon shooting, archery, falconry, even whisky-tasting at the country's newest distillery, in nearby Hawick.

The tower was formerly the home of the Liberal politician Lord Steel, who restored it in the 1990s and won a number of architectural awards. Now under the stewardship of his son Rory, it is the perfect place from which to explore the gorgeous Borders countryside (though you're going to need a car to do it). There's plenty to keep you occupied nearby, from walking in the Ettrick Valley and Forest to shopping in the local market towns of Peebles or Selkirk. Just half an hour away, Glentress forest park is known for its superb mountain biking while those with a head for heights can also head for the local branch of Go Ape's treetop adventures.

SCOTTISH BORDERS Selkirk TD7 5HJ
01750 700500 aikwoodtower.com
HOW MUCH? Between £2050 and £2950 a week, depending on season; weekends £750–£2550; midweek stays from £500 per night (2-night minimum).

"Our 500-year-old walls have countless stories to tell – we love that so many people are able to be part of its story."

Rory and Vicki Steel, Aikwood Tower

What's nearby?

SELKIRK Perhaps the quintessential Borders market town, with an ancient medieval centre that's awash with cafés, pubs and restaurants.

GLENTRESS FOREST PARK Scotland is one of the world's top mountain biking destinations, and this is one reason why – easier green and blue trails plus more challenging red routes.

ETTRICK VALLEY Who said the Highlands had all the best scenery? There are glorious walks galore in the wooded valleys and moorland of the Ettrick Valley.

BEER

"If you're not happy at first, just wait a bit" says Stuart Woodman – forager and brewer of Woodman's Wild Ale, a Cornwall-based brewery that specialises in beer brewed and flavoured with wild plants. It's a patient approach that has led to a growth in demand for his unusual, seasonal beers, all of them based around foraged ingredients or on the natural yeasts found in the air. It's Cornwall... but with a bit of Belgian beeriness thrown in.

Woodman used to lead outdoor experiences for local outfit Seventh Rise and dabbled a bit in brewing at the same time, and in 2016 he started creating his own beers. His first, the tart and fruity Kea Porter, is a typical Woodman brew – made like a regular dark ale but with the addition of native kea plums – and he has gone on to produce several brews each season, steeped and flavoured with whatever is available at the time – blackberries and rosehips in autumn, dandelions in spring, elderflowers in summer, even sea yarrow grass in winter. Try his Mermaid's Kiss, subtly salty with the taste of the sea, or his Redruth Red, flavoured with wild strawberries, bilberries and other forest fruits. He even produces a Christmas ale, flavoured with local honey (though we're unsure where the frankincense and myrrh come from).

Woodman's ales are available in bottles, casks and kegs, and can be found at specialist shops and beer festivals. When Stuart is not making beer he's running walks and open days and generally talking up the joys of beer, foraging... and, well, life in Cornwall. Catch him if you can.

WOODMAN'S WILD ALE Viaduct Works Frog Hill Ponsanooth Cornwall TR3 7JW woodmanswildale.co.uk

The Den, Husthwaite Gate

By a former train station, The Den at Husthwaite Gate is a hard place to categorise – a sheltered barn retreat that can sleep 6 but which has the bonus of a grassy space outside for a couple of tent pitches, an electric hook-up for a campervan and and a separate shower and toilet cabin. It's well suited for friends' get-togethers or families, who can have the whole site to themselves, and is thoughtful, quirky and green in equal measure: electricity is generated by a wind turbine, and the building is very well insulated – warm and cosy in winter and cool in hot weather. There's a high-spec kitchen and bathroom, open-plan living area, smart TV and fast wifi. The site has a cute little honesty shop and self-service café that you share with the odd hiker, and a BBQ with picnic table, firepit and comfy benches from which to watch the sun go down. On clear nights you can stargaze from the comfort of your own wood-fired hot tub before retreating to the quirky ship-cabin-style sleeping pods. Kicking back and relaxing is the order of the day, and it's an eminently tranquil spot to do just that.

NORTH YORKSHIRE Old Station House Husthwaite Gate YO61 4QF 07745 057807 husthwaitegate.co.uk **HOW MUCH?** £375–£750 a week, weekend and midweek stays also available.

Smugglers Cove Boatyard

Situated in a former slate works overlooking the beautiful Dyfi Estuary, Smugglers Cove Boatyard has been acting as a hub for local sailors for years. But these days it's much more than just a boatyard, with camping pitches, a glamping boat on the foreshore and 2 self-catering holiday cottages – Chapel House and Quarry Cottage – that can be rented together as a single holiday let. With room for 14–18 people in 7 bedrooms (as well as the possibility of booking the camping pitches and glamping boat as well), it's an ideal venue for family reunions, celebrations and get-togethers. Both properties were renovated by local architects and are furnished in a rustic style that is cosy rather than posh. You can launch your own boat or just enjoy the private beach; the RSPB Ynys-Hir nature reserve on the opposite shore is worth rowing to, or you can stride out into the hills behind on numerous footpaths. There's also Aberdyfi beach at the far end of the estuary, which is a wonderful expanse of golden sand and dunes.

GWYNEDD Frongoch Boatyard Aberdyfi LL35 0RG 0800 023 6489 smugglerscove.info **HOW MUCH?** From £1395 to £1895 most of the year; short (3–4-night) breaks from £995. Dogs £25.

Seascape

Perched on a clifftop, Seascape is aptly named
– a detached house with dramatic views of the
sea from every window. It has room for 10–12
guests in 4 bedrooms and is very well-appointed,
with smart TVs in every bedroom, a large sitting
room with loads of seating and a table that can
host up to 10 people – who can sit and eat while
enjoying the views through the patio doors. It's
a light and sunny property in summer, and a
cosy one in winter, with gas central heating and
a wood-burner, and a contemporary kitchen
equipped with everything you could possibly need
– electric oven and hob, microwave, coffee maker,
a large American-style fridge-freezer, dishwasher
and washing machine, plus table football in the
lounge area. There's a family bathroom upstairs,
a downstairs shower/toilet, while the garden
overlooks the sea and has a 6-person hot tub.
But perhaps the best thing about Seascape is its
location, just a short walk from the sandy beach
at Minnis Bay, and with 3 smaller beaches nearby,
surrounded by chalk cliffs, cliff stacks and caves.

KENT 33 Moray Avenue Birchington CT7 9UN
07739 850975 kent-cottage-holidays.co.uk
HOW MUCH? Two-night breaks from £595.

Elton Old Hall

With 6 double bedrooms and lots of living space,
Elton Old Hall is the perfect place for a family
gathering or friends reunion. Up to 14 people
can sleep in comfort in in this renovated Grade-
II-listed manor house, and it's comfortably rather
than ostentatiously furnished so large groups can
really let their hair down and enjoy this beautiful
part of the country. All of the rooms have king-
size, double or twin beds, and one has a 4-poster
for you to fight over. Three of the bedrooms
have en-suite facilities and there's also a family
bathroom with a bath and walk-in rainfall shower,
plus a downstairs cloakroom. There is also plenty
of room downstairs, so not only can 14 people
sleep here, they can sit down in comfort as well.
There's also a walled garden with a conservatory,
while the house has a Bluetooth music system
and wifi. In short it's the perfect Peak District
country retreat – and if it's not quite big enough
the same owners have Portland House, situated
in the popular and picturesque riverside town of
Matlock Bath.

DERBYSHIRE Main Street Elton Matlock DE4 2BW
01629 734414 eltonoldhall.co.uk
HOW MUCH? From £995 per week.

Great Barn Farm

A perfect rural spot for large groups to relax and unwind

Head to Great Barn Farm to relax and unwind: located on a 1350-acre working farm, it's home to stunning accommodation set across a series of converted outbuildings. Picture gently rolling farmland and woodlands full of wildlife to explore. Owners Sarah and Julian have taken great care with the restoration, and with 5 separate buildings, the site is capacious and inviting – a wonderful spot to spend time with family and friends.

To start with, there's the early-19th century Farmhouse sleeping up to 16, with a lovely garden that boasts a treehouse, tennis court and a set of manicured lawns. Pick some fruit and veg from the kitchen garden, cook a tasty meal in the superb state-of-the-art kitchen and enjoy an al fresco lunch or dinner out on one of the terraces. Next up is the Cattle Shed, a 5-bed space, though the cows are long gone and in their place there's room for 10 guests to enjoy its stripped wood beams, polished concrete flooring, underfloor heating, splashes of colour and quirky decorative touches. The Tack Rooms is a calming one-bed sanctuary, with a modern kitchen decked out using reclaimed materials and with sweeping views. The Piggery and Stables complete the picture: each has room for 4 people and is full of rural yet also contemporary charm, with original brick walls and cosy wood-burners.

There's an added bonus too, in that each of the holiday homes has access to The Sheep Dip – a good-sized indoor swimming pool with jacuzzi and steam room. Swim a few lengths, watch as the kids splash about or simply relax in the warmth of the water, and be glad of the day you heard about the delights of Great Barn Farm.

NORFOLK Gayton Thorpe PE32 1PN
07789 031518 greatbarnfarm.co.uk
HOW MUCH? The Farmhouse from £3500 a week, the Cattle Shed from £2200 a week. Shorter stays are also available.

"There's something magical about the tranquillity of this little corner of Norfolk; we never tire of the beautiful sunrises and sunsets or the silence of the early morning mist over the fields."

Sarah and Julian, Great Barn Farm

What's nearby?

HOUGHTON HALL One of the most impressive stately homes still in private hands in the country, with magnicent interiors, sumptuous grounds and regular interesting exhibitions.

NAR VALLEY WAY Explore a variety of walks along this beautiful chalk stream, taking in Castle Acre's magnificent ruined priory along the way.

GEORGE & DRAGON Known by locals as the 'Newton George', this old inn recently re-opened with a spruced-up interior and an emphasis on good-quality food.

Plane Castle

A fabulous Scottish castle steeped in history

Historic Plane Castle oozes character. It's divided into 2 parts, the Tower and the Manor, that can be rented separately, or you can combine the 2 and sleep up to 18 people (22 if you also take their nearby cottage) for a truly memorable wedding or party venue. Featuring winding spiral staircases, painted beamed ceilings, stone-vaulted rooms, tapestries, thick walls and splendid dining halls, the castle manages to combine atmosphere and history with comfort. At night there's a roaring fire to sit around, while the bedrooms and bathrooms are warm and welcoming. Mary Queen of Scots is said to have visited the castle often, and Bonnie Prince Charlie's Royal Guard was quartered here in 1746; there's even a secret passage, which kids love to explore.

The Manor is the larger section of the castle, sprawling over 3 levels and sleeping up to 10 people in 4 bedrooms. The vaulted ground floor contains the kitchen and dining rooms; the first floor is entirely given over to the Great Hall, with its vast fireplace; while on the second floor are the bedrooms, one with 4-poster bed and en-suite bath, plus 2 further bathrooms. The Tower – self-explanatory really – sleeps up to 8 people over 4 floors connected by narrow spiral stairs. Accommodation is on the second floor, where there are 2 stone bedrooms with medieval alcoves, and at the top of the tower, the Edwardian Crown Room, which boasts stunning views in every direction and can sleep 4 people. Outside, there are 3 acres of gardens offering plenty of room to explore, with ponds, statues and even a hobbit hole.

STIRLINGSHIRE By Airth FK2 8SF 07706 122034
planecastle.co.uk
HOW MUCH? The Manor from £400 a night, from £2300 a week. The Tower from £300 a night, from £1200 a week. Both from £700 a night, from £3500 a week.

"For us Plane Castle is much more than just a place to stay – kick back with friends and family and embrace its unique charm and character."

Steve Shields, Plane Castle

What's nearby?

DUNBLANE CATHEDRAL Quite simply one of the most dramatic ecclesiastic buildings in the country – and with a touching memorial to the children and their teacher who died in the massacre of 1996.

BATTLE OF BANNOCKBURN Located on the site of the famous battle, this immersive 3D battle experience recreates Robert the Bruce's great victory in 1314.

Tregulland Cottage & Barn

A gorgeous Cornwall setting with every luxury to hand

If your idea of heaven is seclusion in a gorgeous setting with every luxury to hand, then Tregulland Cottage & Barn is for you… and your family and friends (and it's dog-friendly too). Set in 16 acres of rolling Cornish countryside, Tregulland boasts the UK's first indoor freshwater swimming pool, its glass-walled pool house and underwater lighting ideal for a sun-drenched or late-night dip; after that, you could maybe try the Steam Room or outdoor Dutch Tub? There is a fishing lake (look out for Doris, the 23lb carp), and you can expect to see kingfishers, buzzards and perhaps even a resident owl. For those who prefer to stay indoors, there is a huge cinema in the granary, super-fast wifi, ample places to curl up with a book, or you can arrange any number of personalised classes, including yoga and pilates, as well as a bespoke in-house dining service provided by local chefs. Perhaps the most compelling feature of Tregulland, however, is its size. The Cottage and Barn are designed to be taken together so the dining room is set up to seat everyone – up to 25 people. Every bedroom has been designed with immense attention to detail, with luxuries such as rainfall showers and the best Egyptian cotton sheets. The Cottage alone can accommodate 12 in 6 en-suite double bedrooms and The Barn sleeps 10 in 5 en-suite double rooms and even has its own home cinema and 'map room' for planning adventures to the coast (about 15 minutes away). To be honest, though, Tregulland is so beautiful you probably won't want to go anywhere. It's a place to really get away from it all and savour your own private corner of Cornwall.

CORNWALL Tregulland Cottage & Barn St Clether Launceston PL15 8QW 01566 770880
tregullandandco.co.uk
HOW MUCH? Prices from £3090 for a 4-night midweek break, and from £7800 to £12,200 for a week.

"We think this is an awesome place to celebrate those big birthdays, anniversaries and reunions… it will seduce you with its luxurious comfort and relaxed elegance."

Ken and Ilona Aylmer, Tregulland & Co.

What's nearby?

TINTAGEL Is this Cornwall's most spectacular ruined castle? It's certainly its most magical, steeped in the mystery and legend of King Arthur.

CAMEL VALLEY VINEYARD Bob Lindo's vines have arguably brought the same recognition to the region's wine scene as Rick Stein has to its food scene.

THE RISING SUN, ALTARNUN Great pub in the heart of Bodmin Moor serving local ales and excellent, locally sourced food, served with their own homemade bread.

Fair Oak Farm

A unique rural estate in stunning East Sussex countryside

Nestled on a private 12-acre Sussex estate, in a protected Area of Outstanding Natural Beauty, this award-winning complex sleeps up to 36 guests across a unique range of accommodation, including a traditional country-chic farmhouse, converted barns, eco-lodge treehouses and luxury shepherds' huts. Owners Ian and Penny encourage sustainable tourism practices and they cater for all manner of occasions, be it a gathering of friends and family, a business group stay or a wellness retreat. Fancy putting your feet up and letting someone else do the cooking? An in-house cook can be provided and the main barn provides capacious communal space. Keen to play a game or watch a film? There's a table tennis table and if the big screen in the main barn isn't enough, you can head over to the cinema barn. There's even a range of activities available exclusively for guests, ranging from wine-tasting with a local producer to photography classes, trout fishing and beauty treatments.

The complex's vast array of accommodation is spread across a large plot of land. The Grade II-listed farmhouse sleeps 10–12, the country-chic converted barns 10–14, while there are also a series of alternative options if you fancy something a bit different – eco-lodges in ancient trees, shepherds' huts with wood-burners and a Hay Barn overlooking a paddock. Each area has its own private parking and scenic views, and there's a BBQ for summer cookouts on balmy evenings, plus a capacious communal dining area large enough to house all 36 guests. Finally there's a play area for children, who might also want to see the alpacas and peacocks that roam the luscious gardens.

EAST SUSSEX Witherenden Road Mayfield TN20 6RS 01435 884122 fairoakfarm.co.uk
HOW MUCH? From £5895 to £7895 a week for the whole estate, weekends from £4650 to £5620, midweek breaks £4240 –£5215).

"We've had the honour of hosting some truly inspirational people, and there is no better reward than providing them with personal memories they can treasure forever."

Ian Ledger, Fair Oak Farm

What's nearby?

MAYFIELD Head into the large High Weald village of Mayfield for its characterful high street, the Middle House pub (for food) – and, if you're here in September, one of the biggest Sussex Bonfire processions of all.

BEDGEBURY FOREST Home to one of the world's finest conifer collections but better known as a place to walk, cycle, run and ride – plus it has a branch of Go Ape.

BATEMANS Rudyard Kipling's home for 34 years, this Jacobean manor is – as he said – a 'good and peaceable place'. It's now owned by the National Trust.

Crofthouse at Roundhouse

The Crofthouse is situated on Roy Abel's farm in an exquisite Highland location, and is kitted out with all mod cons and home comforts. It sleeps 8 people, so is perfect for a large family or group of friends who are looking for a base in the heart of the Cairngorms National Park. Visitors are made to feel very much part of what is still a working farm, and it's dog-friendly too. The Crofthouse itself is almost Scandinavian in feel, pine-clad outside and in, with a large open-plan living area, a family room that sleeps 4, and 4 further beds in 2 separate spaces in the loft. It's no slouch when it comes to state-of-the-art facilities, with underfloor heating, wifi and flatscreen TVs. And remember, it's a farm, so you can watch farmer Roy's herd of Highland cattle from your balcony. There's a separate studio with stunning views if you fancy a doing a bit of painting or a spot of yoga as you take in the woods and mountain views. The location also isn't far from Aviemore, with all its activities and funicular railway, and come night-time clear starry skies are virtually guaranteed.

CAIRNGORMS Uvie Farm Roundhouse Newtonmore
PH20 1BS 07811 322722 myhighlandcroft.co.uk
HOW MUCH? From £132 a night, Fri–Sun £144 a night.
June–August 7-day bookings only – £596–£696.

Portland House

If you're looking for a big place to rent for a large-scale get-together or family celebration, then this 19th-century gentleman's villa, situated in the picturesque Peak District spa town of Matlock Bath, might just be the thing, with no fewer than 12 bedrooms and any number of contemporary quirky touches that perfectly complement its more historic features. You have the option of renting it on an entirely self-catering basis, and the house has a well-appointed (and, frankly, huge) kitchen in which to cook up some family feasts – and how many places can boast a dining room with a table that can seat 24? There's also a large living room that can also seat everyone, a bar and games room with bar billiards, and you can bolt on as much or as little as you like in terms of extras, with options that include everything from catered dinner parties to clay pigeon shooting and spa treatments. The house also has a lovely walled garden with 2 built-in BBQs and a summer house, or you can head up to the Heights of Abraham on foot or by cable car. Basically a delightful place for a party.

DERBYSHIRE New Bath Road Matlock Bath DE4 3PX
01629 734414 portlandhouse1870.co.uk
HOW MUCH? From £2395 for a weekend.

Crispie Estate

Only in Scotland could you find somewhere like Crispie Estate, where 120 acres of pristine coast and ancient forests are yours for the duration of your stay: both properties are right on the beach and the water is so clear. You can sail, walk, cycle, kayak, swim or just explore the place on foot, and there is even a motor boat moored in the bay for guests' exclusive use. There are 2 places to stay – Crispie House, which sleeps 16 people, and Crispie Lodge, a smaller, more contemporary affair, which can accommodate 8 people. Both have their own grounds and beach; Crispie House has an indoor swimming pool and games room while Crispie Lodge features a fabulous hot tub. Just turn up, and throw away the car keys... and tune out. Dogs are welcome at Crispie House, and any time of year the views across the loch to the Mull of Kintyre are stunning, while outside the lawn sweeps directly down to the beach. Otherwise amble through the woods, fish, swim or cycle, or just relax and enjoy the views across the loch to the Isle of Arran.

ARGYLL Kilfinan Tighnabruaich PA21 2ER
07887 408893 crispie.co.uk
HOW MUCH? Lodge from £900 a week, House from £2500 a week.

Incleborough House

This large, luxurious house on the North Norfolk Coast is a rather perfect place for a big get-together – a sumptuous Georgian property that's one of 3 properties owned by Nick and Barbara Davies; the others are Stable Cottage, next door, and The Brambles, nearby. Located at the eastern end of the coast, in the small, pretty coastal village of East Runton, a stone's throw from a long sandy Blue Flag beach, it has 7 spacious, tastefully furnished bedrooms and 6 state-of-the-art en-suite bathrooms – one of which even has a handily placed TV opposite the tub. Outside there's a beautiful walled garden, complete with a bubbling hot tub, while downstairs a well-appointed kitchen boasts an Aga, satellite TV, DVD player, PlayStations, ping-pong and pool tables, and there's super-fast wifi throughout. You're also just around the corner from the main coast road, so there's no excuse for not heading out to explore the area – Cromer and Sheringham are both just a few minutes' drive away.

NORFOLK Lower Common East Runton Cromer
NR27 9PG 01263 822478 luxurious-cottages.co.uk
HOW MUCH? Prices from £1995 for a weekend in low season.

Tapnell Farm

Beautiful holiday cottages on a working dairy farm

Located just outside Yarmouth, on the western side of the Isle of Wight, Tapnell Farm occupies a a beautiful rural setting and has several high-quality self-catering options, from farm cottages to its own manor house. It's a great choice if you're staying with extended family or a group of friends, as the accommodation is very spacious and there's so much to do – its 'Farm Park' complex is one of the island's biggest attractions, with clay pigeon shooting, pedal go-karts, zip wires, and the Cow Co restaurant for sit-down meals. At the heart of the farm, the Dairyman's Cottage has panoramic views of Tennyson Down and sleeps up to 8. It's decorated with a contemporary feel – sea-grass carpets and wood laminate flooring throughout, bespoke fabrics, luxury en-suite bedrooms and an open-plan living area and kitchen. There is a downstairs wet room with disabled access, as well as a garden and patio with BBQ and a wood-fired hot tub that's perfect for soothing aching muscles after a long day's walking. Stockbridge Cottage, on the edge of the farm, sleeps up to 12 and has views down towards Freshwater Bay and a large garden complete with adventure playground. If you need room for a bigger group, East Afton Farmhouse has 8 bedrooms, a roof-terrace hot tub, cinema room, games area and private courtyard, or try Tapnell Manor, with 10 bedrooms, hot tub and games area. The cottages are right on the doorstep of several footpaths and within driving distance of Freshwater and other great beaches, but with all the activities available you could just stay put. You can collect eggs from the free-range hens or head over to the honesty larder for those handy bits and bobs that got left behind. Many people come back here year after year – we bet you will too.

ISLE OF WIGHT Tapnell Farm Newport Road Yarmouth PO41 0YJ 01983 758729 tapnellfarm.com/stay
HOW MUCH? Dairyman's Cottage £800–£1700 a week, Stockbridge Cottage £650–£1675 a week, Tapnell Manor Farmhouse £2600–£4600 a week.

"Our farmhouse and manor are big enough for the largest family, plus you can enjoy our hot tubs, cinema room and games areas."

Chloe Baker, Tapnell Farm

What's nearby?

FRESHWATER BAY A small sand and shingle cove on the southern side of the island's western tip – quiet and less frantic than the east coast resorts.

CALBOURNE The hidden gem of West Wight, arguably the prettiest village on the island, famous for its film-set perfection, babbling brook and thatched cottages.

TENNYSON DOWN Alfred, Lord Tennyson, lived in Freshwater Bay, and this walk is a steep one but the views from the monument at the top are more than worth it.

GLAMPING

Once upon a time in the UK, 'camping' meant a tent in
a field, and life was very dull. And then a glamorous fairy
cast a spell upon all the tents and, because magic is real,
you can now have a cosy, comfortable stay in a yurt, pod,
tipi, bell-tent, shepherds' hut, safari tent or treehouse
– heck, even a hobbit hole – and that's why we love
glamping at Cool Places.

Longlands Glamping, Devon

Top Of The Woods

Boutique glamping in a beautiful part of Wales

It's easy to get lost at Top of the Woods. Not literally – owners Soo and Jon give you a map on arrival – but in a do-as-you-please kind of way. The atmosphere is so laid-back it's almost horizontal, with various glamping options spread over 27 rolling acres; you'll be soothed and charmed by the sights and sounds of birds and wildlife and the white-grey wisps of campfire smoke. In the adjoining Ffynone Wood – a vast 325-acre forest – you might be lucky enough to spot a resident of the largest badger population in West Wales; you'll definitely see rabbits, and maybe even an otter or two slipping into Afon Dulas, a peaceful stream that runs along the southern edge of the site. Top of the Woods is part of Penrallt Farm, a quaint 18th-century farmstead that has won awards for being a thoroughly eco-friendly place to stay, with a variety of glamping styles – 5 fully furnished bell tents, 4 luxury safari lodges and 9 so-called pioneer camps (basically posher, more spacious, bell tents). It's all pretty high-spec, but the feeling and style is very definitely back to nature. A Dutch Barn serves as a picnic and meeting area for the site, with tables, hammocks, phone-charging points and a stash of games. It's also a handy place to mull over the route that leads you to the enchantingly named 'secret waterfall'. Soo and Jon offer hot breakfasts at weekends and hosted dinners in the evenings, and a mobile fishmonger visits weekly. There are usually any number of activities going on, from a weekend yoga breakfast club to bushcraft sessions and other events, including their excellent 'Woof Weekend', held in May, when dogs and their owners get even more pampered than usual.

PEMBROKESHIRE Penrallt Farm Capel Coleman Boncath SA37 0EP 01239 842208 topofthewoods.co.uk
HOW MUCH? Bell tents from £60 a night, Pioneer Camps from £75 a night, Safari Lodges from £90 a night – 2-night minimum stay.

"Pembrokeshire has something for everyone who loves nature and the outdoors – we love it here!"

Soo and Jon, Top of the Woods

What's nearby?

TEIFI GORGE & MARSHES The deep chasm of the Teifi Gorge is perfect for canoeing and kayaking, plus the top of the estuary is a nature reserve, home to countless birds, otters and even the occasional water buffalo.

MWNT BEACH Cardigan Bay is home to some of the finest beaches in the UK and Mwnt is at the top of the pile: slightly off the beaten track, but the drive there is spectacular.

DOLPHIN WATCHING Trips with Marine Safari take in everything from seals, whales and porpoises to the largest resident dolphin pod in Europe.

Cosy Under Canvas

Never underestimate a woman's glamping touch

Twisting and turning along the winding country lanes, it's almost impossible not to get childishly giddy about what awaits you at Cosy Under Canvas. As you roll into the car park, offload your bags into a wheelbarrow and walk across a wildflower wetland, it quickly becomes apparent that when it comes to glamping, you can never underestimate a woman's touch.

Owner Emma has been running Cosy Under Canvas for 10 years now, and her attention to detail resonates throughout the site – from the little welcome boards with your names written in chalk to the homemade cakes left out for your arrival. There are 7 pitches, spread out in a small private woodland and cleverly hidden from each other by the trees – 5 spacious geodesic dome tents and 2 cosy domes, all with their own wood-fired hot tub, firepit, chiminea, compost loo, indoor wood-burner, sheepskin rugs, super comfy double or king-sized beds, raised double futons, wood and kindling, lanterns and tea lights. There's a 'cosy corner' filled with board games and activities for kids, a 'cosy lounge' with comfy chairs and low tables for adults to chill out, and a large communal sheltered kitchen. There's also fresh drinking water and a handful of gas stoves in case the rain puts a dampener on things. The 2 communal showers are heated by the large wood-fired Aga in the kitchen, but if you fancy a proper power shower (heated by a biomass boiler) then pop up to the main house. All in all it's a thoroughly green woodland retreat like no other. The kids will never want to get out of the hot tub, and couples will only want to cosy up by the fire and stare up at the starry dark skies above.

POWYS Dolbedwyn Newchurch Kington HR5 3QQ
01497 851603 cosyundercanvas.co.uk
HOW MUCH? Domes from £160 for 2 nights, from £255 a week.

"Cosy Under Canvas is a complete digital detox, just what our busy brains need these days! The Beech Dome Hot Tub is perfect for a night of steamy relaxation under the stars or a date with the dawn chorus!"

Emma Price, Cosy under Canvas

What's nearby?

HAY BLUFF Straddling the border of Wales and England, this is a favourite climb of ours, with beautiful views from its windy summit.

HAY-ON-WYE It's just 5 miles to this iconic border town, with its plethora of bookshops, annual literary festival and fabulous revamped castle.

WYE VALLEY The place for local outdoor adventures – try paddling downstream in a canoe, strolling the Wye Valley Walk or a bit of wild swimming at The Warren.

Ivy Grange Farm

Cosy glamping in the heart of the Suffolk countryside

London media world refugees Kim and Nick Hoare have created a real slice of rural bliss a few miles inland from Southwold, just outside the small Suffolk town of Halesworth – a gorgeous spot where 4 yurts and a romantic shepherd's hut form the nucleus of their thoughtfully planned glamping site. It's a place where attention has been given to every sort of detail, and the enthusiasm of the owners shines through at every turn. The yurts are beautifully furnished, with wood-burners, big comfy double beds and pull-out futons, and outside decking with gas hob and fire pit – great for taking in the big skies and glorious sunsets with a glass of wine each evening. There are cauldrons and cooking pots in the shed and a wonderfully well-appointed open kitchen for more ambitious dining. In addition to the 3-acre field, there's a restored barn with tables and chairs, and a lovely woodland shower, supplied by solar-heated water.

As for the location, it's very rural, and right on National Cycling Route 1, so great for exploring the flat and intensely quiet roads nearby – they have a selection of bikes to borrow. If, on the other hand, you just want to stay put and enjoy the peace of the camp, you could join one of their Full Moon Walks at night. The site is a haven for wildlife, and among other birds you can spot yellowhammers, buzzards and bullfinches. The meadow also has butterflies, hedgehogs, dragonflies and even hares throughout the year. Quite honestly, there's nothing better than sitting round your campfire as the sun sets, enjoying an al fresco meal as you watch the swallows, then as dusk settles the bats, and finally the owls hooting in the trees around.

SUFFOLK Butts Road Westhall Halesworth IP19 8RN
07802 456087 ivygrangefarm.co.uk
HOW MUCH? From £190 for a yurt for 2 nights, with discounts for longer stay. Minimum 2 night-stay."

"Relax, recharge, explore or just do nothing in a tranquil spot with birdsong all around."

Kim and Nick, Ivy Grange Farm

What's nearby?

DUNWICH HEATH A special spot, with dazzling circular walks taking in beach, heath and woodland, a ruined monastery and finishing up at the National Trust café at Coastguards Cottages for tea.

ST PETER'S BREWERY The brewery's distinctive bottles hail from this renovated farmstead, which has a shop and restaurant and is open for weekend tours.

KING'S HEAD, LAXFIELD A celebrated pub with no bar, just a load of barrels and several wood-panelled little rooms that make it cosy on a winter's night.

Longlands Glamping

Luxurious glamping in glorious North Devon

Bella, Bugsie and the kids left London 8 years ago to set up their perfect glamping location, and Longlands is the result. They had some very specific requirements when searching for their ideal location: they wanted it to be conveniently close to the sea (to be able to sneak in a lunchtime surf), have breathtaking views and plenty of space to create the ultimate rural retreat. And this delightful destination on the western border of Exmoor, 5 minutes from the coastal village of Combe Martin, pretty much ticks all the boxes. Five thoughtfully positioned safari tents (each sleeping 6) come furnished with vintage leather sofas, luxurious linen and a fully equipped kitchen with a wood-burning stove, keeping the cosy interior warm in all weathers while also providing a means of cooking. Not only that, each has its very own shower room with flushing loo and basin, plus a wide range of natural aromatherapy products.

After spending a memorable day exploring North Devon and its many delights (Exmoor in one direction and the fabulous beaches of Woolacombe and Croyde in the other), Longlands is a comforting enclave to return to each night. Bella and Bugsie have done their hosting homework, pre-empting every need with the 'Longlands Larder', stocked with hard-to-resist, local produce (milk, jam, chutney and cheese) 24 hours a day. Guests can also cook using their private BBQ, and there is a beautiful hot tub on its own terrace, with a changing room and outdoor shower, and with views out across the valley and towards the sea and setting sun. Allow your days to float by effortlessly, while enjoying the simplicity of field living in a luxury canvas lodge.

DEVON Longlands Farm Coulsworthy Combe Martin EX34 0PD 01271 882004 longlandsdevon.co.uk
HOW MUCH? Midweek breaks (Mon–Fri) from £525, weekends (Fri–Mon) from £545.

"We want our guests to return home refreshed and revived, having enjoyed amazing adventures, and with memories to cherish forever."

Bella Given, Longlands Glamping

What's nearby?

HUNTER'S INN There's something very special about this comfy old pub, situated deep amid the rolling wooded hills of Exmoor. It's a perfect place for a pint after walks in the Heddon Valley.

BROOMHILL SCULPTURE GARDEN There's a surprise at every turn in these hillside hotel gardens, filled with contempoorary sculptures of all shapes, sizes and styles.

VALLEY OF THE ROCKS This fabled local beauty spot makes an easy but spectacular walk into Lynton/Lynmouth through a bizarre dry rocky valley, populated by goats.

The Quiet Site

Eco-friendly glamping that's a real family favourite

This hideaway camspite above Ullswater is a real family favourite, set amid the fells on an old Cumbrian farmstead, with dramatic views to all sides. It has pitches for caravans and campervans, grassy pitches for tents and a number of timber-built pods, which offer more comfort and weather protection than mere canvas – all you need to bring is your camping gear, minus the tent. Their eco-hearts are in the right place too, manifest in their unique 'Hobbit Holes', large underground living spaces with awesome views that are insulated and energy efficient – and virtually invisible unless you know where to look. They can accommodate up to 6 people each and some also take dogs, plus they have their own separate WCs and basin. The site also has a couple of holiday cottages, sleeping 6–9 people each.

The site's water is solar-heated and they have a specially created wildflower meadow, while at the same time boasting what they describe as 'The best campsite bar in Britain'. Quite a claim, but we like what they've done with the converted 18th-century Cumbrian long barn, from the toasty wood-burning fireplace to the local ales on offer at the bar. There's a shop on site too, while children get the run of an adventure playground, playroom and games room – or you can wear them out on local walks right from the campsite, including the one to the rather wonderful Aira Force waterfall, situated in a woodland park owned by the National Trust. Ullswater itself is a mile and a half down the hill, with the nearest pub the Brackenrigg Inn (at the turn-off for the campsite), which not only does good food but is also home to its own microbrewery.

CUMBRIA Ullswater CA11 0LS
07768 727016 thequietsite.co.uk
HOW MUCH? Camping pods £35–£50 depending on season; hobbit holes £55–£80 a night.

"The Quiet Site' continues to pioneer the glamping experience, with camping pods, hobbit holes and probably the best campsite bar in Britain."

Daniel Holder, The Quiet Site

What's nearby?

ULLSWATER STEAMERS The crowds go to Windermere but those in the know visit Ullswater, traversed by steamers from Glenridding to Pooley Bridge.

CUMBERLAND PENCIL MUSEUM Let's face it, most people come when it's raining, but this is more than a wet-weather stand-by. The world's biggest pencil, anyone?

RHEGED Europe's largest grass-covered building is pretty much invisible on Google Earth, but inside is a family-orientated mix of film, play and gift and food outlets.

Grasmere Glamping

We've always liked the cosy accommodation at Broadrayne Farm in the heart of the Lake District but Grasmere Glamping takes things to a new level, with 2 bespoke handmade pods designed for couples wanting a romantic retreat. Situated on a former farm, it enjoys a lovely position, surrounded by some of the Lakes' best scenery, and instant access to many inspiring walking routes. Grasmere village is a short stroll away and there is a decent pub – the Traveller's Rest – just 2 minutes' walk down the road. As for the pods, they're equipped with everything you might need for a luxurious stay while sacrificing none of the closeness to nature that makes glamping so special – there's a lounge area with a large sofa, a wood-burning stove, dining table, flatscreen TV, kitchen with oven, hob and fridge/freezer – plus wifi and Bluetooth. As if that wasn't enough, it's eco-friendly too – fully insulated for year-round use, with a biomass boiler providing all your hot water, and LED lighting throughout. If there is a cosier country bolthole for loved-up Lakeland walkers, then we have yet to find it.

CUMBRIA Broadrayne Farm Grasmere LA22 9RU
01539 460978 grasmereglamping.co.uk
HOW MUCH? £225–£325 for midweek and weekend breaks.

Pinewood Park

Yeehah! Camp Pinewood goes one better than all the other tipi sites, offering cowboy shacks and Wild West wagons along with a host of other wonderful glamping options, so that folk who want a more low-key stay are also welcomed along – as are well-behaved dogs. As well as a number of pitches for your own tent, there are a dozen pre-pitched tipis, shacks and cabins with double beds and modern furnishings. A number of the glamping lodges and a couple of the tipis have their own private hot tubs, and the cowboy camping shacks – large pods, really – have their own verandahs, while the fantastic Woody's Western Wagons are old-fashioned caravans just like you see in all the Westerns. For families it's a perfect escape: kids disappear off into the wooded area at the bottom of the site, which has paths weaving around the trees and is perfect for hide-and-seek, while a great little gift shop at reception sells Wild West toys for little and big kids too. For those looking for a family holiday on the Yorkshire Coast, there are few more well-appointed spots.

NORTH YORKSHIRE Racecourse Road Scarborough
YO12 5TG 01723 367278 pinewoodpark.co.uk
HOW MUCH? Tipis £80 a night, Cowboy Shacks £90, Woody's Western Wagons £90, Glamping Lodges £125.

Graywood Canvas Cottages

Inspired by a spot of glamping in California, Stephanie Wakeham-Dawson and her husband returned to their family farm in Sussex determined to bring the Californian dream to England, in the form of 3 unique double-decker yurts with huge picture windows and lots of natural light, and a staircase leading to a clear dome to the sky – perfect for viewing the stars. Each has its own hot tub and can comfortably sleep 5, in a ground-floor bedroom with super-king Hypnos bed and a galleried first-floor with space for 3 more. There is a proper bathroom with flushing toilet, shower, plenty of hot water and toiletries, a kitchen with washer/drier, fridge/freezer, dishwasher, microwave, oven and hob, toaster and kettle. A separate sitting room has custom-made sofas, TV and DVD and a dining table, with chairs for 6 and everything else you could possibly need to make you feel right at home. There's also outside furniture, a firepit and BBQ. The farm itself enjoys a great location in the heart of East Sussex, with plenty of birds and wildlife around and lovely walks into the surrounding countryside.

EAST SUSSEX Graywood Farm East Hoathly BN8 6QT
07715 630665 graywoodcanvascottages.co.uk
HOW MUCH? £650–£850 a week, weekends and mini breaks £490–£640.

Red Kite Tree Tent

Calling all campers: we've officially entered the era of the tree tent, a spherical canvas structure suspended by rope high up in the trees. Sounds ominous? Actually it isn't. Instead it's sort of beautiful, in a futuristic orb kind of way. The tent is located on the outskirts of a dense woodland, and as you walk down the hill, your new accommodation starts to take shape before your eyes. First you'll see the handmade wooden bridge, then the babbling brook followed by the wooden stumps leading up to your very own kitchen and shower. Turn around, and you'll be face-to-face with the tree tent, which comes with a super comfy circular bed and wood-burning stove. We could bore you with the facilities and practical aspects, but all you need to know is that this is an experience like no other. There's a firepit next to the brook, and at night the tree tent gently rocks you to sleep, although the gentleness depends entirely on how windy it is that night. The next day, you might feel that similar wobbly sensation you get when you've been on a boat.

POWYS Newbridge-on-Wye Builth Wells LD2 3SG
07951 957067 chillderness.co.uk
HOW MUCH? From £330–£425 for 3 nights to £550–£710 for 7 nights.

Wardley Hill Campsite

Relaxed back-to-basics glamping in Norfolk

Deep among the birds and bees, bushes and trees of the Waveney Valley, Wardley Hill is a lush, 6-acre space of long wild grass, ageing oaks and trickling streams – a beautiful bucolic retreat on the outskirts of Bungay, with a mixture of car-free pitches for tents and campervans and a handful of glamping alternatives. It's an eco-friendly sort of place: the main field has been sown with wildflower seeds, boosting the butterfly numbers; there are 3 composting loos and a waterless urinal housed in a shelter made from reclaimed timber along with a gas-powered shower; and the site is as populated by wildlife as it is by people, with woodpeckers in the trees and buzzards overhead. Three small ponds offer muddy adventures as well as a small stream where there is potential to spot a stickleback. Mown areas provide practical pitches for tents, and you can also pitch in the small wooded areas surrounding the site, using your own tent or the ready-made 'tree-tent' strung between the boughs. Among other glamping options there is a family bell tent plus a smaller 'Lotus Belle Stargazer' along with Hilda the Shepherd's Hut, sleeping up to 4 in double beds. Furnishings give a sense of warmth and comfort, and they have some purpose-built 'little houses' on the way. Chairs are provided for evenings around the firepit – actually ingeniously converted washing machine drums – and the site is also well placed to enjoy the river, drifting by canoe, kayak or sailing boat. You would be excused, however, for not being in a rush to go anywhere, kicking back instead to enjoy the pleasures close at hand: nature, seclusion and a crackling campfire.

NORFOLK Wardley Hill Road Kirby Cane NR35 2PQ
07733 306543 wardleyhillcampsite.com
HOW MUCH? Lotus Belle Tent £70 for 1 night, £110 for 2 nights, £250 a week; Traditional Bell Tent £140 for 2 nights, £190 for 3 nights, £300 a week; shepherd's hut £200 for up to 3 nights, £250 for 4 nights, £380 a week); hammock hut £55 a night; tee tent £40 a night.

"The Waveney Valley and surrounding areas are full of delights and subtle beauty… a stay at Wardley Hill is an antidote to the everyday."

Joe and Holly, Wardley Hill Campsite

What's nearby?

THE LOCKS INN A boat trip with a pub at the end? Perfect. Get here on the Big Dog Ferry from Beccles to enjoy its unique mix of riverside drinking, hearty food and live music.

NORFOLK & SUFFOLK AVIATION MUSEUM Just outside Bungay, this collection of aircraft is a bit of a surprise in the Suffolk countryside, but worth a look.

SUFFOLK STONEHOUSE Decent pizzas in the heart of Bungay, from the same people who run the excellent nearby Castle Hotel – also a good place to eat.

Comrie Croft

As good as glamping gets – and it's a B&B too!

Situated a few miles north of the charming town of Dunblane, on the edge of the Loch Lomond and Trossachs National Park, Comrie Croft is as good – and as convenient – an introduction to the natural glories of Scotland as you would wish for. An eco-friendly Highland oasis, it's got a bit of something for everyone, and accommodation of all kinds from 3 cosy rooms in a farmhouse and dormitory beds in a converted farmstead to brilliant camping either in the safety of a field with other campers close to all the excellent amenities or the wilder hillside and forest pitches. You can also cheat a little by hiring one of their Nordic katas, 7 sumptuous tipis replete with wood-burning stoves, throws, cushions and solar-powered lighting. There are hot, solar-powered showers by the car park, along with bike hire, a bike and biking equipment store, cycle training, bike trails and a bike skills park. The Tea Garden, meanwhile, satisfies hungry campers with everything from breakfast rolls and freshly made sandwiches to irresistible home baking.

Comrie Croft is in a great location, with fabulous walking and cycle trails in every direction, so even if you arrive by car, you can tuck your keys away for the duration of your stay. It's also extremely eco-friendly, with an emphasis on self-sufficiency, recycling and rural regeneration – not to mention a brilliant farm shop stacked full of local produce. And whatever kind of accommodation you choose, you can sleep to the sounds of the owls and deer outside. Who said campers and glampers had to rough it?

PERTHSHIRE Braincroft Crieff PH7 4JZ
01764 670140 comriecroft.com
HOW MUCH? Private rooms £27–£30 per person per night, dorm beds £20–£22 a night. katas £99 per night, £229 per weekend (Fri–Sun), £499 a week.

"We love our wee bit of Perthshire and love sharing it with our friends and guests too. It's full of hidden places to swim, spot deer or just to see no one at all for an hour or two."

Andrew and Malize, Comrie Croft

What's nearby?

LOCH EARN This gem of a loch at the end of Loch Lomond is a real outdoor playground, with canoes, cycle paths and an abandoned 19th-century village to explore.

FAMOUS GROUSE EXPERIENCE With its interactive exhibits, immersive cinema and excellent restaurant, this is a cut above many distillery experiences.

AUCHINGARRICH WILDLIFE CENTRE A safari park with a lovely café and views to die for. Meet the otters, handle the chicks and feed the Scottish wild cats.

Aros yn Pentre Glas

In the foothills of the Preseli mountains, Aros yn Pentre Glas is a handsome property that's home to 2 special places to stay: Y Caban Bach, a cosy wooden cabin, and Y Panorama, a 1968 converted Bedford Plaxton bus. The bus has a kitchen kitted out with all of the essentials and a wood-burning stove for warmth on a cold night, and a double bed and large futon. Y Caban Bach comes complete with power, double bed and a verandah for making the most of balmy evenings, and there's a fully equipped kitchenette next door. Both units have private al fresco space, so you can light up the BBQ, soak up the stunning scenery and enjoy some star-gazing with your food. Ablution-wise, there's a communal block with 2 shower rooms and a well-maintained compost toilet. On rainy days, there's a cow shed to take refuge in and play a game of pool or table tennis, as well as a chill-out area and courtyard garden during the spring and summer months. Or why not book in a session with on-site yoga teacher, Gilly?

Snowdonia Glamping

Nestled in the hills above the pretty village of Betws-y-Coed, this rather magical glamping spot is home to some off-grid shepherds' huts and a barn that takes glamping to a whole new level. Divided into 2 units, each sleeping 4, it's ideal for both a family holiday and couples seeking a romantic break. Inside, wood-burning stoves, underfloor heating, super king-sized beds and free-standing baths will make you wonder where the camping aspect of glamping comes in. Head outside and there's your answer – each unit has a fully equipped outdoor kitchen, firepit and BBQ. Nothing is too much trouble for Hazel and Richard – they'll put together a hamper, provide binoculars for wildlife watching and maps for trip planning. The location is fab, with Snowdonia National Park's forests, lakes and mountains right on your doorstep. Come evening, if you don't fancy cooking, Ty Gwyn Coaching Inn is a great local place. Then it's back to your peaceful retreat for some star-gazing.

CARMARTHENSHIRE Hebron SA34 0YP 07444 847143
facebook.com/arosynpentreglas
HOW MUCH? From £40 to £85 a night.

CONWY Plas yn Rhos Rhydlanfair Betws-y-Coed
LL24 0SS 01690 710067
snowdonia-glamping-holidays.co.uk
HOW MUCH? From £220 for 2 nights, £320 3–4 nights.

Graig Wen

Graig Wen is one of the smartest operations in the book; not only a campsite and B&B but also a great place for glamping, with 2 cosy yurts, a bell tent sleeping 4, a couple of other 'pop-up yurts' that move around the site according to the season, and a shepherd's hut that comfortably accommodates 2 people. Like the yurts, this has a wood-burning stove (a basket of logs is provided), crockery and cutlery and a comfy bed covered with warm blankets. The great thing about Graig Wen is that there's so much to do nearby, with or without your car. Intrepid walkers could tackle Cader Idris, the spectacular mountain right at the back of Graig Wen, plus bikes are available to hire and using the estuary cycle path you can cycle all the way to Barmouth without even seeing a road – and virtually the entire route to Dolgellau in the other direction. Is there anywhere that has such a wide choice of high-quality holiday accommodation as Graig Wen, and also makes such a great base for exploring Snowdonia? We doubt it.

Middle Stone Farm

Right on the edge of Exmoor, these 6 safari lodges are at the upper end of the luxury glamping scale, with a wood-burning stove to cook on, a fridge-freezer, unlimited hot water and an en-suite shower room, plus a sun deck with a private hot tub and BBQ. One of the lodges ('Stag') sleeps up to 8 people while the others sleep 6, with a king-size bed, a pair of singles and a quirky 'cupboard bed' – a 2-person cubbyhole that children (and adults) adore. There's no wifi but a good 4G signal, and the accommodation isn't confined to glamping: there's a whitewashed cabin in its own corner of the farm (the Deckhouse), sleeping up to 4, also with its own wood-burner and hot tub and glorious views; and Stable Cottage, which sleeps up to 4 and has a small raised patio, has a seating area and BBQ, plus wifi throughout and heating provided by the farm's biomass boiler. All in all this is a lovely spot run by nice people, deep in the Somerset countryside – perfect for couples, families, or groups. Watch this space for their wood-fired pizza oven...

GWYNEDD Arthog Near Dolgellau LL39 1YP
01341 250482 graigwen.co.uk
HOW MUCH? Large yurts from £499 a week, caban £240–£285 a weekend, bell tents £65–£75 a night.

SOMERSET Brompton Ralph TA4 2RT
01984 248443 middlestonefarm.com
HOW MUCH? Safari tents from £120 a night, cabin from £80 a night, cottage from £70 a night.

Knotlow Farm

Back to nature but not back to basics

Bringing a bit of central Asian steppes style to the undulating hills of Derbyshire is the Long Valley Yurts operation at Knotlow Farm, a family-run site bang in the middle of the Peak District National Park. The 4 cosy yurts are set within a whopping 100 acres of rolling English farmland, with not a car, road or streetlight in sight – brilliant for a relaxed getaway in breathtaking countryside.

The yurts are spacious and airy (sleeping up to 6), and sturdy as you like, equipped to fight any unpredictable weather. But it's back to nature rather than back to basics, and they're all lovingly furnished in warm Moroccan hues, with futon-style beds, fairy lights, a wood-burning stove and oven, and a central skylight for star-gazing on those crisp Peak District nights. They also come with everything you're likely to need, from gas hobs and grill, cutlery and crockery to bedding and firewood. Toilets and hot showers are a short walk away but the clinchers for us are the 2 Scandinavian wood-fired hot tubs, set on a decking platform with stunning views over the Derbyshire Dales. The site also allows open fires, so you can do the whole backwoods marshmallow experience whenever you feel like it. There's breakfast available and evening pizzas on site, and there are pubs within easy walking distance.

This part of the Peak District is also fantastic for hikers and bikers, with easy-going footpaths right from the campsite. It's the kind of location that's great for a family break or a couples' retreat, where you can be as relaxed or as active as you like, knowing that you have a fabulously cosy base to come back to each day.

DERBYSHIRE Long Valley Yurts Knotlow Farm Flagg Buxton SK17 9QP 07884 315298 luxury-yurt-holidays.co.uk
HOW MUCH? Short breaks £299 – including exclusive use of a hot tub – to £525 in peak season. Whole weeks £575–£835.

"Furnished with a distinctly Moroccan style, our yurts are comfortable and definitely different, guaranteed to make you feel completely away from it all."

John and Richard, Knotlow Farm

What's nearby?

BAKEWELL PUDDING SHOP Many have tried but nobody has succeeded in copying the Bakewell pudding – a wonky oval pastry case with a soft, jammy, almondy filling, best eaten warm straight from the bag.

CHATSWORTH HOUSE Talk about grand designs. Completed in 1707, and home to the Devonshires since then, visits take in stunning galleries and state rooms full of family jewels.

DEVONSHIRE ARMS Pilsley is chocolate-box pretty, and its pub doesn't let you down, mixing traditional elements with a coolish vibe and great food.

Wheems Organic Farm

Yurts, pods, bell tents – and a cosy cottage!

There's something otherworldly about the Orkney Islands. The land here has been smoothed over by the prevailing winds, and the resulting views are of rolling hills and water, water everywhere between the 70 islands that make up the archipelago. Many visitors arrive on the short ferry hop from Gills Bay, between Thurso and John O'Groats, to the charming port village of St Margaret's Hope, from where it's just a couple of miles to Wheems Organic Farm, where they have a simple and fitting ethos – to keep things small, simple and eco-friendly, but most of all to share the beauty of this ethereal setting. As well as camping, Wheems has 4 solid wooden bothies or pods, insulated with sheeps' wool and with long double-glazed doors that open onto a deck overlooking the bay and sleeping 3 in comfort; a yurt sleeping 3–4 with beautiful latticework walls and a toasty log-burning stove; and 2 bell tents equipped with a wood-burning stove and space for 3 on a double futon and single futon. Finally, there's a wee one-bed loft space above a barn and a small vintage cottage, renovated like the rest of the farm buildings with local, traditional and sustainable materials, and equipped with solar and ground-source heating. Connected to the main farmhouse and also sleeping 3 people, it has sliding doors on to its own sea-view patio and terrace. If the hens are playing ball, fresh eggs are available, along with other homegrown produce and fresh bread, and you can help yourself to the herbs and salad leaves in the garden. There are geese and sheep, and a sandy beach 5 minutes away.

ORKNEY Wheems Eastside South Ronaldsay KW17 2TJ 01856 831 556 wheemsorganic.co.uk
HOW MUCH? Bell tents £30 a night, £180 a week; pods £40 a night, £240 a week; yurt £50 a night, £300 a week; cottage £70 a night, £420 a week, loft £50 a night..

"In Orkney you can find nature, peace, space and sky – we offer our guests a lovely time on our organic farm overlooking cliffs and beaches."

Islay Roberts, Wheems Organic Farm

What's nearby?

SKARA BRAE Among Europe's finest Neolithic sites, this 5000-year-old village lay preserved under layers of sand until a violent storm revealed it in 1850. Not to be missed.

THE ITALIAN CHAPEL One of the most unlikely churches you will visit, and maybe one of the most moving too, built during WWII by Italian POWs.

GYPSY CARAVANS

Have you ever dreamed of trundling around the Lake District in your own gypsy caravan, stopping off at makeshift riverside campsites where you can paddle in cool waters before cooking dinner on an open fire and then staring up at the stars for a while before climbing into your cosy bunk for the Mother of All Sleeps?

Well, with more than a decade's experience making, restoring and travelling in traditional horse-drawn gypsy caravans, Barny Maurice can make your dream happen. His Cumbria-based Wanderlusts outfit – run by him and his musician partner Katus – offers everything from full-on guided gypsy caravan holidays in the Lakes to wild camping by pack-pony, horse-drawn carriages for weddings and music for all sorts of events. Being transported gently through beautiful countryside is a magical way to spend time, great for couples and families alike: the caravans are wooden, well insulated affairs and very cosy. Inside there's a double bed (with bedding) and sleeping mats for children (for whom you need to provide sleeping bags). There's a gas hob, all the kitchen utensils that you need, and a water container. Light is provided by a wind-up torch, candles and some small 12v lights; hot water by heating water on the fire; and a compost or outside loo is never far away.

It's not for everyone, but a few days of living like this make a holiday that is hard to forget – and the kids love it. Not only that, they take you on routes you wouldn't otherwise follow – the quiet lanes of the Lyvennet Valley, between Penrith and Appleby-in-Westmorland, home of the Appleby Horse Fair.

WANDERLUSTS GYPSY CARAVANS **Nutwood Melmerby Cumbria CA10 1HF 07815 439130 wanderlusts.co.uk**

The Hideaway @ Baxby Manor

Off-grid countryside glamping

Get right off-grid at this countryside glampsite in a beautiful farmland setting, where peace and quiet and deep, dark skies await. You can pitch a tent or campervan on the rustic 6-acre site at 700-year-old Baxby Manor – everyone gets a campfire pit, and there are hot showers, sinks and loos in a modern, spotless, heated facilities block. Three chalet-style wooden eco-pods and some cute hobbit houses take care of the glamping end of the market, and there's a brand-new treehouse (accessed by a suspension bridge) with a log-burner, terrace and bean bags, TV, games console, movies and popcorn machine for nights in! It's all very low-key and eco-friendly – BBQ or camping-stove cooking only, solar-powered fairy lights provided, and showers heated by a biomass boiler. Peace and quiet is what you're promised and it's what you'll get too; it's definitely not for big groups, party people or late-night revellers, and there's a strict keep-it-down policy between 11pm and 7am.

It's the extras that really make this place – like the alpacas that sometimes come to visit, the farm eggs that you can buy or the fact that the local butcher calls every Saturday morning to sell bangers, bacon and BBQ packs. Every weekend and daily in school holidays, there's breakfast, barista coffee and home-bakes from a vintage caravan-café. It's also an amazing wedding venue, if you're that kind of couple – think marquees among the wildflowers or a tipi in the vintage apple orchard. You're a short walk from Husthwaite village where there's a pub, and nearby attractions include Coxwold, Thirsk and Sutton Bank, so the location couldn't be better for the west side of the North York Moors National Park.

NORTH YORKSHIRE Baxby Manor Husthwaite YO61 4PW 01347 666079 thehideawayatbaxbymanor.co.uk
HOW MUCH? Pods £25–£50 (2-night minimum stay at weekends); hobbit houses £47.50–£95.,

"The Hideaway offers R&R... and R! It's a place to Relax, Recoup and Revive!"

Barney, Felix and Rufus, The Hideaway

What's nearby?

KILBURN WHITE HORSE The white horses of southern England might be more famous, but the North York Moors' version at Kilburn has size on its side – at 300-ft long and 220 -ft high, it's the biggest chalk horse in the country and can be seen from miles around.

HOVINGHAM VILLAGE MARKET Boasting a fistful of awards, Hovingham's monthly market is a must, with fantastic local produce, food, crafts and gifts.

HELMSLEY CASTLE The region's most significant fortress, with grounds that positively beg to be charged around, preferably with sword in hand (available in the gift shop!).

Loose Reins

This is a glamping destination with a difference, with luxurious cedar-clad cabins and canvas lodges, from which you are taken out to discover the countryside on horseback. We reckon it's a winning formula, though the hand-crafted pioneer lodges and ranch cabins make for a unique place to stay whether you're a riding enthusiast or not. There are 3 cabins and 3 lodges, each sleeping 4–6 people in comfort, with Hypnos mattresses, luxury linen, proper plumbing and electricity, kitchens and wood-burners and outdoor fire bowls. An on-site shop sells essentials, plus dogs are welcome. The owners specialise in Western Riding, with Western tack and American-trained horses but if you're more into the idea of walking or cycling, it's good to know that the site is within easy reach of some of the best paths and bridleways in the Southwest; and the Loose Reins folk will always provide a picnic to take with you. Failing that, you could just hang out on your front porch and watch the buzzards circling.

DORSET Ridgeway Farm Shillingstone DT11 0TF
01258 863533 loosereins.co.uk
HOW MUCH? Cabins from £745 a week in low season
to £1065 a week in peak season; lodges £995–£1145.

Lower Keats Glamping

Situated in the heart of the Axe Valley, this is the ultimate destination for luxury glamping in this part of Devon, with 6 canvas safari lodges that are a perfect place to escape the hustle of everyday life without roughing it too much, with en-suite toilets and showers with hot running water and a kitchen with wood-burning stove to keep you snug and warm. You can wake up and have your morning cuppa, as each lodge is fitted with a double-burner gas hob, while outside a firepit and tripod BBQ offer the chance to cook up an feast while overlooking the voluptuous vales and verdant hills of East Devon. The site itself is great for kids, with a wildflower meadow and pigs and lambs plus chickens to collect eggs from in the morning. They are dog-friendly, and it's also an environmentally friendly place to stay, with locally made natural bathroom products, eco-friendly toilets and lots of recycled materials. They also have an honesty shop selling local produce. It is, as they say, 'a little bit of paradise' – and we're grateful they invited us along.

DEVON Broom Lane Tytherleigh Axminster EX13 7AZ
07540 367386 lowerkeatsglamping.co.uk
HOW MUCH? One week £748–£1375; 3–4 night
breaks £495–£795.

Swallowtail Hill

'Idyllic' doesn't do this East Sussex hideaway justice. Nestled in the High Weald, Swallowtail Hill Farm is 40 acres of tranquil wildflower meadow, ancient woodlands and vibrant wetlands, cultivated for your off-grid glamping pleasure – the result of owners Sarah and Christopher Broadbent's 25 years of hard graft and an acute understanding of the local environment. Sustainability is a central tenet of the Swallowtail ethos, which is why they still produce farm-reared meat, fruit, vegetables and copious quantities of timber for building, fuel and fencing. Little wonder then that TV architect George Clarke featured the Swallowtail site as one of his Amazing Spaces. There are 2 cosy timber cabins perfect for a family of 4, complete with wood-burning stove, kitchenette and firepit, and 2 whimsical wooden cabins on wheels, straight out of the Brothers Grimm, masterfully crafted by using locally sourced timber. A truly special time is assured, and it's a great place for a party too, a unique site in a stunning location. Ticks all boxes really, doesn't it?

EAST SUSSEX Hobbs Lane Beckley TN31 6TT
01797 260890 swallowtailhill.com
HOW MUCH? Cabins from £97 a night, cottages-on-wheels from £107.

Aviemore Glamping

High on the northern fringes of the Cairngorms, Aviemore is a year-round base for outdoors enthusiasts of all persuasions, a veritable smorgasbord of epic features waiting to be explored. However, while there's a refreshing lack of exclusivity about Aviemore, accommodation is often on the pricey side, so it's a treat to find this charming glamping site and B&B, whose 4 ingeniously designed pods comfortably sleep a couple on a fold-out double bed. There's an immaculately maintained shower/wet room, and, most importantly, these cosy cabins stay nice and toasty on teeth-chatteringly cold Highland evenings. They're kitted out with everything you could need, including bedding, cutlery and utensils, and although they don't have full cooking facilities, there's access to a microwave, toaster and hot-water boiler. Or you can nip across the gravel path to join your indoor B&B buddies for a full-on Scottish breakfast, courtesy of hostess Pat. Rufus the resident lurcher is quite a character and always keen to get to know new guests.

CAIRNGORMS Eriskay Craig Na Gower Avenue Aviemore PH22 1RW 01479 810717 aviemoreglamping.com
HOW MUCH? Glamping pods £60–£80 per night, self-catering cabin £220–£500 for 3 nights.

Camp Kátur

Sublime glamping on a beautiful North Yorkshire estate

When Kerry Roy was made redundant in 2012, she took it as a sign to follow her dreams and, along with her partner, decided to set up her own glamping site. We're glad she did, because Camp Kátur – named after the Icelandic for 'happy' – now has one of the most diverse selections of glamping accommodation in the country – nestled within the sprawling 250-acre Camp Hill Estate, North Yorkshire. It's an off-grid glamping experience that brings together a diverse array of native abodes, thrilling outdoor activities and some excellent eco-friendly facilities. They have the UK's first 360-degree panoramic Unidome, brilliant for star-gazing from under the duvet, hobbit pods in the trees, cosy cabins for groups of 4, and 3 safari tents that will each happily sleep a party of 8, complete with a private toilet and shower area. A tipi sleeps 4, and 2 bell tents sleep 5, plus 2 geodomes sleep up to 4 guests, and have their own kitchen, toilet and hot shower facilities.

With such an array of accommodation, you could be forgiven for thinking that things might get a little cramped. But the site is large enough to ensure plenty of seclusion, and there are lots of quirky extras too, from an outdoor hot tub and sauna to the woodland Nordic BBQ pod ('The Podfather') where you can produce your own flame-grilled feast. Glampers have their run of the first-rate adventures on offer on the estate – segways, quad bikes, putting and zip wires. As Kerry puts it, "it's one big playground for big and little kids alike." The Camp Kátur mantra is 'Discover Your Outdoor Happiness'. Thanks to that boss who gave Kerry her marching orders, you can now discover yours.

NORTH YORKSHIRE The Camp Hill Estate Kirklington Bedale DL8 2LS 01845 202100 campkatur.com
HOW MUCH? Hobbit pods from £35 per night; tipis and bell tents from £60; unidome from £70; safari tents from £90.

"We want to help our guests escape reality, reconnect, rekindle and relax among one of life's best remedies... nature."

Kerry Roy, Camp Kátur

What's nearby?

RIPLEY CASTLE Home to the Ingilby family for 700 years and worth an all-day visit, starting with a tour of the house before seeing the walled gardens and grounds.

BLACK SHEEP BREWERY The tour at this Masham brewery gives visitors the full lowdown before ending up at the (well, they couldn't resist it...) baa'r.

BRIMHAM ROCKS Yorkshire's very own Canyonlands, and a most un-English natural phenomenon – more like something you'd find in America's Southwest.

Moss Howe Farm

Charming Lake District yurt glamping

When we say Lake District, you think lakes and mountains, but there's a quieter, gentler side too, as typified by the Long Valley Yurts site at Moss Howe Farm. Set near Witherslack in the little-known Winster Valley, it's about as charming an introduction to glamping as you could wish for – a secluded, rustic location, although also close to the honeypot sights of Windermere for day trips, cruises and activities. There are 4 yurts, all kitted out with all the cosy comforts you need – proper futon beds on wooden floors, wood-burner/oven, fully equipped kitchen, plus Moroccan-style throws and rugs, fairy lights, a games chest, and a central skylight for stargazing. What's more, you can book exclusive use of a Scandinavian wood-fired hot tub that's big enough for 6 to share or for a couple to add a bit of romance to a Lake District break.

Toilets and hot showers are a short walk away, there's a farm shop on site and an excellent local pub, the Derby Arms, within walking distance (try and eat here at least once during your stay – it's great). All told, it's a pretty excellent set-up for not doing very much at all except lounging, reading, eating and drinking, although England's largest lake, Windermere, is close enough for all sorts of more active adventures, from stand-up paddle-boarding to wild swimming and kayaking. The Long Valley team can help book you on to various activities, while back at the site each evening you've got plenty of chance to have a BBQ, roast marshmallows and knock back a glass or two of wine in the hot tub. 'A country mile from anywhere' they say about this place, and we can't argue with that.

CUMBRIA Long Valley Yurts Moss Howe Farm Witherslack Grange-Over-Sands LA11 6SA

01539 733044 luxury-yurt-holidays.co.uk

HOW MUCH? Short breaks £299 – including exclusive use of a hot tub – to £525 in peak season. Whole week £575–835.

"A truly magical experience is how some of our guests have described staying in our yurts."

John and Richard, Moss Howe Farm

What's nearby?

LOW SIZERGH BARN No surprise that the Lake District is full of farm shops. But no others have a tea room looking down on the milking parlour and shop stalls housed in the ancient byres.

LAKELAND MOTOR MUSEUM A fascinating collection of classic cars and vintage vehicles, not to mention boneshaker bikes, tin toys and a recreated 1930s garage.

CARTMEL Formerly known for its medieval priory, Cartmel is an upmarket gourmet retreat these days, due partly to its Michelin-starred L'Enclume restaurant.

Forest Holidays, Blackwood Forest

LODGES & CABINS

You want a holiday cottage... OK, not a cottage, it has to be made of
wood... in a forest, or perhaps by the sea, and you definitely want a
deep double bed, en-suite shower and a morning espresso? I think we
can help, because luxury lodges and hideaway cabins of every shape
and size are some of our favourite Cool Places of all.

The Original Hut Company

Cosy shepherds' huts in the heart of Sussex

Just an hour's drive or train journey from London, close to the East Sussex village of Bodiam, the Original Hut Company makes for a perfect romantic retreat from the hustle and bustle of city living. It's a top choice for shepherd's hut holidays, and the lovingly decorated huts here are a comforting cocoon of cosiness, with wood-burning stoves to keep glamping couples warm, and also separate huts with pristine showers and eco loos. The huts are spread around the large site, some grouped among trees, others in bucolic meadows, and the site also has its own shop, café and meeting place, The Hub, where they have free wifi, as well as a nearby hut given over to massages and other treatments – though naturally these cost extra. There are foraging courses and a summer forest school for your little pioneers – the kids can spot woodpeckers, deer and maybe even the odd badger if they're lucky – and the fairytale Bodiam Castle is just a short stroll from the site, with its magnificent panoramic views over the Weald.

The area is a wonderful part of southeast England, with lots of great walking and cycle trails nearby to explore the gorgeous surrounding countryside on 2 wheels – plus the Kent & East Sussex Steam Railway links you with Tenterden in Kent. It's also a bit of foodie hub, with the Lighthouse Bakery School around the corner and the fine-dining Curlew restaurant as well as several decent country pubs in the vicinity. They also have a sister self-catering cottage in East Sussex – be sure to check it out on p.168.

EAST SUSSEX Quarry Farm Bodiam TN32 5RA
01580 830932 original-huts.co.uk
HOW MUCH? Huts from £82–£99 a night plus a surcharge of £7 per person.

"On the outer reaches of the commuter belt we're in a region that is blessed with an unspoilt rural-ness."

Anna Eastwood, The Original Hut Co

What's nearby?

BODIAM CASTLE Every inch a proper castle, with a wide moat and turreted towers bristling with arrow slits. Winding staircases lead up to the battlements.

GREAT DIXTER Planted by the late garden writer Christopher Lloyd, and surrounding his beautiful 15th-century home, this is worth visiting for its Long Border alone.

KENT & EAST SUSSEX RAILWAY You can explore the Rother Valley by train from Bodiam to Tenterden on this venerable old steam railway.

Forest Holidays Beddgelert

Forest Holidays have cabins in around a dozen peaceful woodland locations around the country, but one of its latest to open is perhaps its most intimate and certainly its most tranquil, with just 16 cabins dotted through the woods. The Colwyn river wraps around one side of the site while on the other you can hop on to one of the steam trains of the Welsh Highland Railway, which whisk you up to Caenearfon or down to Porthmadog through some of the UK's most picturesque mountain scenery. Above all, it's a perfect place to return to after exploring the wilds of Snowdonia, with 1-, 2- and 3-bed cabins that come equipped with everything you need, including hot tubs that are the perfect place to relax after a hard day's hiking. Some of the cabins are dog-friendly, while at the centre of the site, the Forest Retreat and Bakehouse have a café and bar, shop and play area, plus bikes for hire and the chance to go wildlife-spotting and do some bushcraft activities with Forest Holidays' own Rangers.

GWYNEDD Beddgelert Wales LL55 4UU
0333 011 0495 forestholidays.co.uk
HOW MUCH? Prices from £350.

Buttercrambe Hut

Tucked away in an orchard on a working farm, this shepherd's hut is a cosy spot for a loved-up couple, with vintage wall lamps and a retro feel. There's lots to see and do in the immediate area – Castle Howard and the Howardian Hills AONB lie just to the north, but really it's the sort of place you might just want to stay put. It has basic cooking facilities and a breakfast basket is delivered each morning, your own shower room is just a short stroll across the garden, where you'll also find additional cooking facilities. There's a day bed to relax on, an iPod docking station and radio, and in the autumn/winter months a flask of hot soup and bread is provided on arrival. Come evening, you can relax under the stars by the BBQ and firepit or cosy up inside before retiring to your comfy double bed. There is no mobile reception (hooray!) and no TV either, but you can use the wifi in the farmhouse if you're desperate. But this is a such a romantic and homely retreat that you'll soon be oblivious to the world beyond the walls of your cosy hut.

NORTH YORKSHIRE York YO41 1AP 01865 594349
sheepskinlife.com
HOW MUCH? Prices range from £300 for 3 nights to £500 for 7 nights – plus £20 for pooches.

Denmark Farm

Situated in the heart of rural Ceredigion, Denmark Farm is the ultimate eco-retreat, a farm and nature reserve running courses in sustainable living that also has a campsite, yurt, bunkhouse and a self-catering eco-lodge. The great thing about the lodge is that it's flexible: you can occupy as much or as little space as you like, from 2 people to 16, so it's ideal for everyone from couples and families to large groups of friends or extended families. The accommodation is crisp and clean, almost Scandinavian in feel, and is situated in the middle of the farm's 40-acre nature reserve, complete with woodland trails and hides, ponds, lakes and meadows. All profits go to help fund the work of the centre's nature and biodiversity charity, but it's no hair-shirt enterprise – holidays here are both a comfortable and affordable way to enjoy this special environment; and bear in mind also that you're in a fabulous part of Wales, with countless great walks on your doorstep. The beautiful Hafod Estate and the Devils Bridge Falls are nearby – as is the university town of Lampeter.

CEREDIGION Betws Bledrws Lampeter SA48 8PB
01570 493358 denmarkfarm.org.uk
HOW MUCH? Eco Lodge £395–£685 a week for 4 people. Midweek breaks, long weekends available.

Stoke by Nayland Lodges

From the Copella juice family behind the Stoke by Nayland Hotel Golf & Spa – deep in the heart of the Suffolk countryside – come these beautiful self-catering lodges, each full of light and fitted with high-spec kitchens and furnishings. They are an ideal alternative to the hotel, built on the site of the Women's Land Army hostel that used to be at the centre of the family estate. You can choose anything from a 1-bedroom to a 4-bedroom lodge, and all have large living rooms, contemporary kitchens and large wooden decks. Some of them overlook the hotel's golf course, while others have a more secluded, woodland feel. The nice thing is that you can use all the facilities of the hotel while retaining a bit more privacy in what is a lovely, secluded location. You can also order in via a 24/7 porter, or hire your own chef to come over and serve a private dinner. Guests receive a welcome hamper on arrival containing tea, coffee, fresh milk, biscuits, wine – and a bottle of the Peake family's own Copella juice! All in all a great spot for a peaceful weekend in the country.

SUFFOLK Keepers Lane Leavenheath CO6 4PZ
01206 262836 stokebynayland.com
HOW MUCH? From £172.50 a night for a 1-bedroom lodge, from £245 for 2 bedrooms – 2-night minimum.

Cairngorm Lodges

Eco-friendly lodges deep in the woods of Aberdeenshire

There's something special about waking up deep in a forest: sleeping in the woods engenders a cosiness that can't quite be replicated anywhere else, and the truth is that staying in a wooden lodge in some of the Cairngorms National Park's deepest, darkest woodland is about as far away from most people's day-to-day existence as it's possible to get.

Situated on the 750-acre Blelack Estate, Cairngorm Lodges offers a real get-away-from-it-all break, with no wifi and no reception building or additional facilities. The lodges are very well equipped, though. Each has 2 bedrooms – one double, one twin – so is perfect for a family; they each have a sitting room/kitchen and bathroom, outside decking with BBQ, and are heated by a wood-burning stove, and logs are laid on in generous supply. Everything is done with the environment in mind: the lodges are built from sustainable wood and the forest sustainably managed; they recycle everything, and, perhaps most importantly, they are passionate about encouraging the local flora and fauna, running beekeeping courses and offering lots of advice on where to spot local wildlife – red squirrels are daily visitors to the lodges, there are red deer in the woods, and among an abundance of birdlife you will be able to spot kestrels, sparrowhawks and pine martens. The only real difference between the lodges is their location. For example, Osprey Lodge overlooks a small loch, while Red Squirrel Lodge is sited deepest into the woods. All the lodges are dog-friendly, and the forest has a multitude of marked paths it would take weeks to walk. It's the perfect place for both an active holiday and a peaceful contemplative one – or, even better, a mixture of the two!

ABERDEENSHIRE Logie Coldstone Aboyne AB34 5PQ 07583 436040 cairngormlodges.com
HOW MUCH? The 4 newest lodges cost £530–£740 a week; midweek or weekend breaks are £390–£455. The original Woodcutter's Lodge is £450–£620 a week, short breaks £340–£455

"We hope guests will make our forest hideaway their own and are delighted that so many choose to return to us each year. This Scots pine forest is such a special place."

Sarah Leahy, Cairngorm Lodges

What's nearby?

TARLAND TRAILS This set of short mountain trails are suited to everyone from families to more experienced riders. Choose from the Spiky Hedghog or Slinky Fox!

BALLATER ROYAL STATION Recently reopened as a restaurant and museum, this was until the 1960s used by the Royal Family travelling to Balmoral Castle.

ROYAL LOCHNAGAR DISTILLERY A Deeside distillery that produces a silky smooth dram and is open for tours all year. Tie it in with a visit to Balmoral Castle, just a mile away.

The Lodges at Artlegarth

If you're looking for your own private Eden, you might have just found it – well, Eden Valley in Cumbria anyway, where Jennie and Neil's 6 luxury log cabins – each with their own hot tub – sit in 7 acres at the foot of the Howgill Fells. Beautifully constructed in solid pine, these are high-end, luxury lodgings for sure, furnished in a contemporary-country-chic style and each with a private hot tub looking out over fields and fells, spectacular sunsets and the deepest of dark skies. Kitchens and dining areas are not just an after-thought but spacious and fully equipped to rustle up anything from snacks and canapés to a full gourmet dinner for a family or group, and there's plenty in the grounds to keep families happy, from a woodland walk and play area to a wildlife pond and even native red squirrels. The local village has a choice of 2 award-winning pub-restaurants, and you're perfectly sited for both the Lake District and Yorkshire Dales national parks, so walking, cycling, country pursuits and wildlife-watching are all right on the doorstep.

CUMBRIA Artlegarth Ravenstonedale Kirkby Stephen CA17 4NW 07548 668152 lodgebreaks.co.uk
HOW MUCH? Lodges from £399–£799 for 3 nights, £599–£1199 a week.

Woodman's Huts

In the small village of Haverthwaite, where steam trains whistle to a halt outside a quaint old station, this is a glamping site with a quintessentially English setting, made up of just 2 wooden shepherd's huts, insulated with sheep's wool and furnished inside to a seriously comfortable standard. Rough and ready camping this is not – the huts even have underfloor heating, and are as ergonomic as you could ask for. One sleeps 2 people, the other 4, and each has its own en-suite bathroom with a powerful shower, sink and toilet and a few toiletries provided. Together they make for an exclusive stay for small groups, or you can book just one, socialising with your neighbours in the communal 'Arctic Hut' – a hexagonal pine lodge with an indoor BBQ and firepit in its centre. For all its glamping supremacy, though, it's the location that really makes this place a cracker – you can set off into the national park from your doorstep, with several excellent footpaths nearby. Walking is, after all, the best way to bring out your inner shepherd.

CUMBRIA Lanes End Haverthwaite LA12 8AB
07809 402484 facebook.com/woodmanshuts
HOW MUCH? 2-berth hut £80 per night, 4-berth hut £95 per night.

Rowan Lodge

We reckon there are few nicer parts of the country to stay in than the region around the North Yorkshire town of Richmond – and few more appealing towns than Richmond itself. The Scandinavian pine lodges at Flowery Dell are comfortable in the extreme – double-storey in some cases, with well-appointed accommodation for between 2 and 6 people and situated on the edge of the Yorkshire Dales National Park. The natural wood throughout works wonderfully well, and the lodges are thoroughly Scandinavian too in the sense that they are equipped with saunas and in some cases hot tubs. Rowan Lodge sleeps 2–4 and is perfect for a romantic break in the country, with a luxury double room with king-size bed and its own en-suite bathroom plus a twin room, a hot tub on the balcony, a gas BBQ, a wood-burning stove and a beautifully equipped kitchen and a sitting room with 40-inch flatscreen TV. You can also treat yourself to a range of beauty treatments, dressing gown and slippers hire and flowers on arrival for an extra fee.

NORTH YORKSHIRE Hudswell Lane Richmond
DL11 6BD 01748 822406 flowerydell-lodges.com
HOW MUCH? From £467 for a 3-night weekend or 4
nights midweek to £667–£1255 a week.

Harvest Moon Holidays

If mere glamping is not enough for you then you can literally take a step up – into your very own treehouse. These palatial hideaways recline in a blissfully rural corner of East Lothian and boast a massive elevated wooden decking area complete with a sturdy table and chairs. There are two buildings on the deck, one a cosy sleeping space with 2 bedrooms and a proper toilet and shower. The other is an open-plan family-friendly living area, with a wood-burning stove – which you'll need as there's no electricity. Time slows right down when mobiles are not bleeping and the kids are not plugged into tablets, and the entertainment here is charmingly old school, with a set of swings and the chance to feed the on-site lambs and chickens. Or you could just lose hours bashing around on the massive beach just over the sand dunes or admiring the stars from your deck. They also have 7 luxury safari tents on the same site – and a brand-new self-catering cottage for those who want a few more home comforts.

EAST LOTHIAN Tyninghame Near Dunbar East Lothian
EH42 1XP 07960 782246 harvestmoonholidays.com
HOW MUCH? Midweek short breaks £480–£790,
weekends £400–£750, full weeks £600–£1250.

Hidden River Cabins

Log cabins with hot tubs in ancient woodland

We love everything about these luxurious log cabins – think *Cabin Porn* for softies... Staying here, you have all the magic and romance of living in a cabin by a river in an ancient forest without having to forgo 21st-century comforts. There are modern bathrooms, wood-burners, fitted kitchens, TVs with Freeview and a DVD player. We also like that there is no internet or phone reception: having to climb the hill to make a phone call or walk to the estate reception building for internet helps to separate you from the rest of the world. What's more, each cabin is beautifully crafted, and each has its own very gorgeous hot tub on a deck overlooking the river. And, if you don't feel like cooking at all, the estate has its own café and restaurant, Hidden River Café, where prime ingredients – fantastic smoked salmon, Westmoreland black pudding, Cumberland sausage – make breakfast a treat. And dinner is not too shabby either.

There are 5 cabins, set far enough apart from each other to give the impression that yours is the only sign of human habitation for miles around. Inside, the decor preserves exposed log walls – a glass-fronted wood-burner, king-size beds, flagged floors and wooden furniture with clean contemporary lines. There are also fully fitted kitchens, complete with freezer, should you be lucky enough to need to store the day's catch. The cabins can sleep 6–10, but the atmosphere within is intimate and *hygge* enough for romantic breaks for couples. If you do fancy fishing – the river Lyne is famous for its sea and brown trout – there are rods for hire, and for a small extra charge you can rent a state-of-the-art BBQ.

CUMBRIA Hidden River Cottage Longtown Carlisle CA6 5TU 01228 791318 hiddenrivercabins.co.uk
HOW MUCH? Prices start from £190 per night for 2 people in Roe Deer, Otterstone or Kingfisher cabins. Prices for the larger Bluebell cabin start from £210 per night for 2 people. 3-night minimum stay.

"Our concept was to create a space where every cabin feels secluded, with a river view in beautiful Cumbrian countryside."

Rachel Faulkner, Hidden River Cottages

What's nearby?

VINDOLANDA This old garrison fort is the greatest visitor attraction on Hadrian's Wall – and a place where Roman Britain really comes to life.

GRETNA GREEN For a long time this was home to the UK equivalent of the quickie Vegas wedding – and they've been milking it ever since...

CARLISLE CATHEDRAL Norman structure that is second smallest of UK cathedrals, but makes up in beauty what it lacks in size, with amazing Gothic stained glass.

Clippesby Hall

About a mile from the river at Thurne, in the heart of the Broads National Park, this site, fashioned by John Lindsay out of the wooded grounds of his home at Clippesby Hall, pretty much has it all: a wonderful location with lots of trees for secluded camping, and a position that's perfect for cycling and walking, and exploring the Broads by boat. It has great facilities too – its own pub, a very nice outdoor pool hard up against the hall, mini golf, bike rental and a well-priced café; and, what's more, the people who run the place are passionate about their site and the region, for which they have lots of suggestions for cycle routes, boat trips, walking routes and more. They have also built some great wooden lodges in the trees, each sleeping up to 6 people and with their own private hot tub, while managing to keep the sheltered, marvellously bucolic feel of the site. They offer trips with the CanoeMan too (see p.73), so you can easily get out on the water, while the coast at Winterton is just a short distance away.

NORFOLK Hall Lane Clippesby NR29 3BL
01493 367800 clippesbyhall.com
HOW MUCH? Lodges from around £400 for a short off-season break to around £1100 for a week in high season.

Shank Wood Log Cabin

This little house in the big woods is the perfect solution for parents wanting to give their kids a taste of life without a touch-screen, or for couples seeking a romantic forest retreat. Set in a gloriously secluded spot by a river, and built from local timber sourced from a variety of trees, the cabin could easily feature in a Scandinavian lifestyle book, but the only luxuries are a wood-burning stove, hot tub, an outdoor pod with a shower and a comfortable sofa on which to curl up and meditate on the art of chopping wood. Electricity is supplied by solar panels, there's no phone reception, wifi or internet connection, and you sleep on 2 double beds parked back to back; cooking is on a BBQ on the verandah, and the lighting solar-powered. If the sun is scarce the electricity may run out, but living by candlelight only adds to the adventure. Kingfishers, otters and roe deer are all regular visitors. Lying in bed or soaking in the hot tub listening to the sounds of the forest and watching the river flow past is magical.

CUMBRIA Longtown Carlisle CA6 5TU
01228 792489 fishinghideaway.co.uk
HOW MUCH? From £150 to £210 a night for up to 4 people.

Crowtree Wigwams

Call us old-fashioned, but we reckon that there aren't many things to beat sitting nursing a cup of tea on your own verandah while gazing out across an endless vista of cow-dotted fields as a good way to unwind. Located on the banks of the river Welland in the heart of rural Lincolnshire, this farm-based glamping site makes an ideal place to do just that, under a vast and atmospheric Fenland sky. However, let's be clear – these are not wigwams, but well-constructed, heated cabins: dead cosy, with space for 4 people in 2 double beds, and equipped with en-suite toilet and shower, hob, microwave and fridge and all the cooking utensils and crockery you need. You can either bring your own towels and bedding or use theirs for a small extra cost. The site also has wood-fired hot tubs and you can hire a firepit for BBQs. Plus there's a tennis court, croquet and a games room for rainy days. Owners Patrick and Anne are friendly hosts, and you're bang in the middle of some gloriously unspoilt countryside, with a ton of walks on hand. And did we say you can bring your dog along too?

LINCOLNSHIRE Crowtree Farmhouse Wragg Marsh Spalding PE12 6HF 01406 373 341 crowtree-glamping. co.uk
HOW MUCH? Cabins £55–£85 a night for 2 adults.

Lazy Duck

If you want quirky, elemental living then this is the place for you – just a short drive from Aviemore, with a variety of accommodation options that includes a waterside lodge, an eco-cabin, a lambing bothy, and even a funky bunkhouse, as well as 4 pitches for campers. It's a compact, friendly site set amid hulking Scots Pines with the Cairngorms providing an epic backdrop. The name, incidentally, comes from the resident Aylesbury ducks – just spend a few minutes watching them around the pond and you'll see why. The Lambing Bothy, Woodman's Hut and The Duck's Nest each sleep 2 in romantic seclusion; the Hut is completely off-grid, with just candles and low-level battery-powered lighting; the Bothy and Nest have limited mains supply, while all 3 have wood-burning stoves. Outside, there are hammocks in the heather, a Tarzan swing, a wood-fired hot tub with essential oils, a sauna with chill-out tunes and bush showers. There are mountains and walks in all directions, including the long-distance Speyside Way and a hotel bar within walking distance.

INVERNESS-SHIRE Nethy Bridge PH25 3ED
0131 618 6198 lazyduck.co.uk
HOW MUCH £105–£125 a night for 2 people (min 2-night stay); hostel from £95 a night.

Log Cabin Scotland

Log lodges in a spectacular woodland location

Beautifully located on the edge of Loch Awe, in the wilds of western Scotland, these log cabins offer a fabulous chance to get away from pretty much everything if that's what you're keen to do. Their location in the heart of the Inverliever forest (indeed the tiny village of Dalavich is itself a Forestry Commission creation) is perfect for both waterside and woodland holidays: each lodge enjoys fishing rights on the loch (Scotland's longest, and renowned for its trout fishing) and where the water ends, the forest begins, with all manner of scenic walks and cycle routes and any amount of wildlife to spot along the way, from red squirrel and deer in the woods to osprey and otters on the loch. As for the lodges, there are 4 in all, each with its own secluded space (at least a quarter-of-an-acre) so that you would hardly know the others were there. They vary in size, sleeping from 4 to 6 people, and you can choose between a woodland or waterside location. But all come complete with open-plan living area with kitchen, 2–3 bedrooms, family bathroom, a TV and DVD player and wifi, a wood-burning stove and large verandah and eco-friendly wood-burning hot tubs – plus they are all pet-friendly, so you can bring the family hound along as well. Fern Lodge is deep in the woods by a babbling brook but still only 150m from the loch, while the other woodland lodge – Orchy – is not much further from the shore. The other two – Crannog Lodge and Lochside Lodge – both overlook the water. They're all fully insulated, double-glazed and warm and cosy at any time of year, but obviously sitting in the hot tub enjoying a glass of wine while looking out over the loch on a summer's evening is pretty hard to beat!

ARGYLL Dalavich PA35 1HN 07706 122034
log-cabin-scotland.co.uk
HOW MUCH? Fern Lodge and Orchy Lodge from £275 for 2 nights, £300 for 3 nights, £350 for 4 nights, £495 a week; Crannog Lodge from £250 for 2 nights, £330 for 3 nights, £395 for 4 nights, £495 a week; Lochside Lodge from £300 for 2 nights, £425 for 3 nights, £475 for 4 nights; £545 a week. Prices include all linen and 3 bags of logs for the wood-burner and hot tub.

"We are passionate about the wild and tranquil beauty of this region – and hope our cabins provide the perfect retreat from the strains of modern living."

Steve Shields, Log Cabin Scotland

What's nearby?

LOCH FYNE The original and best, the place where the UK-wide seafood chain began. The reputation may have grown but the recipe remains blissfully simple. They cultivate their own oysters in the waters just outside the restaurant, they smoke their own fish on site and the lobster is landed just down the road at Tarbert.

KILMARTIN GLEN One of the most intriguing and dramatic historical sites in the UK, with over 350 monuments, including Bronze Age cairns and standing stones.

Tom's Eco Lodge

Comfy glamping near the Isle of Wight's south coast

Putting the glam in glamping, Tom's Eco Lodge – the sister business of Tapnell Farm Cottages – boasts a mixture of luxurious safari tents, well-appointed cabins and cosy pods, each nestled away in the glorious surroundings of Tapnell Farm on the Isle of Wight. The roomy safari tents offer accommodation for up to 8 people and have log-burners, and 2 have wood-fired hot tubs. Each wooden cabin sleeps up to 10 and has its own west-facing terrace to soak up the afternoon sun and capture the spectacular sunsets, and comes complete with a spacious dining room, cosy beds with electric blanket, bunk beds and cabin beds for the kids, plus hot showers and a flushing loo, a firepit to toast your marshmallows a log-burning stove – and its own hot tub. The pods, meanwhile, are perfect for a couple, or snug for a family of 4, with a double bed and a sofa bed. Each one features a well-equipped kitchenette, BBQ area and private shower room. Finally, there are bespoke cabins – called 'modulogs' – inventive pods for up to 6 people with the best views on the farm and their own private hot tubs. The cabins, modulogs and pods all have heating and insulation so can be rented year-round as warm and cosy winter retreats. Elsewhere on site there are picnic tables, a communal pizza oven and lawned area for games, while a restaurant-bar occupies a converted Swiss barn in the middle of the farm. On a clear day you can see down to the north coast, while a long-distance footpath passes right through the grounds. All in all this is the perfect place for a family glamping holiday.

ISLE OF WIGHT Tapnell Farm PO41 0YJ
01983 758729 tomsecolodge.com

HOW MUCH? Safari tents with hot tubs from £800 a week, from £495 for a 3-night weekend, from £400 for 4 nights midweek – without hot tubs £30–£40 cheaper. Cabins from £600 a week, from £450 for a 3-night weekend, from £310 for 4 nights midweek. Pods from £80 a night, £550–£775 a week, from £300 for a 3-night weekend, from £250 for 4 nights midweek. Modulogs from £300 for 2 nights.

"Boutique glamping with stunning views, spectacular sunsets and space to roam –the perfect farm stay for an adventurous family holiday, relaxing group get-togethers, and even a romantic hideaway'"

Chloe Baker, Tom's Eco-Lodge

What's nearby?

THE DAIRY DELI A short drive east from the site, fantastic local creamery produce is sold at this farm shop 'like no udder' (well somebody had to use it). The cheese scones alone are worth a visit.

DIMBOLA LODGE Hard to believe but the former home of Victorian photographer Julia Margaret Cameron has an eye-popping feast of her photographs.

Destinations

ARGYLL
Crispie Estate 275
Greystones 152
Laggan 236
Log Cabin Scotland 326
Lower Polnish 223
St Hilda Sea Adventures 134

BIRMINGHAM
Staying Cool at the Rotunda   60

BRECON BEACONS
Cosy under Canvas 282
Felin Fach Griffin 92
Red Kite Tree Tent 291

BRISTOL
Bristol Harbour Hotel 64
Brooks Rooftop Rockets 77

BUCKINGHAMSHIRE
The Pointer 94

CAMBRIDGESHIRE
University Rooms Cambridge 59

CENTRAL WALES
Aros y Pentre Glas 296
Denmark Farm 317
Fforest Fields 237

CORNWALL
Artist Residence Penzance 130
Atlantic Hotel 142
Barford Beach House 166
The Beach at Bude 126
Blue Hayes 140
Bosinver Farm Cottages 248
Bryn Cottage 227
Buddha Beach House 169
Budock Vean Hotel 150
Cohort Hostel 149
Costislost 185
Falmouth Lodge 148
Filter House 82
The Greenbank Hotel 138
Gurnard's Head 101
Halzephron House 176
Leskernick Cottage 250
Little White Alice 241
Marine Point 174
The Old Coastguard 131
The Old Quay House 130
The Olde House 238

Pebble House B&B 158
Pentire Penthouse 168
Poltarrow Farm 241
Rick Stein's Café Rooms 160
The Rosevine 144
St Enodoc Hotel 131
The Seafood Restaurant 118
Solomon's Island 175
Talland Bay Hotel 30
Tregulland Cottage & Barn 270
Woodmans Wild Ale 262

CUMBRIA
Another Place, The Lake 203
Applegarth Villa 210
The Barefoot Shepherdess 194
Brimstone Hotel 37
Brownber Hall 48
Fawcett Mill 258
Grasmere Glamping 290
Hidden River Cabins 322
Lakeside Hotel 216
The Lodges at Artlegarth 320
Moss Howe Farm 310
The Quiet Site 288
Randy Pike 32
Shank Wood Log Cabin 324
Wanderlust Gypsy Caravans 302
Woodman's Huts 320
YHA Black Sail 214

DERBYSHIRE
Dannah Cottages 224
Elton Old Hall 265
Knotlow Farm 298
Portland House 274
Manor House 202
Sett Cottage 226

DEVON
The Cricket Inn 113
Hotel Endsleigh 207
Fingals Apart 234
The Horn of Plenty 208
Longlands Glamping 286
Lower Keats Glamping 306
The Nest Treehouse 76
The Old Rectory Hotel 38
The Salutation Inn 100
Saunton Sands Hotel 132
Soar Mill Cove Hotel 136
The 25 36

DORSET
Laverstock Farm 240
Loose Reins 306

EAST LOTHIAN
Harvest Moon Holidays 321

EAST YORKSHIRE
Tickton Grange 212

EDINBURGH
Brooks Hotel Edinburgh 59
Holyrood Cottage 226
94DR 56

ESSEX
The Alma Inn 100
The Pier at Harwich
Maison Talbooth 119
The Pier at Harwich 162
Seven 161
The Sun Inn 96

GLOUCESTERSHIRE
The Bull Hotel 112
Calcot Manor 210
Crestow House 198
The Old Stocks Inn 112
The Painswick 207
The Sheep on Sheep St 118
Symonds Yat Rock Lodge 223
YHA ST Briavels Castle 88

HAMPSHIRE
Careys Manor Hotel 211
Montagu Arms 199
Solent Forts 83

HEREFORDSHIRE
Abbots Lodge 180
Brooks Country House 196
Brooks Vintage Horseboxe 68
Cruckbarn 244

HERTFORDSHIRE
The Farmhouse at Redcoats 199
The Fox at Willian 95
Number One Port Hill 40

ISLE OF SKYE
Three Chimneys 34

ISLES OF SCILLY
Flying Boat Cottages 168

ISLE OF WIGHT

The Little Barn 236
Tapnell Farm 276
Tom's Eco Lodge 328

KENT

Alkham Court Farmhouse 200
Driftwood Beach House 57
The Duke William............................... 217
The Gate House 227
Green Farm Kent 246
The Hadlow Tower 70
House of Agnes 45
Number 1 Wavecrest 175
Rocksalt Rooms 116
Seascape 265
A Secret Garden 82
The Wife of Bath 108

LANCASHIRE

Number One St Luke's 156

LINCOLNSHIRE

Crowtree Wigwams 325

LONDON

Artist Residence London 52
London Honey Company 54

OXFORDSHIRE

Artist Residence Oxfordshire 37
The Greyhound Inn 109
Heath Farm 252
Red Lion Pub & Kitchen 109

NORFOLK

The Angel Inn.. 95
Bank House 44
The Boathouse.. 98
The Buckinghamshire Arms 94
The Canoe Man 72
Cley Windmill 80
Clippesby Hall 324
Deepdale Backpackers 149
East View Farm 237
Great Barn Farm 266
The Grove Cromer 146
Incleborough House 275
Magazine Wood 184
Maids Head Hotel 58
The Rose & Crown 104
Stone's Throw Cottage 170
Strattons 36
Wardley Hill Campsite........................ 292
The Waveney Inn 122
The White Horse 110

Wiveton Bell 101

NORTH YORKSHIRE

The Angel Inn at Hetton 114
Buttercrambe Shepherd's Hut......... 316
Camp Kátur 308
The Den, Husthwaite Gate 264
The Hideaway @ Baxby Manor 304
Low Mill Guest House 28
Millgate House 204
Pinewood Park 290
Real Staithes 172
Rowan Lodge 321
Split Farthing Hall............................... 216
Stow House 186
YHA Boggle Hole 148
YHA Grinton Lodge 76

NORTHUMBERLAND

Lord Crewe Arms 184
YHA The Sill, Hadrian's Wall 217

ORKNEY & SHETLAND

Wheems Organic Farm 300

PEMBROKESHIRE & SOUTH WALES

Caerfai Farm Cottages 169
Manor Town House 154
Top of the Woods 280
Penrhiw Priory 44
Roch Castle 74
Treberfedd Farm 230
Twr y Felin Hotel 62
Ty Mamgu 222

SCOTTISH BORDERS

Aikwood Tower 260
Roulotte Retreats 84

SCOTTISH HIGHLANDS

Achmelvich Beach Hostel 160
Aviemore Glamping 307
Cairngorm Lodges 318
The Crofthouse at the Roundhouse 274
Huntingtower Lodge 190
Lazy Duck.. 325

SHROPSHIRE

The Castle Hotel 188
Old Downton Lodge 192
Walcot Hall Glamping 77

SNOWDONIA

Ffynnon 45
Forest Holidays Beddgelert.............. 316
Graig Wen 297
Henfaes Isaf 232

The Slate Shed 182
Smuggler's Cove Boatyard 264
Snowdonia Glamping 296
YHA Pen-y-Pass 206

SOMERSET

The Chapel 78
Godney Arts House 242
Middle Stone Farm 297
Mill Stream Loft 222
Park Farm House 211
Swallow Barn 206
Tilbury Farm 240

STIRLINGSHIRE & CENTRAL SCOTLAND

Comrie Croft 294
East Cambusmoon Farm 254
Plane Castle 268

SUFFOLK

Bildeston Crown 102
Crossways Farm 185
Fen Farm Dairy 106
Five Acre Barn 42
Ivy Grange Farm 284
Milsoms Kesgrave Hall 46
The Oaksmere 202
Rectory Manor 203
Salthouse Harbour Hotel.....................58
The Sail Loft 128
Sibton White Horse 120
Stoke by Nayland Hotel Lodges 317
The Swan Long Melford 119
The Windmill Suffolk 86

SUSSEX

The Cavalaire 156
Fair Oak Farm 272
Graywood Canvas Cottages 291
The Old Rectory 156
The Original Hut Company 314
Railway Retreats....................................83
Swallowtail Hill 307
The Warrens 174
YHA Brighton 161

WARWICKSHIRE

Hampton Manor.................................. 113
The Townhouse Stratford 108

WILTSHIRE

Howard's House 198

WORCESTERSHIRE

Cider Mill Cottage 220

Inspire me

ADULTS-ONLY

The 25 Boutique B&B 36
Applegarth Villa 210
Blue Hayes................................... 140
Costislost...................................... 185
Dannah Cottages.......................... 224
Five Acre Barn...............................42
The Hadlow Tower..........................70
Millgate House   204
The Old Quay House 130
Pebble House B&B 158
Roulette Retreat............................84
A Secret Garden 82

BUDGET STAYS

Achmelvich Beach Hostel   160
Cohort Hostel............................... 149
Crowtree Wigwams........................ 325
Deepdale Backpackers   149
Falmouth Lodge   148
YHA Black Sail............................... 214
YHA Boggle Hole 148
YHA Brighton 161
YHA Grinton Lodge..........................76
YHA Snowdon Pen-y-Pass 206
YHA St Briavels Castle.....................88
YHA The Sill at Hadrian's Wall........ 217

FAMILY-FRIENDLY

Bosinver Farm............................... 248
Budock Vean Hotel....................... 150
Harvest Moon Holidays 321
Heath Farm 252
Laverstock Farm 240
Little White Alice.......................... 241
Lower Keats Glamping................... 306
Middle Stone Farm........................ 297
The Olde House 238
Pinewood Park.............................. 290
Poltarrow Farm............................. 241
The Quiet Site 288
Railway Retreats............................83
The Rosevine................................. 144
Saunton Sands Hotel 132
Soar Mill Cove Hotel 136
St Hilda Sea Adventures 134
Tapnell Farm................................. 276
Top of the Woods 280
Treberfedd Farm 230

FOODIE BREAKS

The Alma Inn................................ 100
The Angel at Hetton 114
Artist Residence Oxfordshire 37
The Bildeston Crown 102
Bristol Harbour Hotel......................64
The Bull Hotel 112
The Cricket Inn 113
The Duke William.......................... 217
The Farmhouse at Redcoats........... 199
The Felin Fach Griffin   92
The Greyhound Inn......................... 109
The Gurnard's Head....................... 101
Hampton Manor 113
The Horn of Plenty......................... 208
Howard's House 198
Lord Crewe Arms.......................... 184
Maison Talbooth 119
Montagu Arms 199
Old Downton Lodge....................... 192
The Old Quay House 130
The Old Rectory Hotel 38
The Old Stocks Inn 112
The Pier at Harwich 162
The Pointer....................................94
Rick Stein's Café Rooms................. 160
The Red Lion Pub & Kitchen 109
Rocksalt Rooms 116
The Rose & Crown......................... 104
Salthouse Harbour Hotel..................58
Sibton White Horse 120
Strattons.......................................36
The Swan at Long Melford............... 119
Tickton Grange 212
Twr y Felin Hotel............................62
The Wife of Bath 108
Wiveton Bell 101

HOT TUBS

Alkham Court Farmhouse 200
Another Place, The Lake 203
Applegarth Villa 210
Atlantic Hotel............................... 142
Atlantic Hotel............................... 142
Barford Beach House........................ 166
The Beach at Bude   126
Buddha Beach House...................... 169
Budock Vean Hotel........................ 150
Camp Kátur.................................. 308

Careys Manor Hotel 211
Cosy Under Canvas........................ 282
Crowtree Wigwams........................ 325
Dannah Cottages........................... 224
The Den at Husthwaite Gate   264
Driftwood Beach House.................. 157
Ffynnon...45
Flying Boat Cottages, Tresco 168
Forest Holidays Beddgelert............ 316
Graywood Canvas Cottages 291
Green Farm Kent........................... 246
Hidden River Cabins 322
Incleborough House 275
Knotlow Farm............................... 298
Lakeside Hotel............................... 216
Lazy Duck..................................... 325
Little White Alice.......................... 241
The Lodges at Artlegarth 320
Log Cabin Scotland 326
Longlands Glamping....................... 286
Maison Talbooth 119
Middle Stone Farm........................ 297
Moss How Farm 310
Number One St Luke's 156
The Olde House 238
Pentire Penthouse......................... 168
Roulotte Retreat............................84
Rowan Lodge 321
Seascape...................................... 265
A Secret Garden 82
Shank Wood Log Cabin 324
Soar Mill Cove Hotel 136
Solent Forts...................................83
Stoke by Nayland Hotel Lodges..... 317
Tapnell Farm Cottages 276
Tilbury Farm................................. 240
Tom's Eco Lodge – Tapnell Farm..... 328
Treberfedd Farm 230
Tregulland Cottage & Barn 270

OFF-GRID, REMOTE & ECO

Cairngorm Lodges.......................... 318
Crossways Farm............................. 185
Cruckbarn..................................... 244
East Cambusmoon Farm 254
East View Farm 237
Fforest Fields................................. 237
Godney Arts House......................... 242
Hidden River Cabins 322

The Hideaway @ Baxby Manor 304
Ivy Grange Farm 284
Laggan 236
Leskernick Cottage   250
Little White Alice 241
Log Cabin Scotland   326
Lower Polnish   223
Number One St Luke's 156
The Olde House 238
Solomon's Island   175
Tilbury Farm 240
Treberfedd Farm 230
YHA Black Sail 214
YHA Boggle Hole 148
YHA The Sill at Hadrian's Wall 217

POOLS, SPAS & SAUNAS

Another Place, The Lake 203
Atlantic Hotel 142
Brimstone Hotel 37
Bristol Harbour Hotel 64
Brooks Country House 196
Brooks Vintage Horsebox Glamping 68
Budock Vean Hotel 150
Calcot Manor 210
Careys Manor Hotel 211
Cider Mill Cottage 220
Clippesby Hall 324
Crestow House 198
Crispie Estate 275
Fingals Apart 234
Flying Boat Cottages, Tresco 168
Great Barn Farm 266
The Grove Cromer 146
Lakeside Hotel 216
Maison Talbooth 119
The Olde House 238
Park Farm House 211
Poltarrow Farm 241
The Rosevine 144
Saunton Sands Hotel 132
Soar Mill Cove Hotel 136
Solent Forts 83
St Enodoc Hotel 131
Stoke by Nayland Hotel Lodges 317
Tregulland Cottage & Barn 270
The Waveney Inn 122

ROMANTIC RETREATS

Another Place, The Lake 203
Blue Hayes 140
Brimstone Hotel 37
Brooks Rooftop Rockets 77
Bryn Cottage 227

Buttercrambe Shepherd's Hut 316
Cider Mill Cottage 220
Crestow House 198
Dannah Cottages 224
Hotel Endsleigh 207
Ffynnon 45
Grasmere Glamping 290
Holyrood Cottage 226
Howard's House 198
Low Mill Guest House 28
Mill Stream Loft 222
Millgate House 204
The Nest Treehouse 76
The Painswick 207
Randy Pike 32
Red Kite Tree Tent 291
Roch Castle 74
Roulotte Retreat 84
St Enodoc Hotel 131
Talland Bay Hotel 30
The 25 36
The Windmill Suffolk 86

WEDDING VENUES

Aikwood Tower 260
Another Place, The Lake 203
Atlantic Hotel 142
The Bildeston Crown 102
The Boathouse 98
Bristol Harbour Hotel 64
Brooks Country House 196
Budock Vean Hotel 150
Calcot Manor 210
Camp Kátur 308
Careys Manor Hotel 211
Cley Windmill 80
Fair Oak Farm 272
The Farmhouse at Redcoats 199
The Greenbank Hotel 138
The Grove Cromer 146
The Hadlow Tower 70
Halzephron House 176
Hampton Manor 113
Hidden River Cabins 322
The Hideaway @ Baxby Manor 304
The Horn of Plenty 208
Hotel Endsleigh 207
Howard's House 198
Lakeside Hotel 216
Lord Crewe Arms 184
Maids Head Hotel 58
Maison Talbooth 119
Milsoms Kesgrave Hall 46

The Oaksmere 202
Old Downton Lodge   192
The Old Rectory   156
The Painswick 207
Plane Castle 268
Roch Castle 74
Roulotte Retreat   84
The Salutation Inn 100
Saunton Sands Hotel 132
Solent Forts 83
Stoke by Nayland Hotel Lodges 317
Talland Bay Hotel 30
Tickton Grange 212
Tregulland Cottage & Barn 270
YHA St Briavels Castle 88
YHA The Sill at Hadrian's Wall 217

WELLNESS, YOGA, CREATIVITY

Abbots Lodge   180
Another Place, The Lake 203
Applegarth Villa 210
Budock Vean Hotel 150
Careys Manor Hotel 211
Costislost 185
Fair Oak Farm 272
Ffynnon 45
Fingals Apart 234
Flying Boat Cottages 168
Green Farm Kent 246
Halzephron House 176
Huntingtower Lodge   190
Little White Alice   241
Maison Talbooth 119
Montagu Arms 199
The Old Rectory 156
Saunton Sands Hotel 132
Soar Mill Cove Hotel 136
Split Farthing Hall 216
St Enodoc Hotel 131

Places

A

Abbots Lodge 180
Achmelvich Beach Hostel 160
Aikwood Tower 260
Alkham Court Farmhouse B&B 200
The Alma Inn 100
The Angel Inn 95
The Angel at Hetton 114
Another Place, The Lake 203
Applegarth Villa 210
Aros yn Pentre Glas 296
Artist Residence London 52
Artist Residence Oxfordshire 37
Artist Residence Penzance 130
Atlantic Hotel 142
Aviemore Glamping 307

B

Bank House 44
Barford Beach House 166
The Beach at Bude 126
The Bildeston Crown 102
Blue Hayes 140
The Boathouse 98
Bosinver Farm 248
Brimstone Hotel 37
Bristol Harbour Hotel 64
Brooks Country House 196
Brooks Hotel Edinburgh 59
Brooks Rooftop Rockets 77
Brooks Vintage Horsebox Glamping 68
Brownber Hall 48
Bryn Cottage 227
The Buckinghamshire Arms 94
Buddha Beach House 169
Budock Vean Hotel 150
The Bull Hotel 112
Buttercrambe Shepherds Hut 316

C

Caerfai Farm Cottages 169
Cairngorm Lodges 318
Calcot Manor 210
Camp Kátur 308
Careys Manor Hotel 211
The Castle Hotel 188
The Cavalaire 157
The Chapel 78
Cider Mill Cottage 220
Cley Windmill 80

Clippesby Hall 324
Cohort Hostel 149
Comrie Croft 294
Costislost 185
Cosy Under Canvas 282
Crestow House 198
The Cricket Inn 113
Crispie Estate 275
The Crofthouse at the Roundhouse 274
Crossways Farm 185
Crowtree Wigwams 325
Cruckbarn 244

D

Dannah Cottages 224
Deepdale Backpackers 149
The Den at Husthwaite Gate 264
Denmark Farm 317
Driftwood Beach House 157
The Duke William 217

E

East Cambusmoon Farm 254
East View Farm 237
Elton Old Hall 265
Hotel Endsleigh 207

F

Fair Oak Farm 272
Falmouth Lodge 148
The Farmhouse at Redcoats 199
Fawcett Mill 258
The Felin Fach Griffin 92
Fforest Fields Cottages 237
Ffynnon 45
Filter House 82
Fingals Apart 234
Five Acre Barn 42
Flying Boat Cottages 168
Forest Holidays Beddgelert 316
The Fox at Willan 95

G

The Gate House 227
Godney Arts House 242
Graig Wen 297
Grasmere Glamping 290
Graywood Canvas Cottages 291
Great Barn Farm 266
Green Farm Kent 246

The Greenbank Hotel 138
The Greyhound Inn 109
Greystones 152
The Grove Cromer 146
The Gurnard's Head 101

H

The Hadlow Tower 70
Halzephron House 176
Hampton Manor 113
Harvest Moon Holidays 321
Heath Farm 252
Henfaes Isaf 232
Hidden River Cabins 322
The Hideaway @ Baxby Manor 304
Holyrood Cottage 226
The Horn of Plenty 208
House of Agnes 45
Howard's House 198
Huntingtower Lodge 190

I

Incleborough House 275
Ivy Grange Farm 284

K

Knotlow Farm 298

L

Laggan 236
Lakeside Hotel 216
Laverstock Farm 240
Lazy Duck 325
Leskernick Cottage 250
The Little Barn 236
Little White Alice 241
The Lodges at Artlegarth 320
Log Cabin Scotland 326
Longlands Glamping 286
Loose Reins 306
Lord Crewe Arms 184
Low Mill Guest House 28
Lower Keats Glamping 306
Lower Polnish 223

M

Magazine Wood 184
Maid's Head Hotel 58
Maison Talbooth 119
Manor House 202
Manor Town House 154

Marine Point 174
Middle Stone Farm 297
Mill Stream Loft 222
Millgate House 204
Milsoms Kesgrave Hall 46
Montagu Arms 199
Moss Howe Farm 310

N

The Nest Treehouse 76
94DR 56
Number One Port Hill 40
Number One St Luke's 156
Number One Wavecrest 175

O

The Oaksmere 202
The Old Coastguard 131
Old Downton Lodge 192
The Old Quay House 130
The Old Rectory 156
The Old Rectory Hotel 38
The Old Stocks Inn 112
The Olde House 238
The Original Hut Company 314

P

The Painswick 207
Park Farm House 211
Pebble House B&B 158
Penrhiw Priory 44
Pentire Penthouse 168
The Pier at Harwich 162
Pinewood Park 290
Plane Castle 268
The Pointer 94
Poltarrow Farm 241
Portland House 274

Q

The Quiet Site 288

R

Railway Retreats 83
Randy Pike 32
Rectory Manor 203
Red Kite Tree Tent 291
Red Lion Pub & Kitchen 109
Rick Stein's Cafe Rooms 160
Roch Castle 74
Rocksalt Rooms 116

The Rose & Crown 104
The Rosevine 144
Roulotte Retreat 84
Rowan Lodge 321

S

The Sail Loft 128
Salthouse Harbour 58
The Salutation Inn 100
Saunton Sands Hotel 132
The Seafood Restaurant 118
Seascape 265
A Secret Garden 82
Sett Cottage 226
Seven 161
Shank Wood Log Cabin 324
The Sheep on Sheep St 118
Sibton White Horse 120
The Slate Shed 182
Smugglers Cove Boatyard 264
Snowdonia Glamping Holidays 296
Soar Mill Cove Hotel 136
Solent Forts 83
Solomon's Island 175
Split Farthing Hall 216
St Enodoc Hotel 131
St Hilda Sea Adventures 134
Staying Cool at the Rotunda 60
Stoke by Nayland Hotel Lodges 317
Stone's Throw Cottage 170
Stow House 186
Strattons 36
The Sun Inn 96
The Swan at Long Melford 119
Swallow Barn 206
Swallowtail Hill 307
Symonds Yat Rock Lodge 223

T

Talland Bay Hotel 30
Tapnell Farm 276
Tickton Grange 212
Tilbury Farm 240
Tom's Eco Lodge 328
Top of the Woods 280
The Townhouse Stratford 108
Treberfedd Farm 230
Tregulland Cottage & Barn 270
The 25 36
Twr y Felin Hotel 62

Ty Mamgu 222

U

University Rooms Cambridge 59

W

Walcot Hall Glamping 77
Wabderlust Gypsy Caravans 302
Wardley Hill Campsite 292
The Warrens 174
The Waveney Inn 122
Wheems Organic Farm 300
The White Horse 110
The Wife of Bath 108
The Windmill Suffolk 86
Wiveton Bell 101
Woodman's Huts 320

Y

YHA Black Sail 214
YHA Boggle Hole 148
YHA Brighton 161
YHA Grinton Lodge 76
YHA Snowdon Pen-y-Pass 206
YHA St Briavel's Castle 88
YHA The Sill at Hadrian's Wall 217

Acknowledgements

COOL PLACES: Britain's Coolest Places to Stay, Eat, Drink,... and More

Published in the UK by Punk Publishing, 81 Rivington Street, London EC2A 3AY

© Cool Places Ltd 2019

www.coolplaces.co.uk

A catalogue record of this book is available from the British Library
ISBN 978-1-906889-69-2

CREDITS

Editors: Martin Dunford and Jules Brown
Assistant Editor: Lauren Ash
Contributors: Martin Dunford, Jules Brown, Laura Evans, Hayley Lawrence, Pat Kinsella, Robin McKelvie ,Amy Sheldrake, Ros Belford, John Fisher. Thanks also to the many other UK writers who have contributed to Cool Places along the way.
Design & layout: Diana Jarvis and Kenny Grant
Proofreading: Leanne Bryan
UK Sales: Compass IPS Limited, Great West House, Great West Road, Brentford TW8 9DF; 0208 326 5696; sales@compass-ips.cio.uk
Printed by 1010 Printing International Limited, China

This book has been printed on paper made from renewable sources.

PICTURE CREDITS

Images used are used with permission from the property owners or the establishments themselves, except for those listed below:
Cover photograph: Paul Massey for Artist Residence, Penzance
p 1 The 25 B&B, Torquay, Devon
pp 2-3 Tea and Cakes, Lakeside Hotel
p 5 Artist Residence, London
p 6 Cushions, 94DR
pp 8–9 Cley Windmill, Norfolk
pp10–11 Falmouth Harbour, The Greenbank Hotel, Devon
pp12–13 Bourton-on-the-Water, Gloucestershire
pp 14–15 Hotel Endsleigh, Devon
pp16–17 Filby Broad, Norfolk ©Diana Jarvis
pp18–19 Nidderdale, Yorkshire ©Diana Jarvis
pp20–21 The Warrens, Folkestone, Kent ©Diana Jarvis
pp22–23 Maidens Harbour, Ayrshire ©Diana Jarvis
pp 24–25 Hay Bluff, Wales ©Diana Jarvis
pp 26–27 Randy Pike B&B, Cumbria
pp 50–51 Staying Cool at the Rotunda, Birmingham
pp 54–55 London Honey Co ©Julian Winslow
pp 66–67 Roch Castle, Pembrokeshire
pp 90–91 Artist Residence, Oxfordshire
pp124-125 Hemsby Beach, Norfolk ©Diana Jarvis
pp 164–165 Barford Beach House, Cornwall ©Brownhill Photography
pp178–179 The Horn of Plenty, Devon

pp 218–219 Ty Mamgu, Ceredigion
pp 228–229 Godney Arts House, Somerset
pp 256–257 Portland House, Derbyshire
pp 312–313 Longlands Glamping, Devon
pp 330–331 Forest Holidays, Blackwood Forest, Hampshire
Tebay Services ©Tebay Services; Artist Residence ©Paul Massey for Artist Residence; Burrator ©www.visitdartmoor.co.uk; Auchingarrich widlife ©Emma Robertson; Emmetts ©Stuart Hollis/Osborne Hollis Ltd; Cregennan Lakes ©Gwynedd Council; Hatfield Forest ©Paul Burland; Clearwell Caves © TomFKemp; Chastleton House ©MiloBostock; Batemans ©Charlie Dave; Harbour Ferries Robert Orr; Loch Fyne ©David Jones; Vault Beach ©Andrew; Berrington Hall ©Glen Bowman; Brown Willy ©Donald Macauley Dunwich Heath Nick Rowland; Fishpool ©David Harris; Goodrich Castle ©Dave Snowden; Gretna Green ©Nick Amoscato; Gunwalloe Beach ©Tim Green; Hatfield Forest ©Paul Burland; Ludlow Castle ©bvi4092; McCaigs Tower ©Martin Abegglen; Morwenstow ©Steve Bittinger; Stirling Castle ©Dominic Mitchell; St Just ©Tim Green; Sudbury Hall ©Daniel Thornton; Summerleaze Pool ©Tom Bastin; Westhay Moor ©Amanda Slater; Widemouth Bay ©Dawn Robinson-Walsh; Battle of Bannockburn ©Tom Parnell; Bedgebury Forest ©Loz Pycock; Valley of the Rocks ©James Johnstone; White Cliffs ©Tobias von der Haar; K&ESR ©John K Thorne; Lyn Can, Cader Idris ©Graig Wen; Ring O' Bells ©The Chapel; Ettrick Valley ©AikwoodTower; Heath Farm ©Andrew Ogilvy Photography; Sail Loft ©Foyers Photography; Gyllyngvase © Adam Gibbard; Hatfield House ©Gary Bembridge; Henry Moore Studio & Garden ©Stuart Burns. Plus pictures from Halzephron Inn; Hunter's Inn Exmoor; Kings Head Laxfield; Locks Inn Geldeston; Rising Sun Altarnun; Rising Sun St Mawes; The George Hubberholme; Lea Gardens; The George Inn St Briavels.

SMALL PRINT